I0640680

WITHDRAWN
UML LIBRARIES

The
BLOOMSBURY
REVIEW®
BOOKLOVER'S®
GUIDE

Books by *The Bloomsbury Review*®

Living In Words: Interviews from The Bloomsbury Review (1981–1988)

The Colorado Book Guide

Books by Patricia Jean Wagner

Building Support Networks for Schools

The
BLOOMSBURY
REVIEW®

BOOKLOVER'S®
GUIDE

A Collection of Tips, Techniques, Anecdotes, Controversies & Suggestions for the Home Library

WRITTEN & EDITED BY

Patricia Jean Wagner

ILLUSTRATED BY
Sherry L. Watson

Copyright © 1996 by Owaissa Communications Company, Inc., dba *The Bloomsbury Review*
Illustrations Copyright © 1995, 1996 by Sherry L. Watson.

"The Book as Beloved," Copyright © 1996 by Clarissa Pinkola Estés, Ph.D. All performance, derivative, adaptation, anthology, musical, illustrative, theatrical, film, pictorial, electronic, and all other rights reserved.

Book Lover's® is a registered trademark of Barnes & Noble, Inc.

Names mentioned in the text are real, and all quotes are published with the written permission of the contributors.

Editorial policy:
The Bloomsbury Review separates the functions of advertising and editorial in all of our publications. Products, services, and organizations mentioned in the text of this book did not pay for the publication of their information and names; in most cases, the editorial department did not know until publication time who was buying ads. Advertisers were informed that buying an ad did not guarantee mention in the text of the book.

The Bloomsbury Review
1762 Emerson Street
Denver, CO 80218-1012

ISBN 0-9631589-3-7
ISBN 0-9631589-4-5 pbk.
ISBN 0-9631589-5-3 ltd. ed.

10 9 8 7 6 5 4 3 2

Manufactured in the United States of America

ref Z 987.5 .U6 W34 1996
Wagner, Patricia Jean.
The Bloomsbury review
  booklover's guide

Dedication

To Karl Young, Douglas Stone, and Irene Mitkus,
who showed me the difference between passion and competence.

Liberty is the possibility of doubting, the possibility of making a mistake,
the possibility of searching and experimenting,
the possibility of saying "no" to any authority
—literary, artistic, philosophic, religious, social, and even political.

Ignazio Silone, novelist

from *The God That Failed.* Edited by Richard H. Crossman.
Copyright © 1949 by Richard Crossman
Reprinted by special permission of Regnery Publishing, Inc., Washington, DC

Warning: Read This Before You Read This Book

Two important themes are emphasized in this book: ensuring the physical safety and health of people (and their pets), and maintaining and improving the condition of books, photos, paper records, etc.

Before you follow the advice given in this book, please do your homework. This book is not a substitute for using the advice of a professional who will know your special situation, be it an allergy to wheat paste or the geneaology of a rare mold infecting a rare book. For reasons stated in this book, it is impossible to guarantee what will happen when you take apart a book or treat it with what you assume are benign chemicals.

Therefore, the information provided in this book should only be used with caution. If you misinterpret the information contained in this book, you may be seriously injured or your property damaged as a result of your misunderstanding.

There are no express or implied warranties that this book contains accurate and reliable information. There are no warranties as to fitness for a particular purpose. Your use of this book expressly indicates your assumption of the risk of serious injury or damage to your property as a result of risks that may be inherently dangerous in maintaining and improving the condition of books, photos, paper records, etc., and is an acknowledgment of your own responsibility for your safety and condition of your property.

Neither the publisher of this book, the editor, nor the contributors assume any liability for any injury or property damage that may result from any attempt on your part to use any method, procedure, or product as described or implied in this book for maintaining and improving the condition of your books, photos, paper records, etc.

Personal Acknowledgments

To my husband and best-beloved friend, Leif Smith, who keeps the e-mail running and who reads me to sleep;

To my parents, Esther and Harold Wagner, who let me read instead of wash dishes and who bought me every book I ever wanted;

To my sister, Aileen Wagner, who introduced me to the Encyclopedia Britannica and let me keep her horse book;

To the extraordinary folks at *The Bloomsbury Review*, who made this book real, with special thanks to Lori D. Kranz and Caryl Riedel for their editorial artistry and to Tom Auer and Marilyn Auer for their insightful questions. Their attention to the details made this a much better book;

To the dozens of booklovers who responded to our request for stories and information, and to the many experts who lent their valuable time to this project. The genius is theirs; the mistakes are all mine.

And, finally, to Dr. Mark D. Solano and Dr. Michael H. Hitchcock and their staffs, who got me back in working order; to Leslie Aguillard and Steve Carney, who helped me heal; and to the many loving friends and family who supported me through the dark days, so that we could enjoy the sunshine together.

Response Note

"Because of space limitations ..."

"As of this writing ..."

These are the two most frustrating phrases in the book business. Because of space limitations, I had to leave out 85 percent of the print material I had gathered and could use less than one percent of what would be relevant and available on the Internet about the book community. As of this writing, I knew some of what was happening with electronic bookstores, the cost of paper, the conventional wisdom on glue sticks, and the financial health of the independent booksellers versus the superstores, but these facts can change in a matter of days.

So, when this book lands in your lap, it will be incomplete and slightly outdated. It is a snapshot on paper, not a live feed from a satellite. I hope to use some of the overflow in my column, "The Practical Bookshelf," in *The Bloomsbury Review*. And, of course, we all hope that the book will sell well enough to warrant a new and larger edition in the future.

Writing this book has been part of a dialogue with booklovers from all over the country that I will miss. Feel free to call, mail, fax, or e-mail. I don't have a secretary, but I promise to do my best to respond promptly. Criticisms and complaints are welcome, as are compliments and contributions. Tell me what you would like instead of or in addition to what I have presented, or what I left out that you missed, and what has been most useful to you.

You can reach me at:

Patricia Jean Wagner (aka Pat Wagner)
The Bloomsbury Review
1762 Emerson Street
Denver CO 80218-1012
(303) 863-0406, fax: (303) 863-0408
e-mail: pat@pattern.com

Table of Contents

Foreword

Chapter I — Introduction
Being a Revelation of the Origins of This Book,
the Controversies That Were Encountered During the Research
of Same, and an Introduction to Resources for the BookLover.

Chapter II — The History of the Book and the Library
Being an Introduction to the Past,
Present, and Future of the Book and the Library.

Chapter III — The Book Arts
Being a Discussion of Some Aspects of the Craft of the Book
and Some Resources to Tickle the BookLover's Artistic Palate.

Chapter IV — Analysis and Evaluation
Being a Grand Tour of Your Home Library and the Books Within,
With an Emphasis on Saving the Best of What You Have.

Chapter V — Acquisitions
Being a Discussion of Better Ways to Find
Current Books, Especially the Good Stuff.

Chapter VI — Collecting Books
*Being a Chapter About the Economics, Secret Handshakes,
Diseases, and Joys Associated With the Conscious Collecting
of the Book, and Sources for Used, Rare, and Antiquarian Books.*

Chapter VII — Display and Storage
Being Suggestions on Managing and Manipulating the Physical Environment of Your Home Library, With Information on Critters Who Like to Homestead in Your Books.

Chapter VIII — Classification and Cataloging
Being an Orderly Collection of Stories and Admonitions Concerning the Classification and Cataloging of Your Home Library, With Musings on Insurance, Appraisals, and the History of the Bookmark.

Chapter IX — Repair
Being a Recipe Book of the Basic Care Procedures for New and Old Books, Without Resorting to Tactical Nuclear Weapons.

Chapter X — Weeding

Being an Exposé of Phobias About Weeding; Loans and Theft (Which Are Two Ways to Weed Your Collection); Disposing of Your Collection After Your Death; and the Truths Most BookLovers Don't Want to Hear About Landfills and Composting.

Chapter XI — Other Libraries
Being a Guide to the Diverse Flora and Fauna
That Inhabit the Greater Library Ecology Outside the Walls of Your
Own Book Zoo and Some Advice About Creating a Real Library.

Chapter XII — Electronic and Online Books
Being a Snapshot of the Internet and Computer Resources,
for Those Who Regret the End of the Gutenberg Era.

Chapter XIII — Children and Books
Being a Guide for Parents and Other People Who Love Children and
Who Want to Infect Them With a Passionate Love for Books.

Chapter XIV — The Home Archives
Being a Revelation About the Differences Between Home Libraries and Home Archives, and Why You Should Care, With Special Resources for Preserving Your Personal History.

Foreword

The Book as Beloved
By Clarissa Pinkola Estés, Ph.D.

The Bloomsbury Review BookLover's Guide is a splendid idea in ever so many ways, but especially for those of us who are sometimes semi-witless about how to organize and care for our home libraries. The folks at *The Bloomsbury Review*, and the editor of this book, Pat Wagner, know whereof they speak. They have dealt with the stacks in one way or another for years. Accordingly, in this informative tome, one will find much advice borne of experience—all by kindred spirits who have tried every imaginable method "in order to keep order" amongst their precious volumes.

One will find valuable hints and tips on the often painful necessity of weeding out books before the house joists collapse. In this fine manual, one will find advice about animals and books, loan policies, children's libraries, where not to store books, insights about the art of crafting books, and much more.

It seems that once one has more than two books to rub together, like the genie let out of the bottle, the desire to buy, eat with, and sleep with books is unleashed. Oh yes, and the desire to read them, too. However, it is not by accident that librarians stand in the top ten of those I most admire on the face of this earth, for they, unlike most of us, know exactly how to select, preserve, shelter, and mend books. Those in library science always know where Strunk and White is when they need it. And most often, it is exactly where they put it—instead of propped up under one corner of the dog's bed, or in with the kitty pajamas and other assorted animal-to-human costumes left over from last year's Halloween party, or in the pocket of the trench coat one bought last year when in love with that mysterious writer person. So, it is a relief that this almanac aims to make us better home librarians, at the very least able to describe our lyceum by more than color of spine.

Although my research library aims to be organized according to the Dewey decimal system—minimal confusion there—my personal volumes are organized by other means. Which means? Er, "The Pinkola Estián means." Someone once said that I had put an invisible padlock on my personal library—only those who know me very, very well are able to follow its organizational logic.

Here, paraphrased, is a conversation between a friend and myself about my personal library.

"Why do you have Hedda Gabler *in with the psychology books?"*
"Because Hedda was profoundly depressed."

1

"Well, why is Totus Tuus *on Pope John Paul II's plea for reconsecration of the world to the Blessed Mother in the Theravada Buddhism section?"*

"The dialogue between Christians and the East needs to continue."

"You think by putting books together, this will build political bridges?"

"No, but hopefully reading these together will provide me with the pylons and ropes just in case ... "

"And books on Dia de los Muertos, *the Day of the Dead, why are they in the children's section?"*

"Because on *Dia de los Muertos,* we teach our children the stories of their ancestors' lives, their failures, and triumphs."

"What is this little stack of white paper in the Medieval section?"

"Oh, that's a photocopy that I made at the library of an out-of-print book on mathematics. I put it in the Medieval section because it was copied from a copy—the way manuscripts were copied from copies during Medieval times."

And so on. It is clear to me as a poet and psychoanalyst that a library is not just shelf after shelf of books, but, at least in our home libraries, a gigantic thought system—whether organized by the brain stem of passions or the "higher" centers of thought seems to depend on the individual—and the day of the week for some.

The best suggestions I have for others are these:

• Keep children's books for grown-ups, and on occasion, grown-ups' books for children. There are parts of Buber and Eliade that delight children. I have read from Elie Wiesel's *Night* to fifth graders whose hearts are still so very open. Teenagers, who are often wasting away from "terminal cool," are boggled to be read Hershey's *Hiroshima* or Hemingway's *The Old Man and the Sea.* Do you really think that *Catcher in the Rye* was meant only to be read silently to oneself? Teenagers love to laugh together over it. And adults? So many have never been read C. S. Lewis's *Chronicles of Narnia.*

• Let there be disorder to a point—it is wonderful to find Heshel's *I Asked for Wonder* when you are trying to figure out your taxes with Jane Bryant Quinn.

• Read aloud whenever you can—when you are alone, as well as when you are with others. There are many ways to use a library.

• If you have only one loaf of bread, give away half in order to buy a book you desire—for yourself or for another.

• Care for old books. Some of my books are ancient, many having been purchased at garage sales. Like the old people in my family, I try to embrace them more and more gently, more and more tenderly, as time goes along. I have to turn the pages of several books with a hairpin, so delicate are they. I have cried when a corner of a page cracked in two like a dry cracker and fell to the floor. But I repair, prop, and strengthen them wherever I can. It does not matter what they look like—only that their richness of word and image is kept alive.

• Build as many bookcases as possible. Once I ran out of bookcase space, so I put bookshelves over the toilet, over every doorway, in the hallways, along all load-bearing walls. I lifted the bed so low bookcases could range around its perimeter. (I have slept with Shakespeare, Galeano, Lorca, and other fine authors.) I put up so many "instant" bookcases of cinder block and pine boards that the floor in my apartment sagged slightly. Glasses in the kitchen cupboards began to tremble when anyone walked across the floor. I have put up so many bookcases that we had to put timbers in the cellar to bear the weight of the books on the floor above. I have this mad plan—that if I weatherproof some of my books—(Giant baggies? Dip them in paraffin? Fashionable Kevlar® jackets?)—I can store them in bookcases on the front porch in all kinds of inclement weather, and they will be safe.

What shall I do with my library when I die? I write all over my contemporary books, both outside and inside. I draw pictures in them. I bend them, crease them. A couple are a little war-wounded from falling. One treatise on the ruling class' right to dominate all others once threw itself across the room. I don't think any respectable library would want my library. Maybe there's a disreputable library that would like them. My sense is that my illustrated books might serve as outsider art.

I have had this persistent fantasy that began in the days of my childhood when we had no books. We couldn't afford them, and couldn't have read them had we had them. The fantasy has changed gradually through five decades. I see a library with chairs that don't make any part of the back or hips hurt, that have arms just right for holding a book. There are 500 pairs of reading glasses scattered all over the place. (No need to explain this strange desire to those who buy reading glasses at Walgreens, as I do.)

There would be many alcoves and little desks and chairs in each alcove and perfect light for reading, and every beloved friend I have, or would have in the future, would spend time there, reading and researching. And I would bring them tea and sharp pencils, and treat them in an old fashioned way. There would be a resident ghost for those who stayed late, an old poet *cantadora* from the family. And late at night, the sound of *canto llano* would sometimes be faintly heard off in the far distance. This library would be so fine and it would create memories so deep, that everyone who had been there, each person who had ever worked there on a sultry day or on a wintry night, would, when they were very, very old, write about their experiences, their hauntings, and the yearnings that passed through them there in that library of eld.

I have lettered a sign about lending books. It reads: "My books are the tools of my trade, they cannot be lent." But now there are a few trusted souls, who, over the years, have shown they are kind to books and creatures, and they come to my library to carry on their research on the premises. In this sense, for those who have shown themselves thusly, this long-lived fantasy library has indeed come to life—kept alive as always by all the myriad voices in the books, and all those who love, hate, harbor, understand, fear, witness, and care for those voices in books, and who believe, as I do, that each volume, in its own way, regardless of blemish or age, is an excellent consort, a most worthy Beloved.

❖

Clarissa Pinkola Estés, Ph.D., is a poet, scholar, Jungian psychoanalyst, and *cantadora* (keeper of the old stories in the Latina tradition). Her published works include *Women Who Run With the Wolves* (published in twenty languages world-wide); *The Faithful Gardener; The Gift of Story;* and the forthcoming *The Dangerous Old Woman* and *La Pasionara* by Alfred A. Knopf.

*When Pat reads that the best way
to preserve a book is to not read it,
she realizes that she does not have
the properly reverent attitude.
page 8.*

Chapter I — Introduction

Being a Revelation of the Origins of This Book, the Controversies That Were Encountered During the Research of Same, and an Introduction to Resources for the BookLover.

Genesis

Somewhere in the world, someone has just rolled over in bed, opened her eyes, and said, "I don't remember buying 5,000 books. Do you remember buying 5,000 books?" Let us call this someone Pat.

Her cheek is embossed with the edge of the trashy spy paperback she fell asleep reading. Scattered throughout the bedclothes are mystery novels, classic science fiction, biographies, humor anthologies, and one children's book with a torn cover.

The walls of the bedroom are a canyon of pulp. A geological survey would reveal layers of paperbacks with fading covers and fragile pages ripening to sepia.

Outside the bedroom, books on economics and history fill the house. Classic novels, rescued from the free shelf at the neighborhood coffeehouse, spill into hallways and lurk on staircases. More books nap under pillows in the living room. They sulk under magazines, and they pout, draped with cobwebs, in the attic and basement, in the unheated garage, and in the trunk of the station wagon.

> *I sleep with my friends. Books are my friends, so I sleep with them.*
> —Elaine Ricklin, artist and art educator, Denver, CO

In boxes sealed since the last move, reference books mutter mutiny among themselves. And the library books on the dining room table shiver with fear: Will they be absentmindedly filed in the floor-to-ceiling bookshelves under "oblivion," along with the orphaned loaners and never-read bargain books?

Pat is not a scholar who locks rare books in temperature- and humidity-controlled storage cases as if they were fine cigars. Her hardbacks are not swathed in Mylar™. Her paperbacks have not been deacidified and rebound with archival-quality paper and glue. She does not collect all the books written by any single author. Pat does not salt away books for investment purposes. Her home library does not follow the cataloging guidelines of the Library of Congress.

Pat simply loves books. She buys books for pleasure, for lifelong learning, for research, to solve problems in her life, on the spur of the moment, for gifts that are never given, to distract her from pain, to put her to sleep, to make her laugh.

However, she is feeling guilty about her personal library, about whether her mass of books, photos, artwork, and personal papers deserves this lofty label.

Take the matter of book care. Something needs to be done about beloved volumes that are deteriorating. When conscience strikes, Pat buys books on book repair, but she does not understand how preservation differs from restoration or conservation. The names of the chemicals are beyond her. She is overwhelmed by the amount of specialized equipment she must buy and by the glues and cleaners she must stock. The instructions seem vague and contradictory.

Also, to be perfectly honest, she is a klutz and a slob.

When Pat reads that the best way to preserve a book is to not read it, she realizes that she does not have the properly reverent attitude. She wants to use and enjoy her books, but she is aware that too many of her favorites have been lost and damaged by her neglect. Pat needs practical advice she can put into action without breaking the bank, poisoning her cats and husband, or destroying her only decent copy of that racy John D. MacDonald paperback about illicit love in Florida.

The physical care of her books is not the only issue. Pat wants to be better organized. She wants to have a real home library, the kind where the books are in some kind of sensible order. But books on the art of displaying and cataloging books tend to fall into two categories. They are written either by bibliographers who think that cataloging is a theological pursuit or by interior decorators who treat books like collections of china dogs.

To the former, all books and printed documents are part of the Archival Ether, an invisible web of obligation that binds Pat to Its Demands: She must document, catalog, and file every book and scrap of paper that falls into her hands, appropriately annotated in case Pat becomes famous in 350 years, never mind the cost. On Judgment Day, this doctrine implies, God will be revealed to be the Head Archivist, and Pat had better be able to find that Nancy Drew mystery she bought in 1958 and her fifth grade report card from Horace Mann Grammar School.

The interior designers, on the other hand, want to make every home look like a backdrop for a television soap opera, with ancient leather-bound volumes leaning artfully in the background, as Ashley reveals to her new husband Radcliffe that she is really his stepmother. Of course, we don't have ugly books on display, do we? Ugly is for poor people with no taste.

And what if Pat suspects that a few of the books in her collection might be worth something? Is she required to replace her wood planks with metal shelving in order to prevent book lice from nesting in the cracks? To install a computer system to sample temperature and humidity every thirty minutes? To test the pages in each volume for the presence of acid? And must she put away forever the valuable books she loves?

This volume is for Pat and for booklovers like her.

Binding the Words: How This Book Was Created

A book about books and home libraries is an audacious task; I do not pretend to be an authority about topics such as first-edition collecting and fine-book preservation. But I have had the pleasure of working alongside experts from every corner of the book and library communities since the late sixties, from printers to published authors, from book artists to bookstore owners, from literary agents to librarians.

So, I went to those experts. A very few sniffed at the project and refused to help. They could not imagine a book about personal libraries that did not address the issue from the viewpoint of the "real librarian," or the "real scholar," or the "real collector." I thanked them and moved on.

Literature, to me, is a form of companionship, and just as we do not love our friends any less because they may have a darn in their shirts or a crack in their shoes, or a crumple in their suits, similarly I like a book to show signs of life and usage, signs of reasonable wear, if not tear.
—Christopher Morley, bibliographer
from *Ex Libris Carissimis*. A.S. Barnes & Co., Inc., 1961

However, most of my sources were good-humored, generous, and appropriately iconoclastic about their expertise. They told me of personal blunders and cheerfully recounted how many of the sacred book and library cows deserved judicious grilling.

Next, I put out a call to home librarians from Australia to the Florida Keys. I contacted them via flyer, phone call, fax, and e-mail. I ran ads in *The Bloomsbury Review* and in newspapers and magazines. I accosted people at conferences and left brochures at used bookstores. Friends told friends and posted my messages on corkboards and electronic bulletin boards.

I got great advice, not just from experienced researchers with well-organized collections, but from retired teachers and truck drivers, from scientists, poets, professors, and homeschoolers. Total strangers sent essays, poems, photos, and drawings. They shared stories of insect infestations, fires, floods, and chemical holocausts, of neglectful houseguests and mean-spirited relatives. And they poured out their hearts about their great affection for their books.

Finally, I went to the hundreds of volumes available on book care, book storage, book collecting, and the passion for books. I scrounged through new and used bookstores, checked the online version of *Books in Print*, ordered from publishers' catalogs, and asked friends for contributions from their own shelves.

This Is for Everybody

When selecting information for this book, I tried to be inclusive. For example, I refer to different kinds of expert advice for dealing with the physical book. An archivist will recommend the kind of coddling that is necessary to extend the life-spans of rare and fragile books. A librarian who wants to keep a book in active circulation might suggest a more rugged approach.

A third type of expert advice comes from the book artist/historian, who will want you to adhere to a classic discipline of book construction and design. And yet another type of advice comes from the book collector, who is interested in maintaining and enhancing the value of a book by protecting its pristine condition. Sometimes these experts will suggest the same strategies, but more often than not, they don't agree.

Several philosophical controversies rage through the literature and have peppered many conversations I have had with booklovers and home librarians. I have tried to represent all sides fairly. The most notable disagreements include:

1. *The Craft of Books Versus the Science of Information Question.* Are books a sacred cultural treasure being destroyed by neglect and the juggernaut of high technology? Or are they a fragile and expensive way to handle data, which could be better accessed via online services and interactive, electronic multimedia?

2. *The Book as Tool Versus the Book as Icon Question.* Are books meant to be annotated, ripped apart, and physically transformed to suit the uses of the owner? Or should they be treated with religious respect, virgin except for, perhaps, the lightest of pencil marks in the corner of a flyleaf?

3. *The Weeding Versus Archival Question.* Do we dispose of books we don't want? Or are we constrained by the demands of future historians to preserve everything, no matter how outdated, incorrect, trivial, or damaged?

4. *The Accumulation Question.* Should we use interlibrary loan services when we want to read an uncommon or out-of-print volume? Or should we buy those books, so as not to stress shrinking public and academic library budgets?

5. *The Classification and Cataloging Question.* Are there right ways to organize books in a home library? And what should be done with the people who violate the rules? (And what about all these strange stories about Melvil Dewey,

father of the Dewey decimal classification system and library visionary? Did he really let only young women into his classes at what was then Columbia College? Did many eastern university librarians refuse to use his system while he was alive because he was such a jerk? Inquiring minds want to know!)

6. *The Expert Question.* Who should be the final arbiter of what happens to books and libraries? Is it up to librarians, historians, educators, computer programmers, government archivists, readers, or electronic publishers? Should it be up to any one group or committee? Are public, private, and charitable information goals incompatible? If each community of experts and scholars has a different perspective and a different set of priorities, to whom should the home librarian listen?

Robert Stephens, one of the early printers, surpassed in correctness those who exercised the same profession. To render his editions immaculate, he hung up the proofs in public places, and generously recompensed those who were so fortunate as to detect any errata.
—Isaac Disraeli, eighteenth-century booklover
from *Curiosities of Literature*. Bradbury, Agnew & Co., 1839

---

7. *The Collector Versus the Reader.* There are book collectors who never read the books they own and who talk about their books as if they were only investments. There are book readers who have never taken care of their books and who have destroyed priceless volumes. Are the book collectors who treat books like silver bars really booklovers? Are the book readers who systematically let their books die disfiguring, physical deaths really booklovers? Should books of value to the public be sold to private collectors? And who decides what is of value?

Out of the conflicting opinions, patterns emerged, and I learned an important lesson: Even smart, attractive, experienced, and caring individuals can become hysterical about duct tape.

This Is Useful

Another guideline I try to follow is to make this book useful for the average booklover. You do not need a degree in library science or special skills in Japanese papercraft to improve your home library. I have tried to keep the jargon to a minimum, but you might turn to the glossary, where you will find a few terms that are referred to throughout the book.

The Bloomsbury Review BookLover's Guide starts out with introductions to the art and history of the book. Then, after guiding you through a physical audit of your current collections, the *Guide* follows the life cycle of the book and library, from acquisition to arranging for your library to be adopted after your demise. The last four chapters are devoted to several interdisciplinary issues, including your home library's relationship with the larger information world, the online book and library, the special needs of children and families, and finally, some ideas on how to take care of the other "stuff" that clogs the veins of your house, including legal records, manuscripts, artwork, and music.

I never think of it as a collection.
It's more like someone who lives with me.
—Mike Robinson, booklover, Tacoma, WA

Each chapter of this book also contains a sample of booklover and home librarian resources. The books were in print at the time of publication, and the magazines were publishing, but there are no guarantees. The organizations were contacted, and phone numbers updated. Current prices were checked. The online resources were surfed. Products were purchased or their usefulness verified by reputable informants. Mail-order catalogs were scanned; as a typical booklover, I bought too much and stockpiled goodies that I may never use.

This Is Fun

Books are precious, but without the perspective provided by laughter, humans can become inflexible in the face of crisis and opportunity. If it ain't fun, why do it? I include humorous and offbeat entries on book history, neat gifts for booklovers, and, whenever possible, information that is entertaining.

I allow for some sentimentality on these pages, but I also had no problem poking at the hot air balloons of pontification lofted by the bibliographically correct. The banner of perfection is not raised in these pages. I encourage you to sing, dance, and laugh in the temple.

Bibliomancy *is about using books, particularly religious texts, to seek guidance. First, you proclaim the question while holding the closed book. Then, open to any page, and start reading out loud at a randomly chosen point in the text. What you read should provide you with your answer, although it might take you some time to figure out the implications. Besides religious texts, popular bibliomancy tools include dictionaries,* Bartlett's Quotations, *and anything by William Shakespeare, Lewis Carroll, Emily Dickinson, Robert Louis Stevenson, Ayn Rand, Walt Whitman, H. L. Mencken, and Mark Twain. Books by philosophers and poets work equally well. Try your favorite author.* ❖

It All Started With a Woman
By Don McNatt, programmer and poet, Colorado Springs, CO

Sure, I had always loved books, had several lying around with book-marks somewhere between the "dark and stormy night" and the butler's confession. But the Woman gave me the incurable disease, that insatiable desire to have books around me.

It seemed so innocent, meeting clandestinely in a city I shall not name. I thought it was to be a physical and lustful encounter just like the many that occur every day. If only that were true.

I soon found myself being dragged into a rundown brick building. The sign read "BOOKS—Rare—Used." I'll humor her, I thought. She must have some odd notion of saving money by buying the dirty, tattered discards of libraries and garage sales. Weren't there many bookstores, both new and used, in her own city, with more books than she could ever read? She laughed. Much later I knew that it was the same laugh of the dope pusher when giving out a "free" sample of his wares.

Once inside, I was uneasy with the many dark, dusty, musty stacks of books, magazines, and papers. I still did not know, I did not know! I was innocent as a lamb led to slaughter, as trusting as a child to his father. And she betrayed me. She'd planned it all along.

Casually looking from side to side, I had no desire to pick up even a single dirty, smelly volume that had come from God-knows-where. One book was different. I pulled it from its resting place. It was bound in red leather. I opened to "The Rhyme of the Ancient Mariner." I began to read and was transfixed. I could not put it down until I had read the entire poem.

Just then I heard low laughter behind me. The Woman had found me. I then looked down and found I had not one but four books in my hands. There was Masefield, and Donne, and Whitman, too. A fear gripped me. My life was changed, forever.

I find that I judge new acquaintances by their attitude toward books. I've learned subtle ways to ask without revealing my own condition. I've become a closet book bigot, secretly avoiding those who do not read, own, and cherish books the way that I do. Of course, I have only a few friends now.

But I have my books, more than I can ever read. I revel in the knowledge that no sickness, no snowbound prison, no late sleepless night will ever find me without a book to read.

Now, in spite of everything, I can say to the Woman, "I forgive you." ❖

General Resources for BookLovers
Books for Readers

1997 Writer's Market®. Edited by Kirsten C. Holm and Don Prues. *Writer's Digest, $27.99 cloth, ISBN 0-89879-742-X.*

A best-kept secret of professional writers, *Writer's Market* is an important source of insider information about book publishers, awards, national writers' organizations, magazines that review books, and tips on how to get published, which is one way to get paid (albeit poorly) for reading books. The latest edition contains about 4,000 listings; more than 900 are new.

Benét's Reader's Encyclopedia. Third Edition. Edited by Katherine Baker Siepmann. *HarperCollins, $45.50 cloth, ISBN 0-06-181088-6.*

When a character in a novel refers to Lupercalia, how will you know what he means without this book? How will you find the birthday of poet Kenneth Rexroth or learn the importance of the Jindyworobak movement to Australian writers? Browse the entries for enlightenment about literary references and characters, learn about important figures in world literature you never studied in school, and memorize tidbits to dazzle the relatives at the next family party. The latest edition contains about 9,000 entries.

Biblioholism: *The Literary Addiction.* Tom Raabe. Illustrations by Craig McFarland Brown. *Fulcrum, $10.95 paper, ISBN 1-55591-080-7.*

Raabe offers a test to determine if you really love books to excess. I scored an 18 out of a possible 25; however, I do not consider myself a biblioholic. Here are some sample questions from the test, quoted with permission from the publisher:

> *9. Do you have a personal library on an entire subject, none of which you have read?*
>
> *13. Have you ever been fired from a job, or reprimanded, for reading?*
>
> *19. Did you ever lie about how many books you've bought?*
>
> *21. Has your book buying ever embarrassed your family or friends?*
>
> *25. When a bookstore clerk has been unable to locate a certain book in the stacks, have you ever been able to find that book?*

You might wonder why people think the book is funny, because the author has so accurately described your life. Or, you buy a copy for all of your bookloving friends and hope they will realize how sick they are. However, it is more likely that you will be really irritated because several friends have bought copies for you, and all of them underlined the same passages. As if *you* needed to read them. As if *you* had some kind of problem.

14

The Chicago Manual of Style: *The Essential Guide for Writers, Editors, and Publishers.* 14th Edition. *University of Chicago Press, $40.00 cloth, ISBN 0-226-10390-0.*
Since 1906, people in the U.S. book world have relied on this volume to arbitrate decisions about language, grammar, editing, and book production. The current edition contains 900 pages of information about The Book, from how to number the bastard title page (with a lowercase *i*, please) to how to interpret the zero when deciphering handwritten manuscripts.

The Gutenberg Elegies: *The Fate of Reading in an Electronic Age.*
Sven Birkerts. *Fawcett Columbine, $12.50 paper, ISBN 0-449-91009-1.*
With passion and wit, Birkerts writes about how the package in which information comes does change the way it is absorbed and understood. Here are essays about the joys of reading, the power of the spoken word, and the seduction of electronic data.

The Joy of Publishing. Nat Bodian. *Open Horizons, $29.95 cloth, ISBN 0-912411-47-3; PO Box 205, Fairfield, IA 52556-0205; (800) 796-6130.*
Crammed with book lore, personal insights by important authors, and the kind of information about the publishing industry that takes a lifetime to learn, these stories revolve around both the superstars and the average people in the business, from famous novelists explaining how they write their books to the taxicab driver who collected jokes from his passengers and turned it into a book.

Lost in a Book: *The Psychology of Reading for Pleasure.* Victor Nell.
Yale University Press, $42.00 cloth, ISBN 0-300-04115-2.
Booklovers who are looking for research about their affliction can console themselves with this scholarly exposition of reading. There are statistics about the commerce of bookselling, historical notes on reading and libraries, and explanations about why you read instead of making a living. This book may be out-of-print, but it is worth searching for through your local library.

Ruined by Reading: *A Life in Books.* Lynne Sharon Schwartz. *Beacon Press, $18.00 cloth, ISBN 0-8070-7082-3.*
While the rest of womankind were learning basic life skills, like cleaning and cooking, I was reading. This author, who seems to have shared that experience, explains, in lovely prose, what she has learned from words, and why reading is a necessity for those of us who live in and between the latest books on the nightstand by our beds.

General Book Review Magazines for BookLovers

Subscription fees quoted are for one-year subscriptions in the continental United States, and are subject to change without notice. Most of these magazines offer discounts for multiyear subscriptions and charge extra fees for subscribers outside of the continental United States. Some magazines are for the publishing and library industries, which means the average booklover will read the professional insiders' perspectives, and pay extra for the privilege.

American Book Review. Unit for Contemporary Literature, Campus Box 4241, Illinois State University, Normal, IL 61790-4241; (309) 438-2127; fax (309) 438-3523; e-mail: rcrubin@rs6000.cmp.listu.edu; bimonthly; $24/year.

The Bloomsbury Review®. 1762 Emerson Street, Denver, CO 80218-1012; (303) 863-0406; fax (303) 863-0408; e-mail: bloomsb@aol.com; bimonthly; $16/year.

Booklist. 434 West Downer, Aurora, IL 60506; (708) 892-7465); monthly, bimonthly during summer; $65/year.

BookPage®. 2501 21st Avenue South, Suite 5, Nashville, TN 37212; (615) 292-8926; fax (615) 292-8249; e-mail: ellen_myrick@bookpage.com; monthly; $18/year.

The Boston Book Review. 30 Brattle Street, 4th Floor, Cambridge, MA 02138; (617) 497-0344; fax (617) 497-0394; e-mail: bbr-info@bostonbookreview.com; 10x/year; $24/year.

Chicago Books in Review™. 5840 North Kenmore Avenue, Chicago, IL 60660-3721; (312) 561-6280; quarterly; $16/year.

Choice. 100 Riverview Center, Middletown, CT 06457; (860) 347-6933; fax (860) 346-8586; 11x/year. Call for subscription price.

Hungry Mind Review: *A Midwestern Book Review.* 1648 Grand Avenue, St. Paul, MN 55105; (612) 699-2610; fax (612) 699-0970; e-mail: hmreview@winternet.com; quarterly; $14/year.

Kirkus Reviews. 200 Park Avenue South, New York, NY 10003; (212) 777-4554; fax: (212) 979-1352; e-mail: kirkusrevs@aol.com; bimonthly. Call for subscription price.

NAPRA (New Age Publishing and Retailing Alliance) Review. PO Box 9, Eastsound, WA 98245-0009; (360) 376-2702; fax (360) 376-2704; e-mail: napra@pacificrim.net; bimonthly; $50/year.

New York Review of Books. 250 West 57th Street, Suite 1321, New York, NY 10107; (212) 757-8070; fax (212) 333-5374; e-mail: nyrev.panix.com; biweekly; $21/year.

New York Times Book Review. 229 West 43nd Street, New York, NY 10036; (212) 556-1314; fax (212) 556-7088; weekly. Call for subscription price.

QBR, The Black Book Review: *Our Lives, Our Words, Our Stories.* 625 Broadway, 10th Floor, New York, NY 10022; 5x/year; $12/year.

The San Francisco Review. 582 Market Street, 13th Floor, San Francisco, CA 94104; (415) 403-1330; fax (415) 403-1339; e-mail: sfreview@aol.com; bimonthly; $16/year.

Fun BookLover Product Catalogs

Flax Art and Design. PO Box 7216, San Francisco, CA 94120-7216; (800) 343-FLAX.

Flax is filled with attractive blank books, including a German-made scrapbook of seasoned walnut and handmade paper, designer lamps, magnifying glasses, bookends, and various artist tools for making paper and decorating the results of your bookmaking. Prices range from modest to extravagant, and many items target children of all ages.

Levenger®: *Tools for Serious Readers.* PO Box 1256, Delray Beach, FL 33445-1256; (800) 544-0880; fax (800) 544-6910; e-mail: cservice@www.levenger.com.

When you marry for money and your new spouse asks you what you want, hand her this catalog. Circle the photos of the lovely bookcases, the collection of pillows designed to make reading easier, the museum-quality lamps, the leather accessories, the bookstands, the footstools, and the comfortable chairs.

The products are practical, and they are redolent of money and class. The most appealing gift for the home librarian is the library steps, a simple stepladder with three broad rungs and an optional metal railing.

Organizations for Readers

Groups where readers get together to talk about books are hot stuff. The ones sponsored by libraries, churches, schools, and bookstores are often led by a knowledgeable facilitator, who starts out with a short lecture on a book or author, and then runs an open discussion. Other groups meet in homes and operate as loosely knit collectives. Still others are study groups, where participants exchange views on religion or a self-help topic. The best ones are glued together by people who share a great love of fine writing, an interest in human nature, and an addiction to lively conversation.

A list of such groups would be impossible, but here are five handbooks on the topic. Each provides suggestions for running a successful reading group, with much of the advice coming from experienced participants. Each book also has assembled booklists to whet the appetite. Some of the best advice:

1. Knitting and other forms of handiwork can drive people crazy.
2. Groups can deteriorate into social groups where books are never discussed, if the social hour is not separated from the book discussion time.
3. Be prepared to be horrified by other people's opinions.
4. Look for participants who will be open-minded about your own horrifying opinions.

The Book Group Book: *A Thoughtful Guide to Forming and Enjoying a Stimulating Book Discussion Group.* Ellen Slezak. Foreword by Margaret Atwood. *Chicago Review Press, $12.00 paper, ISBN 1-55652-246-0.*

The New York Public Library Guide to Reading Groups. Rollene Saal. *Crown, $11.00 paper, ISBN 0-517-88357-0.*

The Reading Group Book. David Laskin and Holly Hughes. *Plume/Penguin, $9.95 paper, ISBN 0-452-27201-7.*

The Reading Group Handbook. Rachel W. Jacobsohn. *Hyperion, $10.95 paper, ISBN 0-7868-8002-3.*

What to Read: *The Essential Guide for Reading Group Members and Other Book Lovers.* Mickey Pearlman, Ph.D. *HarperPerennial, $9.00 paper, ISBN 0-06-095061-7.*

See Chapter V for information about magazines, newsletters, and reading guides distributed by leading publishers specifically targeted for reading groups.

The Letter Exchange
By Stephen Sikora, founder, The Letter Exchange, Albany, CA

The most important volume among my books would be my list of addresses. That's the one "book" (a file on my computer, actually) that I can't live without. Interaction with other people, especially through correspondence, sends me back to books and gives me reasons to be reading them. Without a fellow traveler or two to keep me going, the books just sit here, unread. Solitary reading no longer appeals to me very much. Most often I fall asleep! Books by themselves do not provide enough company to make the trip through their pages worthwhile. So I write to lots of people about books, chat with other readers on the Internet, and meet a few in person, as I say, for those weekly sessions of collective reading. The interaction makes all the difference in the world.   ❖

The Letter Exchange celebrates the handwritten letter by encouraging people to write to each other. Subscribers receive a booklet that lists hundreds of individuals who want to correspond with each other about ideas. Many of the participants are book-lovers who want to discuss favorite authors and books. This is not a lonely hearts' club, and scam artists are quickly sniffed out. The Letter Exchange has been around for many years and is one of the best-kept secrets in our culture. **The Letter Exchange: A Magazine for Letter Writers.** *Stephen Sikora, PO Box 6218, Albany, CA 94706; 3x/year. Write for subscription price.*

❖

Few civilizations have not created their
own versions of physical memory.
page 22.

Chapter II — The History of the Book and the Library

Being an Introduction to the Past, Present, and Future of the Book and the Library.

A Brief History

A *book* is a piece of physical memory. It has been incarnated as pieces of ivory, notched sticks, wax tablets, and strings with knots. As a pattern of molecules containing information, a book can be as large as the millions of miles of synapses that connect the World Wide Web, or as small as an array on a layer of silicon.

A *library* is a collection of these pieces of memory. It can be public or private, free or accessible for a fee. It can be stacks of shelves, piles of boxes, sacks, or a deep pit. It is, one would hope, in some kind of order, but in the home library, which is the focus of this book, that order is as personal as a haircut. Once the second copy of the very first book was made, and the two were placed side by side, the library was born.

Perhaps these definitions offend you, because you think they are too broad. You argue that a book can only be stacked, fanned, folded, sewn and/or glued leaves of paper, and that the variations in size are limited by what can be grasped by two human hands. You insist that there must be a cover of leather, paper, plastic, or cloth. The pages are printed with ink, you say, and each page has a fixed and replicable image. As for libraries, you proclaim that each is known by its Librarian, who stands at the front door with a fiery sword, testing the honor of those who would enter the Correctly Organized Sacred Stacks.

A book isn't born until someone reads it.
—Christopher Morley, bibliographer
from *Ex Libris Carissimis*. A.S. Barnes & Co., Inc., 1961

I believe this describes only one kind of book, the Gutenberg-era book, and it has existed in this form for only a very few hundred years. And I don't believe libraries are limited to those collections organized by "real" librarians.

Historians have a good idea where the book was born. Usually, the honors are shared by the civilizations that occupy places now called Egypt and Iraq. In Egypt, the papyrus scroll filled libraries with the wisdom of the ages. In Iraq, in which was then called Mesopotamia, clay tablets were used to store and transport economic and administrative records.

In both cases, the books were made from materials common to their regions. The roots of the words that describe the book in contemporary Western languages are found in the ancient names of these materials and those first used in budding European civilizations: bark, beechwood, water reeds, and clay.

However, somewhere, at some time, almost every material found in nature was used to create an artifact that would be recognized by its function as a book. Few civilizations have not created their own versions of physical memory.

How many schoolchildren have learned about the use of raised, block images to produce books in Asia, or of the hundreds of bookstores that flourished in the Islamic Empire during Europe's Dark Ages, decades before the French and English book fairs and centuries before the Gutenberg era?

Who first repeated pictograms on silk, or duplicated a portrait by pressing a coin into the surface of a piece of leather, or employed the cuttlefish as a source of ink? Who first decorated a buffalo skin with images that represented a chronicle of winters? Who first rolled a linen scroll, or used white paint on black cotton?

Except for a few notable landmarks, such as the generally agreed-upon date, A.D. 105, for the invention of paper in China, historians can be vague about benchmarks in book history. The great library of Nineveh, with its 20,000 tablets, existed in Assyria 2,500 years ago—sort of. I found several different years given for when Johann Gutenberg produced his first Bibles with movable type (1450ish, 1455ish, etc.), partly because the task took years, and it is difficult to agree when to mark THE DATE. (Some historians claim that Gutenberg learned the secret of movable type from a man who had worked for a Dutchman named Laurens Janszoon Koster.)

A culture without books is only alive to the edge of the fingertips of an outstretched hand and within the sound of a voice. Oral histories require the physical presence of the historian, priest, artisan, or trader. That limits the acquisition and spread of knowledge to the intimacy of personal relationships.

---

*You can order a handmade wooden replica of a colonial-era hornbook for only $9.75 from: **The Horn Book, Inc.**, 11 Beacon Street, Suite 1000, Boston, MA 02108; (800) 325-1170. The hornbook resembles a square paddle with a handle. It was designed to protect a single sheet of information from dirt and wear by covering it with a transparent, waterproof sheet of material, such as translucent animal horn. You can make your own version of the hornbook. If you don't happen to have a thin slice of translucent animal horn around the house, kitchen wrap or waxed paper will do. For more information about* The Horn Book, *a magazine about children's literature, please see Chapter XIII.* ❖

If you were not apprenticed to an expert, you had to rely on the trained memories of other specialists. And despite the legendary memorization skills of our ancestors, holding complex legacies of religion, art, technology, and commerce in the minds of a few people makes those legacies exceedingly fragile.

Many factors determined whether books flourished in a particular culture. Was there an available source of materials to make the books: beds of reeds, clay banks, sheep, forests, or inexpensive electronic chips? Was the political climate conducive to the conservation and distribution of information? Were the rulers interested in travel, science, and art, or were war and conquest their major goals? If the rulers were into conquest, were they successful at capturing people with knowledge about books?

The worst thing that ever happened to a fairly large collection of books was that my first wife burned them in the backyard after I deserted her in the early 1950s. We had met in a Trotskyite group in Detroit, and I had several hundred radical books collected. After I left her (it was mainly my immaturity, my fault) she renounced her radicalism. A mutual friend observed the bonfire.
—Anonymous (by request)

Was the culture in a location crossed by trade routes, where travelers could exchange new ideas and technologies? Did the local religion support books and libraries? Did an active commercial community need records to conduct its business and financial transactions?

How was language represented? Was there a written alphabet or just pictograms? Was the culture vital? Were there scholars actively studying and teaching? Were there inventors, artists, and philosophers working their trades? Was there a demand for new books? Was there an appreciation of old knowledge?

Were there bookstores and libraries? Were these available to the average, albeit prosperous, citizen or only to a few elite? As book technologies stalled or faded because of a change in the availability of a material or a change in the political climate, did key people seek out new technologies? Were books fashionable, and thus promoted by the leadership and the influential classes?

Were there some kinds of information that could only be put into book form because of custom, religion, or secular law, such as certain types of literature, sacred texts, or census records? Did someone steal the right technology at the right time? Was someone moved to make a buck? Were there vital professions of scribe and author? Were books a dominant technology? Did someone have the dumb luck to figure out how to make a book, do it more than once, and remember to tell someone else?

On the dark side, political and religious book burners have been around for millennia. If you would salt the earth when conquering a people, destroy their libraries. (And, before you feel too smug, please remember that there are few civilizations, few cultures, few religions, few philosophies that can be said to be exempt from the bonfire mentality. Censorship is not new, nor is it exclusive to either the oppressors of the left or the right. It would take a book many times this size to record the histories of the libraries we know of that have been purposely destroyed.)

The book continues to evolve as the result of collisions of technologies and cultural attitudes. In the past, it was escorted across political and geographical boundaries by armies, merchants, religious fanatics, and thieves. Today, it travels at the speed of e-mail and faxes.

And a library, which used to be a elite depository of knowledge, which you had to visit in person (if you were one of the anointed), has evolved, in one of its forms, into a series of electronic pointers to information, accessible while eating dinner at home, catching some rays at a beachside resort, or traveling above the clouds.

The Technology of Printing — Re-Creating History

Tools have limits, based on size, shape, and the characteristics of the materials from which they are made. Tools are also affected by the skill of the toolmaker and the influence of the culture where the technology is created and used. It is said, for example, that Europeans, during the Industrial Revolution, built better machines, but that the Chinese, in the same era, were more concerned with the final product. Consequently, superior European machine technology could not reproduce the superior paper produced by the Chinese.

You can re-create some of the problems the early book artisans encountered by learning the traditional fine book arts circa the Gutenberg era, as outlined in Chapter III. The catalogs listed in Chapter III and throughout this book can supply you with the same materials and tools that manuscript and book conservators use to repair and replicate great works of book art.

Or you can mess around with tools and materials that will allow you to experiment with the technologies of many different civilizations and, in effect, invent your own book history.

In either case, you will need printing tools, printing surfaces, and printing liquids, which you can find in catalogs, a garden, a kitchen, an empty lot, an artist's studio, a toolbox, a beach, and a kid's chest of toys.

Printing tools might include pens, pencils, brushes, chalk, crayons, knives, styli (this pointed tool can be duplicated with a knitting needle), a single-edged razor blade, and quill pens. An old-fashioned fountain pen will also work just fine, if you don't have a garden full of geese. You can also use chips of stone, bamboo, reeds, twigs, sticks, and plant stalks from the garden. Potatoes, turnips, and other vegetables make great block printing devices.

Besides plain writing paper, printing surfaces you might gather up include a piece of soft rock (such as sandstone), different kinds of cloth, heavy aluminum foil, scraps of leather or plastic, clay, the large smooth leaves from common plants like iris, a brown paper shopping bag, and, if you have access, a sidewalk or a dead tree. Floors, walls, ceilings, and the side of a mountain are also acceptable, if you are replicating the book as a civic monument.

Printing liquids include any liquid or squishy substance you have in the house that can leave a stain. (Please avoid the toxic stuff, and don't mix any man-made chemicals together.) Any kind of paint or ink works well, but you can also use leftover Easter egg dye, cranberry juice, chocolate syrup, shoe polish, crushed fruit, herbal tea, fabric dye, etc.

Now comes the fun part. How does printing liquid A, when applied to printing surface B, using printing tool C, work? Can ketchup be used to create a lasting, legible impression on stone, using a brush made of dried grass? Can a piece of bark be carved with a stone chip as easily as with a metal blade? Your experiments will give you a better idea of what it took to evolve the current versions of the book than any lengthy lecture on the history of printing.

You might run into the same challenges that affected the discovery and invention of printing materials and methods. For example, the liquid needs to be thin enough and smooth enough to flow evenly. However, if the printing surface is too absorbent, the printing liquid will spread, obliterating the image. The printing surfaces might need to be treated so that the pigments in the printing liquids can dry on top of the printing surface, or be absorbed only slightly.

Also, the liquid needs to be dark enough to leave a visible and lasting mark. You will discover that simple vegetable dyes are not as effective as the intense blacks found in carbon-based pigments, such as those that originate in burnt spaghetti sauce.

Surfaces that are meant to hold a physical mark, such as stone or wood, need to be soft enough to take a mark, but not so soft that the mark will disappear. That is why cultures in countries such as Korea and India, which developed metal-based book crafts, could not rely on using pure gold, a notoriously soft material.

One advantage of the book and protobooks, such as scrolls, has been their portability. Heavier materials were more suitable for archives and ceremonial pieces; lighter materials were for libraries and commerce. In creating your book, you will have to choose a balance between strength and weight.

Some printing tools are too tough for a printing surface. A very sharp tool will destroy the surface of papyrus and similar materials, so even though Egyptians had plenty of birds whose large feathers were available for making quills, reed pens were used instead. The sharpened quill pen did not come into favor until parchment and vellum replaced papyrus.

Multiply these concerns by the thousands of combinations of tool, surface, and liquid, and you will see why, although most cultures have had their version of printing and the book, only a few succeeded in discovering and developing lasting technologies.

Evolution of the Printed Word

Most typestyles we use today evolved from attempts to work with the restrictive characteristics of particular materials. For example, the finishing stroke that a woodcutter or stonemason used to end a carved line evolved into serifs, which are those extra little marks that accent the ends of the strokes of the letters on this very page. The stroke of a brush, made of soft hair, or the scratch of a sharpened edge of a metal knife, the imprint of a leaf, the grain in a block of wood, the shadow cast from a raised piece of metal: These images inspired the design of type.

Twentieth-century technologies have removed the boundaries of type design; check out advertising art in better magazines to see what is happening at the cutting edge of graphic design. Art school exhibits are a good place to monitor the bleeding edge.

By the way, if you are thinking of inventing a new type of book or book-related product, be aware that books have their own class designation in the U.S. Patent System: Class 281—Books, Strips, and Leaves. Dozens of subclasses include Book or Leaf Holder (045.00), Protectors (020.00), and Scrapbook Binding (022.00).

An Animal Inventory

From animals, humans have used bone, horn, tooth, and ivory, both as materials on which to carve and as tools with which to mark and sew.

Wax was used to coat tablets of wood. Pre-Christian- and Christian-era Roman schoolchildren could smooth out the impressions their styli made and use the tablets over and over.

Fur, hair, quills, and whiskers have been used in different types of book preparations, from the manufacture of felt used in printing and binding to the creation of fine covers. Brushes, still vital tools in bookbinding and repair, are graded by the quality of the animal hair and fur used in their manufacture, with manmade bristles considered a distant second.

The skins of animals have been made into vellum, parchment, and leather. Also, animal hides were used as storyboards, where pigments from clay and ore, together with plant and animal dyes, created images that tracked historical events and weather patterns, recorded the genealogy of a tribe, appeased the gods, honored feats of bravery, or marked a trade route.

Curing processes kept hides supple and prevented them from rotting so they could be used as writing surfaces and covers. Some processes used salt and plant extracts; others used enzymes found in the organs of the same animals that supplied the hides. The fact that many older manuscripts and books are in such good condition is a tribute to the skills of the early tanners.

Books in a home library represent place, created and inhabited.
—Bernadine Clark, author and writer, Winter Park, FL

Blood, milk, and egg have been used to produce ink, paint, and glue. I won't disturb your breakfast with some of the less palatable book manufacturing substances found in living tissues, but there is a documented tradition in the printing trades of using urine and saliva to temper rollers so they are soft enough to deliver ink at the right flow. Also, during my years as a printer, I was advised that using certain bodily fluids was the time-honored method of adjusting the chemistry of liquids used in photolithography.

From silkworms and bees come silk for the fabric used in scrolls and beeswax for treating the fine linen thread used in sewing the best books. The crushed bodies of some insects have been used to make dyes. From mollusks, artists have extracted various inks and dyes, and pearls and mother-of-pearl have adorned the covers of many precious volumes.

Fish parts can be boiled for glue, and their skins have been used as a writing surface, as have, according to one authority, the intestines of serpents. Tortoiseshell has been used to strengthen the points of quill pens, which were harvested from any one of several large birds, such as geese, peacocks, and crows, while feathers have been used in ornamental inlays for centuries.

The End of the Gutenberg-Era Book?

In 1994, a dramatic increase in the cost of paper coincided with an increase in the cost of postage. Some book publishers closed down; others produced fewer new titles on cheaper paper. A stampede of businesses headed toward the online services in an attempt to replace their print catalogs with electronic versions.

The doomsayers were ecstatic. Conventional printing was dead, they announced. As further evidence, they cited the fact that more encyclopedias were being produced in electronic form than were printed on paper. Also, textbooks were being replaced by online services that guaranteed the latest product, and book fairs and library conferences were dominated by computers and CDs. This book was written in 1996. Is the book dead? I contend the book is still evolving, and the definition of *book* is changing, because our choices are increasing. But the book, as defined as a piece of physical memory, will never die.

What Happens to Old Technologies Versus New Technologies?

Here is a list of technological evolutions. In each case, when the new technology was introduced, some people thought that the old technology would disappear. Others thought the new technology was just a fad and that the old technology would maintain its dominance. What did happen in each case?

Old Technologies	New Technologies
Sailing ships	Engines/Powerboats
Horses/Wagons	Engines/Automobiles
Drawing/Painting	Photographs/Film/Videos
Storytelling	Writing/Literacy
Calligraphy	Typography/Printing
Live theater	Movies/Television
Home cooking	Restaurants/Packaged food
Gardening	Farming/Agribusiness
Musical instruments	Records/Audiotapes/CDs
Healing	Medicine
Books/Libraries	Computers/Online services

1. *The old technologies still exist.* Storytelling conferences attract thousands of participants, and garden seed and supply companies proliferate like weeds.

2. *The old technologies are sources of inspiration.* Professional film actors return to the theater to refresh their skills. Regional home cooking and traditional dishes supply the basis for the latest trends in the restaurant industry.

3. *The old technologies require lots of human interaction.* No one has invented a computer that can train a cutting horse. Many naturalists believe that drawings of plants and wildlife are better tools than photographs for identifying individual species, because art can isolate and emphasize specific characteristics, such as shape and relative size.

4. *The new technologies tend to have more power and impact on the economic lives of individuals and institutions.* The latest television series, not the latest winner of a playwriting contest, will dominate the covers of newsmagazines and the

conversations of investment bankers. Millions are made from expensive medical technologies, not from the healing touch of a parent's hand on the forehead of a feverish child.

5. *The old and new technologies coexist.* The same person can appreciate a handmade dulcimer and the latest music synthesizer. A nurse can use both massage and sophisticated drugs to help a patient control pain.

6. *The new technologies have experienced more change in the last fifty years than old technologies experienced in hundreds of years of human history.* Technological innovation influences technological innovation, so that change flickers through the chemical and computer industries at an exponential rate. But a cook is still a cook. A storyteller is still a storyteller. And, even with the electronic boat gizmos that can plot a course and send out distress signals, a sailor still needs to be able to make decisions based on the feel of wind and water.

How does this model apply to books?

Why Books Will Never Die

1. *Books still exist and will continue to exist.* The book arts are flourishing, in universities and galleries, at art festivals, and in private studios. For every publishing house that fails, there seem to be three new ones eager to grow in its place. The used and rare book businesses are booming.

2. *Books are still a benchmark for technological friendliness and are continuing sources of inspiration.* Some claim that one of the paradigms that holds back the development of electronic multimedia is that of the book, in the same way that the efficiency of early automobiles lagged for decades because car designers duplicated the structure of horse-drawn wagons. However, many of those computer programmers who design what appears on a computer screen use the Gutenberg-era book as a standard of beauty and practicality. Also, it is still true that the important ideas that excite people and make a lasting impression still seem to come from books, not from sound bites and computer games.

3. *Books are a human-sized technology and require human interaction.* A book is a teddy-bear technology, dragged along in the dirt by one hind leg. You take it to breakfast, snatch a quick read at stoplights, pack it on picnics, immerse yourself in it on the bus, and prop it on your tummy or knees in the bathtub. You snuggle under a quilt on a cold night with a warm four-year-old on your lap, and the two of you trace with your fingers the blueberry stain you left on your copy of *Curious George* when you were four.

And you don't need batteries.

4. *Books are linked to the higher profile, high-technology industries.* Books are talked about, even though the emphasis is on the celebrity of their authors, the movie rights, the television series, and the amount of the advances paid.

5. *Books and information technology coexist.* Most of the people I know who love computers, love books. A world-famous engineer of my acquaintance, when writing a complicated text on chemistry, spent months making sure the typography of each page of formulae looked good. The computer sections of the bookstores I frequent are growing.

6. *Change affects both books and electronic information sources, but at different speeds.* My home library contains useful books more than 140 years old, and books with texts that are thousands of years young, but I have changed my computer hardware and software three times in the last six years. I don't complain, because each move has provided me with better tools with which to do my work. But it is disconcerting to be forced to discard a software package fresh from the box, only because the software company has come up with a new version and has stopped supporting the old one.

Editor's note: Johann Fust was the man who bought Gutenberg's presses when he was forced to sell them to pay his debts.

The tradition of the Devil and Dr. Faustus was said to have been derived from the odd circumstances in which the Bibles of the printer, Fust, appeared in the world. When Fust had discovered this new art ... he undertook the sale of a considerable number of copies of the Bible in Paris. It was his interest to conceal this discovery, and to pass off his printed copies for [handwritten] manuscripts. [The process] enabled him to sell his Bibles at sixty crowns, while the other scribes demanded five hundred. [Fust] produced copies as fast as they were wanted, and even lowered his price. The uniformity of the copies increased the wonder. Informations [sic] were given in to the magistrates against him as a magician; and in searching his lodging a great number of copies were found. The red ink, and Fust's red ink is peculiarly brilliant, which embellished his copies, was said to be his blood; and it was solemnly adjudged that he was in league with the Infernals. Fust at length was obliged, to save himself from a bonfire, to reveal his art to the Parliament of Paris, who discharged him from all prosecution in consideration of the wonderful invention.
—Isaac Disraeli, eighteenth-century booklover
from *Curiosities of Literature.* Bradbury, Agnew & Co., 1839

And what about the future of the library? Popular media presents public and school libraries as anachronisms; if you believed the newsmagazines, you would assume the physical library is dissolving into a ghostly, electronic vibration, bouncing off satellites and streaming through glass fibers. Even schools are being built without space for libraries. But hundreds of public and university libraries are being built or renovated, even as these words are written.

The book and the library are not going to die. They will survive in many forms. The book will be craft. The library will be place and community. They will both be survival tools, like a penknife or a stout rope. And, to use a current cliché, they will reinvent themselves, as they have for thousands of years, by embracing new technologies and new materials, even though those new materials may not be mud and reeds found along the banks of an ancient river.

Resources for Book Historians

Book Publishers for Book Historians

Oak Knoll Books and **Oak Knoll Press.** 414 Delaware Street, New Castle, DE 19720; (302) 328-7232, toll-free order line (800) 996-2556; fax (302) 328-7274; e-mail: oakknoll@ssnet.com.
Catalogs and newsletter available.

One of the treasures of the book world is Oak Knoll Books and its imprint, Oak Knoll Press. In only twenty years, they have grown to include a leading antiquarian bookstore and mail-order service for books on books, a publishing house, and distribution service. They also run one of the nicest book-related web sites on the Internet. (See Chapter XII for more information.)

If you are interested in almost any aspect of the book, from collecting books about books to learning about papermaking and printing, you will find Oak Knoll a prime source of new, used, and antiquarian books. Here are some examples from their current catalog.

ABC for Book Collectors. Seventh Edition. John Carter. Revised by Nicolas Barker. *Oak Knoll Press, $25.00 cloth, ISBN 1-884718-05-1.*
"All extremes are a bore." *ABC* is an annotated dictionary of more than 400 entries related to books, printing, publishing, and book collecting. Carter's scholarship, combined with Barker's fine-tuning of the most recent editions, would have been enough to make this book important to the bibliophile. But it is the humorous asides, skewing the profession of book collector, that make it a perennial classic. A "must buy" for the booklover.

The Art and History of Books. Norma Levarie. Foreword by Nicolas Barker. *Oak Knoll Press, $29.95 paper, ISBN 1-884718-03-5.*
One blessing of contemporary publishing is the trend toward reissuing classics. Oak Knoll has rescued Levarie's book, first published in 1968, and produced an inexpensive edition. Levarie scrolls through the entire history of book artifacts, with an emphasis on the Gutenberg era. There are dozens of black-and-white reproductions of book artifacts.

Second Impression: *Rural Life With a Rare Bookman.* Barbara Kaye (Mrs. Percy Muir). *Oak Knoll Press, $35.00 cloth, ISBN 1-884718-04-3.*
Many of Oak Knoll's books are personal histories, journals, and annotated bibliographies of people who helped shaped the modern international book community. *Second Impression* is a recent contribution, which offers insights into the creation of the International League of Antiquarian Booksellers and some of the controversies surrounding book collecting after World War II. Many serious U.S. booklovers are Anglophiles, and one of the attractions of the book is the details presented of life in England after the war.

Dover Publications. 31 East Second Street, Mineola, NY 11501. Free catalogs.
I love Dover. Zillions of catalogs, plump with inexpensively reproduced books on zillions of topics. No phone numbers, no credit cards, no fax, no e-mail. You pay the old-fashioned way, with a check in the mail. Many of their books are replicas, which is a nice way of saying Dover saves money by printing from images of the existing pages, rather than resetting the type. Their 1995 catalog boasts more than 5,800 titles. Several more of their book-related books are listed in Chapters III and Chapter IX. Diringer's book (below) is the most significant volume they publish on book history.

The Book Before Printing: *Ancient, Medieval, and Oriental.* David Diringer. *Dover, $12.95 paper, ISBN 0-486-24243-9.*
Someday, some scholar without a distracting personal life will put this monumental work on a computer database and create a decent cross-referenced index of its contents. Until then, I will continue to mutter to myself as I attempt to navigate its dense pages, choked with a kudzu-like knit of historical data about the book and library. Unlike most of the other popular book histories, this is about everything BUT the Gutenberg-era book. The dry, scholarly style allows for the optimal compaction of too much information in a paltry 600 pages.

Other Book and Library Histories

Book. Karen Brookfield. Photographs by Laurence Pordes. *Knopf, $19.00 cloth, ISBN 0-679-84012-5.*

If you don't have children, you might not know about the remarkable Eyewitness Books series. *Book*, like the rest of the series, is meant to be a picture book for children, but it has the substance of an adult text and the artistic flair of a coffee-table museum piece. Each page is crammed with colorful artifacts, photographed against a white background so that the images visually pop out. You can study each item's details without a distracting background. The accompanying text is simple, without condescension. In many ways, *Book* is a full-color summary of David Diringer's monumental text.

The Joy of Books: *Confessions of a Lifelong Reader.* Eric Burns. *Prometheus Books, $24.95 cloth, ISBN 1-57392-004-5.*

Eric Burns chats about books and reading the way you wish your next dinner party partner would chat. He drops names and facts in every paragraph, with all of the gossipy details that make you believe he was there. The highlight is an eyewitness account of a book burning in a midwestern town, which he describes in the clinical fashion of an ex-newsperson. Even when he is most indignant, Burns still remembers that he is talking about human beings.

Printing's Past and Poems for Printers. Frank Granger.
549 Harper Davis Road, Lake Wylie, SC 29710; (803) 831-2614.
Send SASE for more information.

Frank Granger charms readers with his unpretentious way with words. He has created a series of columns on the history of printing and related subjects, which he syndicates for free to magazines and newspapers; he also sells the bound columns in small booklets. He collects provocative quotes, researches historical figures, and, like the beloved columnist in a small-town paper, talks the reader through the story as if he were leaning over the back fence on a late summer day. He is also trying to revive the tradition of printer's poetry and has published a chapbook of poems. This is a "labor of love, not profit" and is funded by the sale of the booklets and chapbooks.

A class of artisans were trained to burnish the pages of the first printed books so that they would resemble the older handwritten manuscripts. The technology of printing was too newfangled for some booklovers; they needed the familiar imperfections of the handwritten book. ❖

The Smithsonian Book of Books. Michael Olmert. *Wings Books, distributed by Random House Value Publishing, $24.95 cloth, ISBN 0-517-14725-4.*
Another case of a rescued book, reissued only three years after the original edition. It pulses with lavish color photos of tools, art, bindings, paintings, and snapshots of the ephemera for which the "nation's attic" is known. It makes a perfect gift for the booklover to give to a "book-liker," with its interesting tangents on culture, politics, and art. The most dramatic examples of the latter are two reproductions from the series of paintings N. C. Wyeth did for the 1911 edition of Robert Louis Stevenson's *Treasure Island.* The brooding images could have been taken from the cover of a contemporary, illustrated, heavy-metal novel.

Book and Library History-Related Organizations

To explore the history of books, start with the resources in your own neighborhood, such as libraries, universities, museums, and historical societies. National organizations often operate on tiny budgets and have over-worked staffs, so be patient. Also, please respect their criteria for membership.

American Historical Association (AHA). 400 A Street SE, Washington, DC 20003; (202) 544-2422.
This organization is the umbrella for dozens of scholarly historical societies. If you have an interest in the history of books that refer to a particular aspect of culture, science, art, politics, etc., this organization may be a place to be referred to a more specific organization.

American Printing History Association (APHA). Executive Secretary: Stephen Crook. Berg Collection, New York Public Library, Fifth Avenue at 42nd Street, New York, NY 10018; $30/individual, $35/institution. Publications: *APHA Newsletter,* quarterly; *Printing History,* biannual.
APHA was founded in 1974 to encourage the study of printing history and its related arts and skills, including calligraphy, papermaking, bookbinding, illustration, and publishing.

American Society of Papyrologists (ASP). Scholars Press, PO Box 15399, Atlanta, GA 30333-0399; fax (404) 727-2348; e-mail: scholars@unix.cc.emory.edu. Annual dues: $40.00.
ASP was founded in 1961 to further the study of ancient Greek and Latin papyri and of the materials contained in them. The Society supports and encourages research in the field, the teaching of the discipline, and opportunities for international cooperation by the scholars in the field.

Bibliographical Society of America. PO Box 397, Grand Central Station, New York, NY 10163; phone/fax (212) 647-9171. Write for current schedule.
Membership is open to all those interested in bibliographical projects.

Institute of Paper Science and Technology. 500 10th Street NW, Atlanta, GA 30318-5794; (404) 853-9500; fax (404) 853-9510.
Printing and graphic arts. A museum of the history of papermaking is at the same address. Historic book collection on printing and papermaking. World's largest library on pulp and papermaking. All open to the public.

Print Council of America. c/o Richard Field, Yale University Art Gallery, PO Box 208271, New Haven, CT 06520-8271; (203) 432-0628; fax (203) 432-8150.
Museum curators' organization for graphic arts.

Society for the History of Authorship, Reading and Publishing (SHARP). Dr. Linda Connors, Drew University Library, Madison, NJ 07940; $15/year.
SHARP is one of the new virtual professional organizations, managed electronically across thousands of miles. It has an inclusive membership policy that spans academic boundaries. The newsletter contains information about international publications, education, research, and conferences.

❖

... you can play with materials and tools
not very different from those used
by a book artist hundreds of years ago.
page 38.

Chapter III — The Book Arts

Being a Discussion of Some Aspects of the Craft of the Book and Some Resources to Tickle the BookLover's Artistic Palate.

A BookLover's Journey

My bibliocentric world changed for the better thirty years ago. Up to that time, I cared only about the brains of a book; its body meant nothing. Then, in my sophomore year of high school, my journalism advisor, Ferne Hoeft, showed our class of budding writers and editors how the skillful choice and arrangement of type could guide the eye of the reader down the page. I had not known until then how to savor the rhythms of beautiful typography. I did not know to look for the extra ink that outlines printed characters in a book printed by a letterpress, or about the almost invisible ridges of ink that run through the center of characters printed using the gravure process. I started thinking about how my words looked, not just what they said.

Three years later, I was suffering through my first and last official college poetry critique. The professor announced that my writing was "accessible and derivative," which is academese for "Go home and marry for money, so that you do not starve as a poet." Having been rejected by the establishment, the only way my poems were going to be published was if I printed them myself. I marched into the shop of the college printer, Jim, and asked to be taught how to run a printing press. Jim obliged immediately by setting me to work.

In China [around the time of the birth of Christ], writers were recording their notes on slips of bamboo. The slips of bamboo were held together with a cord of silk or leather. The intellect of a scholar was judged on how many carts it took to carry all his books when he took a journey.
—Frank Granger, Director of Graphic Arts,
Central Piedmont Community College, Charlotte, NC

Frank Granger © 1994. From *Printing's Past II*. All rights reserved.

A few hours later, I was smeared with oily ink and madly, passionately, hopelessly in love with printing. I was no longer someone who merely read books and aspired to write them. Now I was someone who could create books, even though, at the moment, I only knew how to watch sheets of paper move through a press.

For the next twelve years, I lived the bohemian life of the poet who prints. Sometimes, I took a job outside of publishing to pay the bills, but mostly I wrote books, designed books, hand-bound books, printed books, sold books, and learned what I could about the book arts. My efforts were quite modest, and I never blossomed with artistic talent. But I developed a knack for running a printing press in a commercial shop, and I learned enough about printing and publishing to teach beginner classes and introduce others to the love of making books.

I learned that a book is more than the author's podium. It is an object that has a separate existence from the author and publisher. It can evoke a positive, emotional response, just like any other work of art. Because books traditionally were made from organic materials, the rituals of creating a book by hand give the same soul-soothing satisfaction as throwing a clay pot, sewing a quilt, weaving a blanket, kneading and baking bread, or even planting a garden.

Practicing the books arts was another way to make the magic of books "accessible," to use the same word with which that poetry teacher chastised me almost thirty years ago. I learned how to repair books by making them. Also, knowing about the book arts added a new dimension to my love of books and libraries. The more I knew, the more ways a good book could make me happy. The combination of great writing, lovely paper, elegant typography, graceful illustration, and skillful binding can fill my senses like an English cottage garden on a sunny day or a seven-course meal with rare wine.

The book arts world encompasses calligraphy, illustration, printmaking, photography, typography, painting, sewing, papermaking, paper marbling or marbleizing (a paper decoration technique), leatherwork, and hand-binding. The books arts are about the chemistry of dyes, the discipline of fine engraving, and the construction of paper boxes.

There are several kinds of book craftspeople. Many, for example, have committed themselves to obedience to the discipline of the traditions of bookmaking, starting from the time when scrolls were being replaced by flat sheets, folded and sewn. If you choose this path, you can play with materials and tools not very different from those used by a book artist hundreds of years ago. Linen thread, bone folders, goat leather, cast-iron book presses, beechwood book boards, paper made of 100 percent cloth rags, and gold leaf are available by mail order, and every major city has institutions offering classes. Each time you dip a piece of paper into a pan of swirling color to create tinted endsheets or thin a piece of leather with the edge of a sharp blade, you act out of the heritage of generations of bookmakers.

A subset of the traditional book artists is the elite of the corps of book conservators; they work for the best museums, libraries, and archives. The book artists who care for rare books know the history of the time in which a specific book was created and something about the author and subject matter. Their educations include chemistry and art history, and they must have the intellectual discipline of the scholar and the physical dexterity of the artisan. And the best have that indefinable gift of good taste. Becoming one of them takes nearly a lifetime.

One reason the book arts are so popular is that there really are no rules. Artists influenced by design trends, such as the Bauhaus movement or the campy "atomic" themes of the fifties, and the popularity of nontraditional materials, such as aluminum and nylon, have been driving the purists crazy for decades. How *dare* they, huff huff.

If you are creating a book for yourself, you have many choices. You can use only historically accurate materials, or you can make your book from recycled plastic, tin cans, electronic parts, and synthetic fabric. You can make one-of-a-kind books that are polymorphous toys in the shapes of balls, kites, dolls, and moving vehicles. You can make a book from glass and mirrors, or the parts of an old guitar. You can invite other artists to contribute and construct a book that is a compilation of mail art from around the world. And, as many book artists are discovering, you can create physical memory that is art by manipulating bytes of information on a computer.

Some of the academic book art societies can be a little intimidating. Some of their members will insist that there is only *One Book* and only *One Right Way* to make one. My solution is simple: Learn as much as you want and can about the traditional bookcrafts, so that you can apply that wisdom when you create a book that is truly your own.

The invention of what is now called the Italic letter in printing was made by Aldus Mantius, to whom learning owes much. He observed the many inconveniences resulting from the vast number of abbreviations, which were then so frequent among the printers, that a book was difficult to understand; a treatise was actually written on the art of reading a book, and this addressed to the learned! [Mantius] contrived an expedient, by which these abbreviations might be entirely got rid of, and yet books suffer little increase in bulk. This he effected by introducing what is now called the Italic letter, though it formerly was distinguished by the name of the inventor, and called the Aldine.
—Isaac Disraeli, eighteenth-century booklover
from *Curiosities of Literature.* Bradbury, Agnew & Co., 1839

Even a little knowledge about the craft of books will destroy your innocence. You will flinch from the bad cover art on most bestsellers, which is meant to sell books the way boxes of breakfast cereal are sold. And when you sit down at a restaurant, you may check the menu's typography as a way of determining if the meal will be any good. When one of my printing mentors was handed a magazine of hard-core pornography, his first act was to examine the photographs under a magnifying glass. He was more interested in the quality of the printing than in the provocative images. Rest in peace, Ed.

Devouring Your Library

You will find that many of the most elite products advocated by the traditional book artists are based on plant products so pure that you can probably eat them and suffer little harm. Here is an untried recipe for an edible book that I concocted many years ago. Proceed with caution, however; my lawyer could not advise me on the legal precedents for damage claims from trying to make a book that can be eaten. I have no idea if this will work.

The idea is to imprint the leaves of edible rice paper, the kind found in gourmet, health, or Asian food stores, with edible pigments smeared onto block prints carved from raw veggies. The mess created in your kitchen is forecasted to approximate the level of disaster left behind by an egg-coloring party, so be prepared with lots of cleanup towels and patience.

Assemble the usual implements you use when playing with your food: bowls, potato peelers, small knives, cutting boards, waxed paper, and a couple of paintbrushes that have never been used.

The vegetable of choice is potato, but jicama or any other firm, large tuber or fruit will do. Instead of rice paper, try wonton skins or egg roll wrappers; most grocery stores stock the skins and wrappers near the tofu. Please check if the printing surfaces can be eaten raw, or if they need to be baked or cooked before or after the printing process.

The ink can be made from red beets (a jar of beet borscht is a ready-made source), raspberries, homemade cranberry juice (reduced in a saucepan over low heat to a concentrated ruby glow), or turmeric, the bitter yellow spice that gives yellow mustard its sunny color. Chocolate syrup, maple syrup, and jam have been proposed. (A friend suggests milk-based products, red wine, or any other beverage that has ruined a good blouse or tie.)

After you have carved the appropriate symbols or letters into the surface of the vegetable, dip or paint the face of the image with the dye substance. While the surface is still damp, press it into the surface of the printing material.

Allow the printed sheets to dry thoroughly on waxed paper or your marble candy slab, the same place where you make chocolate truffles. A clean kitchen counter will do. Then, to facilitate folding, moisten each sheet along a line bisecting it in half. The sheets can be stacked and creased along the softened spine. The book is completed by gently pinching the folded edge.

What would such a book say? "EAT ME," of course.

My books and bosom have been subjected to: spaghetti sauce, oatmeal clumps, dustings of all kinds of sugar, hamburger drippage, and burrito debris. The occasional translucent bacon spot. A more unusual fate befell my only copy of Leonid Leonov's The Thief. *At the time of the incident (sixteen years ago), it wasn't that easy to find, either. What spilled all over* The Thief *was a medium-sized bottle of Future® floor wax. It solidified into a book-shaped block that sat in the sun and hardened until I had to chip the pages apart with a chisel, and it made my hands smell awful. I still have the book. What I learned from this is never to wax your floor, no matter what.*
—Robin Chotzinoff, writer, Indian Hills, CO

The World's Largest Book

The word for "book" in English and many European languages, according to some historians, has its origin in the word for beech tree. Beechwood was and is used in making books. You can engage your family in designing a tremendous literary pun by creating a giant group book on the sandy surface of a beach.

Assign each family member a rectangular portion of the beach to mark off as a page, using sticks, reeds, shells, and stones. The pages should have just enough room between them for the authors to work. (Please watch out for broken glass, and do respect the environment, if you are visiting a fragile ecosystem.) Then, with a writing instrument (big toes are recommended), each author fills his or her page with messages, pictographs, and mythic symbols, and adds recycled treasures rescued from the sand. In a project like this, age, experience, and talent are not necessarily advantages.

Depending on the size of the group and the number of pages, this monumental beach book will look quite impressive from a distance and probably confuse both visiting UFOs and black helicopters.

It will fail as book art if you stick to the strict definition of a book, since a beach is hard to transport in a backpack. However, you can cart along a camera and take pictures from some higher vantage point of the individual pages and their authors, then bind them together. (The pages, that is, not the people.)

If it seems a little silly, keep in mind that a New York art gallery would serve white wine and charge audience members $25 a head to participate.

41

Sixteen Ways to Get Started in the Book Arts

Bookmaking

1. Go to an art supply store, or use one of the catalogs listed in this book, and buy a couple of sheets of one of the fancier papers. Cut the sheet into small rectangles the size of an 3" x 5" index card. Stack no more than four of the sheets on top of one another, and fold the entire stack along the middle. (It does not matter which direction you fold.) You now have a *signature*. If you sew the sheets together along the folded edge, you have sewn a small book.

2. Make another book, using different stitches.

3. Make more books, using different kinds of thread, yarn, and string.

Papermaking

4. Make your own paper. The basic recipe is simple. Fill an old blender (to which you do not have an emotional attachment) halfway with water. Add a few postage stamp-size pieces of paper torn from the unprinted edges of a newspaper and blend on low for a few seconds. (Remember to put the cover on the blender.)

Repeat until you get a thin soup of paper fiber. This is called a *slurry*. Pour the slurry through a fine screen, such as a piece of fine mesh metal screen or a piece of muslin drawn taut across an embroidery hoop. Let the mess dry thoroughly and remove the dried fibers. You will have a funny-looking, slightly bumpy piece of dry pulp. This is technically a piece of handmade paper.

5. Add different kinds of plant fiber to the basic slurry, blend, and see what happens. Small snips of fabric, grass clippings, flowers, and plant stalks are favorite ingredients. Avoid adding paper with print, because the pigments can overwhelm the final product and you want to be able to savor the subtle textures made by the different materials. The thread in dyed fabric will usually hold its pigment without bleeding too much. If you want to see pieces of the ingredients intact, they can be stirred directly into the slurry without blending.

Decorative Arts

6. Take a class in calligraphy.

7. Decorate a book cover. Start with a commonly available paperback (so you can experiment with a clear conscience), and glue, staple, or sew a collage of images and materials to the cover. A child might be delighted with a fake fur cover for a favorite copy of *Rabbit Hill*, particularly if you remember to attach button eyes and string whiskers. A science-fiction book might look good wrapped in foil, with wire for antennae bristling from the front. Or, paste your own face on one of those humid bodies on the cover of a romance novel.

8. If there is some other craft at which you excel, you can transfer that set of skills to the book arts. A potter can make a book from clay. A quilter can quilt a cover or create a book that is a wall hanging of open pages. A woodworker can create a book box with a cover that shows a scene from a beloved work of fiction. A gardener can preserve flowers to ornament the cover of a book of love poems.

9. Create an accordion-fold book. Fold a piece of paper as if it were an accordion. (What were accordion folds called before accordions?)

10. Cut some stiff, lightweight material into identical strips, and then sew the strips into a fan. Each strip can contain a line of poetry, a quotation, or a picture.

11. Scrapbooks were once a popular bookmaking technique. Although they are still used to hold memories of a special event such as a wedding or anniversary, the electronic era has eliminated the need to collect information and paste it in a book. (See Chapter XIV for more information about protecting family photos and keepsakes.) And, of course, many of the techniques we once used have been discredited, because the glues and pastes destroyed those precious pictures. But you can construct a scrapbook using archival-quality materials and use it to create a temporary collection. A college student who has no time to read the hometown newspaper from front to back might like the gift of a few months of interesting clippings, presented in book form.

12. Most book artists take formal classes, such as summer residence programs. You can combine a vacation with the challenge of learning a fine craft. Age, gender, experience, and education do not matter.

13. If you are part of a book reading group, encourage the other members to get involved in the book arts. You might be able to find a local book artist, perhaps disguised as a librarian or school art teacher, who would be willing to do a brief demonstration, and lead you and your bookloving friends in a session of bookmaking.

14. You say you are too embarrassed to take a craft lesson or even express an interest in the book arts? If you offer to help out a children's bookmaking class for a scout troop or museum program, you will have the fun of learning how to make a book, under the cover of being a concerned adult who cares about helping youth.

15. Use paper, leather, and cloth to create miniature books to hang from your holiday tree this December. The books can contain blank pages, or you can ask family and friends to contribute art and text.

Book Construction

16. Take an old, worthless, clothbound book apart. See if you can put it back together. Make another book from the pieces you have left over.

Resources for Book Artists

Most of the resources in this section relate to some aspect of the construction of the Gutenberg-era book, and fall under the category of "hand-binding" or "bookbinding." Some address specific interests, such as marbling or calligraphy. Some will be carried by your local art supply store.

The materials and tools used to create books and repair books overlap, so in this chapter I have chosen to include companies that specialize in traditional book arts materials and tools, which are also applicable to book repair.

Chapter IV has a list of general supply catalogs for home libraries, Chapter IX has more information on repair resources and conservation organizations, and Chapter XII discusses the best web site to explore the book arts online. Chapter XIII lists books and kits for children and families, and Chapter XIV focuses on the archival needs of the nonbooks in your library, such as photographs, CDs, sheet music, artwork, and business records.

Catalogs and Directories for the Book Arts

The Book Arts Classified and **Page Two, Inc.** *"The 'town square' of the book arts community,"* bimonthly; $12/year; and **The Book Arts Directory.** $9 annual. Tom Bannister, PO Box 77167, Washington, DC 20013-7167; (800) 821-6604; fax (202) 895-6048, (800) 538-7549; e-mail: 74603.1175@compuserve.com.

Both the newspaper and the directory are small gems of typographical art, and are packed to their paper gills with dozens of listings for both suppliers and small fine book artists. Calligraphy, papermaking, and fine printing are all here, as is contact information for meetings, classes, publications, organizations, and collaborative projects. These two publications are excellent places to start your exploration of the book arts community and to locate book artists, schools, and businesses near you.

Bookmakers. 6001 66th Avenue, Suite 101, Riverdale, MD 20737; (301) 459-3384; fax (301) 459-7629; e-mail: bookmowery@aol.com.

This is the best overall catalog for the hand-binder I have found, with all the supplies you would need to make or repair books. More than a third of this catalog is devoted to the different kinds of paper and leather used in the book arts; this reflects Bookmakers' relationship to Pyramid Atlantic, a center for book arts that shares its physical space. (The other fine catalogs I tracked down are either much broader in scope or focus on one book art.) The catalog is well organized and easy to use. The beginning book artist will also find the source for a variety of educational videotapes from the Guild of Book Workers, available for rent or sale.

Colophon Book Arts Supply. 3046 Hogum Bay Road NE, Lacey, WA 98516; (360) 459-2940; fax (360) 459-2945; catalog $2.

When I ordered a modestly priced book from this supplier and the order was delayed a couple of weeks, I received a friendly call long distance asking if I still wanted the book, and if it was all right for them to cash my check. That kind of personal service is not unique in the book arts world, but it is the hallmark of small firms like Colophon. The focus of this catalog is marbling, both traditional and Oriental, but like the other catalogs in this chapter, there are general hand bookbinding supplies as well. Several of the products offered have been developed by Don Guyot, an experienced paper marbler and teacher whose friendly letters preface the catalog.

John Neal, Bookseller. 1833 Spring Garden Street, Greensboro, NC 27403; (910) 272-7604; fax (910) 272-9015; $3/issue; membership in Letter Arts Book Club (LABC) $7.50/year.

A feature of this mail-order company is its own book club. Join the Letter Arts Book Club and receive four catalogs a year of books, supplies, and book arts–related gifts. LABC also offers discounts for many of their offerings, which will more than pay for a subscription.

The book arts teacher, hobbyist, and professional (particularly the calligrapher) will find what they need to pursue their crafts, including papyrus, inks, paper, pens, and vellum, and technical books on manuscripts, lettering, and the book arts. Beginners will find books on a wide range of book art subjects, and sprinkled throughout are fine booklover gifts, including calendars and, of course, beautiful books on art, history, and literature.

Journal of Artists' Books (JAB). 324 Yale Avenue, New Haven, CT 06515; semiannual; $9/year.

Not all book artists are traditionalists concerned with replicating the efforts of cloistered monks. JAB uses jagged words and images, culled from contributors who seem mostly interested in testing late twentieth-century cultural icons from the mass media, politics, and art, all through the medium of the book.

Keith A. Smith. 22 Cayuga Street, Rochester, NY 14620-2153; phone/fax (716) 473-6776.

Smith focuses on the bare-bones structure of the book: the architecture of folded sheets of paper held together by thread. His books can be purchased bound or unbound and feature dozens of techniques for constructing books that require only paper, thread, scissors, and needles.

Like many book artists, Smith has balanced the merits of tradition and modern technology. Besides publishing technical books and creating one-of-a-kind artist's books, Smith sells an up-to-date list of more than 650 book arts resources on a Macintosh-compatible diskette for a measly $5. Several of the catalogs in this book carry his works, or you can send him an SASE and request a brochure.

Kodansha. Sales Department, 114 Fifth Avenue, 18th Floor, New York, NY 10011; (800) 788-6262; fax (201) 933-2316.

Japanese papercraft is an important field of study in the book arts. Many book arts catalogs carry Japanese papers, and bookbinders use Japanese sewing and box-making techniques in their pieces. Kodansha publishes a wide range of English-language titles of Japanese craft books, including books on design, paper, box construction, paper marbling, and card design.

Lyons & Burford. 31 West 21st Street, New York, NY 10010; (212) 620-9580; fax (212) 929-1836.

In the introduction to their spring 1996 catalog, the publishers explain their philosophy of publishing books that are "small" in scope, with specialized audiences. Thank goodness that book artists are one of their small audiences. You will find some of their books described in Chapters VI and IX. Besides their own fine craft books, they distribute from the lists of Oak Knoll and Design Books.

Organizations for Book Artists

Never try to write a book about an explosively popular topic. You will be overwhelmed by daily reminders, in the form of brochures and letters from newly minted organizations, of how inadequate you are to the task. You are about three phone calls away from any number of organizations devoted to the book arts, from library schools and art programs to craft festivals and small publishing houses. Please see Chapter XII for online sources of current book arts organizations. Also, at the end of Chapter IX is a list of regional book conservation organizations that can lead you to book arts groups. These New York organizations are places to plug into no matter where you live, if you don't know who to call locally first.

American Craft Council. 72 Spring Street, New York, NY 10012; (212) 274-0630; fax (212) 274-0650; $40/year.

Hours: Monday through Friday from 1:00 to 5:00 p.m. Phone calls and visitors are welcome during these hours. Summer hours may vary. Collections of the library include materials on the book arts. In addition to assisting library visitors, the staff responds to mail and telephone inquiries. In-depth research requests cannot be undertaken by library staff; however, library staff will discuss possible solutions and give referral information. Nonmembers are charged $5 per visit. METRO (New York Metropolitan Reference and Research Library Agency) referrals are accepted free of charge.

The Center for Book Arts. 626 Broadway, 5th Floor, New York, NY 10012; (212) 460-9768; fax (212) 673-4635; e-mail: bookarts@pipeline.com; associate membership $35/year.

The Center for Books Arts, founded in 1974, is "dedicated to the preservation of the traditional crafts of bookmaking, as well as contemporary interpretations of the book as an art object." Besides classes and exhibits, the Center offers apprenticeship and internship programs, lectures, and studio rentals.

Guild of Book Workers. 521 Fifth Avenue, 17th Floor, New York, NY 10175; (212) 757-6454. Write for current information or contact the regional chapters listed below. E-mail: Karen Crisalli, president, at karenC5071@aol.com. Bernadette Callery, membership secretary, at bcallery@flounder.com.

The Guild of Book Workers is the national nonprofit organization for all the book arts. It was founded in 1906 and currently boasts more than 900 members worldwide. Areas of interest include bookbinding, printing, conservation, marbling, calligraphy, and papermaking.

Regional chapters include: New England, New York, Delaware Valley, Potomac, Midwest, Lone Star, California, Rocky Mountain, and Southeast.

Books for Book Artists

The average neophyte book artist should expect some challenges when hunting down books on the theory and practice of the book arts. Art supply stores and museum bookstores are likely to carry a better selection of book arts books than your local bookstore. Also, because of the various disciplines involved in the book arts, you might have to hunt through several different sections to find what you need. For example, you will find additional books on the book arts in Chapters IX and XIII. Many of these books are reprinted from originals, some dating back many decades.

Despite my fondness for craft books, I know, from firsthand experience, how frustrating it can be to try to learn a craft from a book, unless you already have training in art and craft techniques. However, once I took instruction under the patient and skilled guidance of an experienced artisan, who also knew how to teach the artistically challenged, the books made sense.

The Art of the Comic Book. Robert C. Harvey. *University Press of Mississippi,*
$22.00 paper, ISBN 0-87805-758-7.
The Art of the Funnies. Robert C. Harvey. *University Press of Mississippi,*
$19.95 paper, ISBN 0-87805-674-2.
Together, the two books provide a serious look at this century's illustrated
storybooks for adults, from a scholar's and practitioner's point of view. Influenced
in part by the adult comic books produced in Japan, by movie art, and by computer tools, more and more book artists are using the storyboard model of the
comic in their works. The line between so-called comic book art and serious
book illustration is fuzzier than ever.

The Art of the Handmade Book: *Designing, Decorating, and Binding One-*
of-a Kind Books. Flora Fennimore. *Chicago Review Press, $11.95 paper,*
ISBN 1-55652-146-4.
This book is earmarked "for the talented beginner" and for "ages 10 and up."
Start with this one if you want some easy and attractive successes right away.
Please note that the author suggests the use of products such as rubber cement,
which do not hold up well over the years.

Bookbinding: *Its Background and Technique.* Edith Diehl. *Dover,*
$16.95 paper, ISBN 0-486-24020-7.
Another Dover reprinted classic, first published in 1946, with 400 pages of
text on the development of bookbinding. For your reference library of historical
book art techniques.

Bookbinding and the Care of Books. Douglas Cockerell. Introduction by
Jane Greenfield. *Lyons & Burford, $16.95 paper, ISBN 1-55821-104-7.*
A master's description of bookbinding and the care of books, first published in
1902. Except for a few dubious practices that would make contemporary book
conservators shudder, such as rubbing Vaseline® and castor oil into leather bindings, this book is surprisingly accessible (there's that word again) to the beginner.
Introduced by my favorite book conservation author.

The Centaur Types. Bruce Rogers. *Purdue University Press, $14.95 paper,*
ISBN 1-55753-076-9.
Rogers was one of the book art gurus of this century. This reprinted replica is
a small gem. Originally self-published as a private press book in 1949, this fresh
edition demonstrates how a master of type and book design pays attention to the
tiniest details to create a work of art.

Cover to Cover: *Creative Techniques for Making Beautiful Books, Journals, and Albums.* Shereen Laplantz. *Lark Books, $24.95 cloth, ISBN 0-93727-481-X.*

Cover to Cover is recommended by a hand bookbinder with decades of experience and some impressive art awards, who wants to make book arts easier for people like me. Lots of pictures and easy-to-understand illustrations.

The Craft of Bookbinding. Manly Banister. *Dover, $7.95 paper, ISBN 0-486-27852-2.*

This is a good introduction to the use of some of the arcane tools of the bookbinding profession. It uses both photographs and illustrations to get its ideas across.

Creative Bookbinding. Pauline Johnson. *Dover, $12.95 paper, ISBN 0-486-26307-X.*

A well-known standard of bookbinding, written very much like a college textbook. For the person who needs lots of structure, but still wants to experiment. This was the very first book on bookbinding I bought, and it provided the background I needed to understand what was happening in the classroom.

The Design of Books. Adrian Wilson. Foreword by Sumner Stone. *Chronicle Books, $14.95 paper, ISBN 0-8118-0304-X.*

When I first become interested in designing books more than twenty years ago, Wilson's book was recommended. It is a combination of designer's manual, with samples of type and page layout, and history book. Although much of the information dates back to the prehistoric era before desktop publishing and computer-aided design, the principles are eternal. Wilson explains the joy of type and the mathematics behind the design of margins, the history of papermaking, and what makes a good page design. (This book may be hard to find, since it seems to have been "remaindered" just before this guide went to print. I was able to find copies for about $6 on the discount shelf of a large bookstore.)

Hand-Made Books: *An Introduction to Bookbinding.* Rob Shepherd. *Search Press, $16.95 paper, ISBN 0-85532-754-5.*

Full-color photographs of a serious-looking human being operating bookbinding tools will benefit many beginners. The British vocabulary (what is *mull?*) might be a little confusing to U.S. readers, but it also adds a little romance. Also, the author suggests practical alternatives, which can be found in the average home, to specific bookbinding tools. This and other fine craft books by the British Search Press are available from Arthur Schwartz and Company, 234 Meads Mountain Road, Woodstock, New York 12498.

Hey Look . . . I Made a Book! *A Step-by-Step Guide to Creating Your Own Notebook, Sketchbook, Dreambook, Anything Book.* Betty Doty and Rebecca Meredith. *Ten Speed Press, $7.95 paper, ISBN 0-89815-686-6.*

An unpretentious introduction to the book arts in a small book format. Unlike the other books listed here, the authors are interested in encouraging you to write books, not just make them.

How to Marbleize Paper: *Step-by-Step Instructions for 12 Traditional Patterns.* Gabriele Grunebaum. *Dover, $2.95 paper, ISBN 0-486-24651-5.* **Techniques for Marbleizing Paper.** Gabriele Grunebaum. *Dover, $2.95 paper, ISBN 0-486-27156-0.*

The lovely, swirly-looking papers you find in finer books are called marbled or marbleized paper. This, I believe, is the most difficult of the book arts, because of the intricacy of the process.

The basic idea is to gently plop colored pigments into a flat pan of water so that the plops float on top, undisturbed. You then swirl the plops around with an object like a steel comb so that they form feathery patterns. Are you still with me? Then, you gently transfer the pigments to paper or cloth, first dipping the sheets into water behind the floating design, without ruining the fragile patterns, and then lifting the sheets.

You cannot imagine all the things that can go wrong. Buy these inexpensive books and drool over the pictures, then find a class or ten to take. And be patient.

Making Paper: *A Look Into the History of an Ancient Craft.* Bo Rudin. *Lyons & Burford, $40.00 cloth, ISBN 1-555821-167-5.*

If you are getting serious about the book arts, you need to get serious about your paper. This book will inspire you past the blender and shredded newsprint stage, with information about historical techniques and paper chemistry.

Type and Layout. Colin Wheildon. Foreword by David Ogilvy. Edited and with an Introduction by Mal Warwick. Afterword by Tony Antin. *Strathmoor Press, 2550 Ninth Street, Suite 1040, Berkeley, CA 94710-2516; (800) 217-7377 (orders only, please); $24.95 paper, ISBN 0-9624891-5-8.*

Although I get a kick out of the no-holds-barred type design of magazines such as *WIRED*, I admit that I prefer books that use type design that is legible, which is not necessarily the same as boring. The problem is that many of the people responsible for making type decisions learned their trade at the keyboard of a PC; the desktop publishing revolution destroyed the typography trade in less than a generation. This book helps plug the gap.

Wendell Minor: Art for the Written Word: *Twenty-Five Years of Book Cover Art.* Edited by Wendell Minor and Florence Friedmann Minor. Introduction by David McCullough. *Harvest/Harcourt Brace, $30.00 cloth, ISBN 0-15-600212-4.*

Book illustrators must read the heart and mind of a book in order to give it a compelling face. This book shares the thoughts of authors who have had that kind of psychic reading performed by Minor, a contemporary master of book jacket illustration. It is a book for inspiration and enlightenment.

Which Paper? *A Guide to Choosing and Using Fine Paper.* Silvie Turner. *Design Press, $24.95 paper, ISBN 0-8306-3967-5.*

Although the focus of this book is fine art papers for the graphic artist, the book artist will find much useful information, with tips about paper care and selection. There is also a handy list of international sources for fine paper, historical information, and explanations of terms and practices. This book is no longer in print, but it is worth hunting for in libraries and used bookstores.

❖

A friend can be a reality check
on how good or bad things really are.
page 59.

Chapter IV — Analysis and Evaluation

Being a Grand Tour of Your Home Library and the Books Within,
With an Emphasis on Saving the Best of What You Have.

The Home Library Audit

Some people boast about the bad condition of their libraries: the disorganization, the strata of dust, the gaggles of cobwebs, the shakiness of shelves, and the inaccessibility of significant parts of the collection. This chapter is not for them.

The difference between a bunch of books and a library is the difference between not knowing and knowing. So long as you are content not to know a better way of physically caring for your books, it is just a bunch of books.

It is also the difference between no action and action. You may know that those leaning art books will eventually warp, that the pretty covers on the children's books in the spare room will fade to nothing in the morning sun, but knowledge does not necessarily translate into action.

Also, it is the difference between blind acquisition and thoughtful discrimination, in the best sense of the word. Do you acquire more books than you can physically and financially care for?

Where and how we keep books often is a balance between will
and serendipity and may relate to the size of our house and
paycheck, the limits of our ego, the length of our life, the height
of our ambition, the depth of our curiosity, the perimeters of our
escape, the shape of our fantasies, the texture of our temperament,
the extent of our family cooperation, and
the amount of time we have.
—Bernadine Clark, author and writer, Winter Park, FL

What is the right amount of money to budget for the care of your books? Protecting the cover or dust jacket of a newly acquired book might cost roughly $.50 to $3.00 per item. Cleaning or replacing the cover of one leather book, replacing the endsheets, repairing torn pages, removing the worst stains, and reinforcing the hinges could end up costing you $300 or more, depending on the extent of the damage, the value of the book, the cost of materials, the skill of the conservator, and your desires.

Replacing a book that is damaged beyond repair might only mean a quick trip to a local used bookstore and the outlay of a shiny quarter or months of searching, with a hefty price tag when you do find the item. Then, of course, there are the minimal costs of cleaning, storage, and insurance.

Most booklovers choose to be unconscious about the cost of managing their collections. "Loving" books is enough for them, until a beloved book is lost forever because of neglect.

The home library audit will help you begin to move from not knowing to knowing, from no action to action, and from blind acquisition to thoughtful discrimination. The purpose of this audit is threefold:

1. *You will establish an overview of the physical state of your collection.* You will be able to choose which books and which parts of your library need emergency first aid, which ones are doing all right but will need surgery and hospitalization in the near future, and which ones will be fine for a long time.

Books in your home library that need immediate assistance might include books that have value to you because:

    a. They have historical or cultural importance to you, your family, your community, or scholars.

    b. They are part of an investment collection.

    c. They contain important information.

    d. You love them.

If you classify every single book you own under one of these four categories, ask yourself which of these books you could not replace; the answer might help you decide which books to check first. What if you have decided that everything you own is irreplaceable? Then decide if your home library, in its current state, is the best place for your books, or if you need to move them to a professionally maintained archive. Meanwhile, start somewhere, even if it is with only one short shelf's worth of books.

2. *You will be able to identify the steps you need to take.* You will create a plan based on your budget and available time, before you frenziedly begin to slap adhesive tape on ripped covers and haul boxes to the dump, only to collapse in a cloud of dust and despair after a few hours. You will be able to create reasonable library improvement projects that have a beginning, middle, and end. You will be in control. You will be able to look people in the eye and say, "My home library is in very good shape." Your posture will improve, and your complexion will clear. You will no longer apologize to your books in the middle of the night. You will sleep better. Trust me.

3. *You will be encouraged to reduce the number of books you live with to a more manageable level.* You will begin to ask yourself some hard questions before you acquire a book, and you will ask some equally difficult questions about what you need to weed from your collection.

Other choices for managing the number of books you buy include winning the lottery and starting your own used bookstore. (See Chapters V, VI, and X for more solutions.)

Depending on the size of your library, this audit can take anywhere from thirty minutes to several hours. However, it will take forever if you forget these three important rules:

1. *This is not the time to fix problems.* At this stage, you are just looking, making notes, and putting paper flags in books and at locations that need immediate attention. If you stop to fix each damaged book, you are doomed never to finish.

If a book is in immediate danger of dissolving in a pool of water or being eaten by active mold creatures from the Planet Xcucon, you can place the book in a resealable, airtight, plastic bag, and put it in your freezer. This will slow down, stop, or kill whatever is destroying the book. Yes, you put the book in the bag while it is still damp. If you stop your home library audit to dry the book the correct way, with pages interleaved with absorbent paper, you will take forever to finish.

Remember, freezing the book will not repair the damage. It just buys you time. As of this writing, a European study shows that freezing and defrosting books does not affect the strength of the paper, even if it is done more than once. See librarian Susan Hartman's exclusive report on this topic later in this chapter.

If the book is dry but falling apart, you can put the book plus any loose pages in an envelope, box, or bag until you get it repaired.

2. *This is not the time to do a complete inventory.* Counting and cataloging books can take weeks, as can dusting, rearranging, building new bookshelves, and moving boxes up and down stairs. The only items you will need to handle are the ones in immediate need of CPR: Compassionate Publication Rescue.

I do not have a home library. I have books stuffed everywhere and hundreds of them in boxes in the basement, under the bed, in closets. Spaces in my house that don't have something specific assigned to them, such as a cat bed, or a blender, or a plant, or clothes, invariably have books lying around.
—Ron Else, Federal Personnel Specialist, Lakewood, CO

If you have an emergency need to inventory your books for insurance purposes, and you do not have the time to create a written list of hundreds of titles, ask your insurance agent about using a still camera or video recorder to create a visual record of your library. Be sure to date the images and have someone witness the process. Such visual records are a common means of keeping track of valuable collectibles. See Chapter VIII for more information about inventories, insurance, and appraisals.

3. *This is not the time to read the books.* Lash yourself to the mast, metaphysically speaking, plug your ears, and ignore the siren call. Be harsh. Be cold. If you succumb, you will forget your goal of taking better care of your library, tempted by the immediate gratification of losing yourself in the addictive pages of your fourth grade geography book. You will tell yourself that you can take the time to just flip through a few pages. This is a bald-faced lie, and you know it. This is the kind of rationalization that got you 5,000 musty books in the first place.

Tools for the Audit

Here is a list of the basic tools for the audit.

1. *A way to take notes.*

If you want to begin the practice of book care correctly, choose a pencil over a pen; you don't need the humiliation of smearing your volumes with ink from a leaky ballpoint. If you are the chatty type, use a tape recorder. If you are facile with the computer, remember that you want to collect data, not design the ideal data collection system, at least not at this point. Instead of using a database program, just open up a document in a word processing program and make a simple list of things to do as you go along.

2. *A tape measure.* You might be surprised at how many linear feet of books you have, and how few linear feet of bookshelves on which to put them. Do you know how deep and long your existing shelves are? How many books per foot, on average, your shelves can hold? How many additional feet of shelving it will take to put on display those fourteen boxes of books stashed in the furnace room? Chapter VII discusses these issues in detail.

3. *White slips of paper.* You will want some physical way to flag both individual books and specific physical locations that need help. White is best, because you do not want to risk pigments from the paper slip staining the pages of a damp or fragile book. Remember that paper is very absorbent.

The experts will tell you to buy expensive acid-free paper; you can find many varieties in the mail-order catalogs listed throughout this book. But unless you are convinced that you have very fragile and/or valuable books in your collection, acid-free paper slips are not necessary.

A good rule of thumb is not to put anything in a book that you would have to worry about causing damage if you forgot and left it in there for a couple of years. Paper clips can rust, rubber bands can turn black, and any object, other than a flat piece of paper, can dent pages.

The kind of white paper or card stock sold for office use is appropriate for home library use. Don't use the excuse of not having the perfect paper slip to keep you from conducting your audit. Plain white index cards are fine.

If you want to be extra careful, don't use the ubiquitous yellow sticky note. It can leave a residue and, in time, its adhesive can discolor whatever it touches.

Also, as I have learned from firsthand experience, sticky notes, when exposed to extreme heat, such as that generated in the trunk of a car on a hot day, can weld to a page. Removing the sticky notes after this happens requires great care, because pages and covers can rip.

4. *Airtight, resealable plastic bags.* During the triage process, as mentioned earlier, you might find a book that is rapidly self-destructing.

    a. The book is wet.

    b. You smell mold, and the mold you can see is damp and looks alive.

    c. The book is inhabited by what are clinically referred to as "ooky, crawling things."

The experts will want you to take the items to a commercial cold storage facility that is designed to accommodate books, or at least some kind of food or chemical storage warehouse with big freezers. Professional disaster recovery experts will use freeze-drying techniques to remove the moisture, but these can be expensive processes and must be applied almost immediately. Chapter IX has information about how to find such commercial sites.

Home refrigerators and freezers, the experts tell us, do not keep items cold enough, and the temperature and humidity fluctuate too much. But these appliances are better than nothing and are a satisfactory place to keep a particularly suicidal volume until you can enlist professional help. The cold temperature can slow down or kill various molds and bugs, and stop the damage.

I prefer to put books into new, resealable plastic bags because they are clean, transparent, and airtight. In a crisis, you could reuse plastic bags from the grocery store, such as those used for produce or bread. These bags, however, are not designed to survive cold, damp conditions. Also, the bugs will like the fact that you left English muffin crumbs at the bottom of the bag, and will take this as a sign of your affection.

The resealable bags made for use in home freezers have a place on them for marking with a indelible ink pen, but if you want to be extra careful, do not use any pen on or near the bag. It is easy to smear ink from your hand to the book, particularly if you have the extra klutz gene.

Instead, make a dated inventory sheet of the books you are putting in cold storage on a piece of paper or on your computer. Or, put the information on one of your white cards, in pencil, and slip it into the plastic bag with the book.

If the book is really wet, there is a slight danger that the card will adhere to the book when it freezes. You can put the card in the freezer in its own plastic bag. Or, wait until the book is frozen solid. Then, open the bag, put the identifying card on top of the book, and close the bag. You can also put a piece of waxed paper between the card and the book. Note that sealed books can still pick up odors from your freezer, particularly if they are left there for many months.

5. *Tyvek® bags.* What if you find a book that is dry, does not smell strongly musty, does not have the local Bug-Faced Benevolence Association picnicking in its pages, but the glue and thread in the bindings have given way? If the book has deteriorated into a pile of pages and you are afraid that the contents will be lost unless something is done right now, you can use a Tyvek bag.

Tyvek, which is made of polyethylene fibers, is what makes those free, oversize envelopes used to send priority and overnight mail pretty much indestructible. I don't think it is reasonable, however, to expect the postal clerk to hand over several hundred of them for a home-improvement project.

You can buy both Tyvek envelopes and flat sheets at office supply stores, commercial paper store outlets, and art supply stores. Tyvek is a very safe material to use around damaged books. It does not interact with moisture or most chemicals, so it will not make the situation worse. I don't recommend the self-sealing Tyvek bags for the freezer, however, because the seals are not very good, and the material is opaque. But if that old book with the damaged pages could be further damaged by contact with regular paper, Tyvek is a readily accessible choice.

Of course, you can dump the book and its loose pages into any kind of bag, small box, or large envelope. It just depends on how reckless you are feeling that day, how valuable the book is, and how long you plan to keep that book in that bag or envelope. Chapter XIV lists some sources for the kinds of boxes and bags used by experts to protect valuable books and papers that have fallen apart and can't be readily repaired or rebound.

6. *Paper towels, garbage bags, dustpan, broom.* You will want your basic cleaning tools for dealing with the dust and garbage you find in your bookcases. This is not to say you are going to clean every shelf right this minute. But if you find something that needs to be swept up immediately and put in the trash—say a dead mouse—it is nice to have these tools ready.

Disposable paper towels ensure that you do not accidentally transfer mold and insect eggs from one part of your collection to another with the careless wipe of a cloth rag. If you prefer to use cloth rags, the experts will tell you to use undyed cotton, to use the rags only once before putting them aside to clean, to wash them in mild soap, and to rinse very well before drying them. (Fanatics will suggest sun-drying as a way to sterilize the fabric.)

Mops, rags, brushes, and dusters that are used around books should be constantly checked for dirt and kept clean, oil-free, and dry. Some cleaning tools are sold impregnated with cleaning solutions, which can stain your books. One-Wipe® cleaning cloths are the preferred choice of some book conservators, because the treated fabric does not leave a residue. When in doubt, check your purchase with a local book expert.

To prevent dirt from falling into the pages, books need to be cleaned before they are removed from the shelf and opened. They can be vacuumed on the shelf, but loose book parts can be accidently sucked up by a vacuum cleaner. A piece of cheesecloth, placed between the brush attachment and the hose, will keep your vacuum from inhaling a loose piece of cover.

> *I no longer keep track of paperbacks. They are free to roam in and out of my library without restraint.*
> —Jonathan Zimmerman, architect, San Francisco, CA

To clean an individual book before it is opened, tip the book so that the dirt falls away from the spine and toward the *fore-edge*, which is the side of the book where the pages open. Wipe away from the spine and toward the fore-edge with a cloth or rag. Some people prefer a soft paint brush or shaving brush.

7. *A sturdy stepladder.* Most of you probably think that you only need to pull out that rickety old kitchen chair with the uneven legs that you use whenever you need to get something down from the top shelf of the ten-foot-tall cabinet in the spare room. That's what most households have for getting things down from high shelves.

It is why those books on the top shelves often turn to topsoil before they are ever read. If you have books out of reach, you need an easy means of getting to them for audits, cleaning, and practical access.

Hardware stores sell sturdy ladders. Buy a ladder tall enough to allow you to reach the very top shelves of your collection without having to stand on the top rung. Ideally, you want a ladder tall enough so that you can scan the top shelf at eye level; otherwise, you can never be quite sure of the condition of the shelf or books. If a colony of Something has staked out a claim in the Himalayas of your collection and if your ladder is too short, you won't be able to tell until it is too late. Short ladders also make cleaning improbable, unless you own extra-long vacuum extensions.

Wooden ladders, in particular, can deteriorate over time. Check ladders for cracks and loose hardware before using.

8. *A friend or relative to keep you on course.* A friend can be a reality check on how good or bad things really are. A friend can hold the ladder. A friend who

does not live with you and is not accustomed to the intense tropical odor emanating from your old newspaper pile can help sniff out rotting books. People can lose their sense of smell as they age. If you are in your silver or golden years, a younger person might be more sensitive to book odors.

A friend should not be another fanatic booklover. Otherwise, both of you will sit down to read together, when you should be measuring, documenting, cleaning, documenting, and measuring. A friend can keep you from losing yourself for hours in old copies of *The Saint* or *Tarzan*.

The Audit Questions

As you scan the shelves, you will be:

1. Removing books at risk and putting them in a safer environment, even if only temporarily.

2. Getting an overview of display and storage problems.

3. Taking measurements.

4. Noting what needs to be done and in what order of importance.

Here are the audit questions. Even if you don't do a formal audit right now, you can use these questions as the basis for the incremental improvement of your home library.

1. *Are there any visibly (or olfactorily) ailing books?* The last time you looked, everything was fine; but Eisenhower was president then, and many of us thought everything was fine. Out of sight, out of mind.

Once the deterioration has started, it will not stop. Your problem will be to decide which books need immediate help and which are valuable enough that they need to be pulled and treated, no matter how small the damage.

You definitely want to remove a book immediately from its surroundings if:

a. *You discover wet books.* Paper loses 90 percent of its strength when wet, so handle damp books very carefully. Resist the urge to open them and flip through the pages; it is likely that the pages have stuck together and your well-meaning efforts will make things worse. Slip each book into the plastic bag and seal it up. Then place the bag in the freezer, after making a note of the name of the volume and the date you put it away, as described above.

Old cloth covers are notorious for bleeding pigment when damp. Check the covers of adjacent books, wooden bookshelves, and any other absorbent surface that might have been stained by contact with the offending fabric. Until the stained surfaces are clean and dry, it is best not to put any books on or near them.

Leather was once living skin, and leather covers can suck in moisture from the air until the damp, dead flesh becomes a breeding ground for microscopic beasties, which feed off the leather and cause permanent damage. Yuck. A book conservator will dry out the leather and treat it with strong chemicals to kill the infection and protect the book from future damage, but there is little he or she can do to restore the book cover to its former state. A new cover, unless unacceptable because of archival concerns, is the best solution.

Unless you are dealing with rare antiquities (which you allowed to GET WET?), you can remove the covers from the books and freeze the pages. The covers can be frozen in separate bags, to save for the person who will be fixing the book, in case there are any parts to salvage or to help replicate historically important artifacts. (You allowed valuable books to GET WET?) If you are dealing with valuable or rare books, call in expert book preservationists. The pages of the rescued books probably will be permanently wrinkled from the moisture.

In the unlikely event of divorce, those books are
(Daffy Duck voice) MINE! MINE! MINE!
—Carol Kimball, artist and puppetmaker, Denver, CO

---

b. *There is a live infestation of insects.* How can I say this tactfully? If you can see things moving among the shelves, you'd better move fast. Where there are insects, there are insect eggs. And larvae. And pupae. And corpses. Vacuum up the invaders and dump the bag in the garbage can outside your home. I am not talking about exotic bookbugs from the Congo: Cockroaches like bookbindings and glue. No more needs to be said.

Refrain from spraying the area with bug poison, at least until you have removed all the books from the immediate area; the ingredients in pesticides can stain, especially the oils. This is also true of the environmentally friendlier products; many contain citrus oils that can mark your books permanently. See Chapter VII for information about cleaner methods to keep insects out of your library.

Be wary of pest control advice from experts who are museum-quality book conservators. These folks can have a zero tolerance for book critters. Museums seek and receive special dispensation from the EPA and other government agencies to bomb their collections with highly toxic chemicals that are totally inappropriate in the home.

If it is the books that are moving, the situation is beyond the help of this modest volume. Ask your library for the number of a book-sensitive exterminator.

If the bodies of the books have been physically invaded, it is time for the deep freeze. While the insects hibernate in comfort, plan your next attack.

c. *There is a strong odor.* I discovered one rack of damaged books during an audit at a friend's house by following my nose. When I opened one old paperback, the stench was overpowering; the mold had literally turned the center of the book to mush; we discovered the whole shelf had become a blue cheese farm.

A visit to my own home library revealed several common problems.

First, many of the older paperbacks were disintegrating. Most were published before 1980; the glue in the spines had dried out or rotted. In the worst cases, pages were spilling out from the covers and dropping to the floor, or drifting behind the shelves.

Second, elderly, clothbound hardbacks were suffering from unraveling spines and covers. The colors of the covers had faded to a uniform reddish brown, and some of the spines were literally hanging on by only a thread. Many were inherited from parents, moved half a dozen times through several states, and were rarely opened.

I went for the books that had discolored covers first. I found about fifteen books that, on closer inspection, smelled like mushrooms. Green mold had autographed the pages. I threw away half of them (after making some hard decisions about replacement costs, etc.) and ripped off the covers of the volumes that were smelly but clean. I put the intact book innards in a dry, clean, dark space and left them to fend for themselves for a few months in our dry Denver climate. When I looked in on them, the odor was gone. I sent them to a professional binder, who refitted them with new cloth covers.

If you have not checked your library in a long time and you live in a damp climate, this first stage of the audit might dishearten you. If it is any consolation, the only book professionals I interviewed who consistently take excellent care of their own books at home are those whose collections are financial investments.

A librarian might tell you that missing pages are a signal to discard the book. A conservator or collector might want you to check each volume for torn pages. You need not take the time to check each book for internal damage during this audit. If you cannot see or smell the problem, it can wait.

In the future, you can mend your books as you use them. Also, you can check your books a few at a time for internal damage as part of your new ongoing maintenance plan. (Did I warn you there was going to be homework?)

2. *Are the books stored so that they are protected from heat and light?* So, you think, first she tells me to watch out for damp, and now I am supposed to look out for heat and light? Make up your mind, Pat!

Sorry to make your life more difficult, but books are affected by heat and light, as well as water. Think of heat and light as radiation damage, as vibrations breaking up molecules and destroying the genetic integrity of your books. Colors fade, paper bakes, fibers tear, glues disintegrate.

What you are looking for during the audit are direct sources of sunlight and heat. Active fireplaces, hot air vents, space heaters, stoves, and shafts of sunlight falling across bookcases are the most common culprits. Sunlight and heat damage cannot really be repaired, but only patched up or treated to prevent further damage, so badly parched books will need special care. The best you can do for your library during the audit process regarding heat and light is to move the books out of harm's way, or move the source of the problem. See Chapter VII for more information about light damage.

3. *Are the books stored so that you can keep them clean and dry?* Every expert I consulted on the subject of book care said the same thing, over and over: It is relatively easy to keep books in decent shape and relatively difficult to get them back into shape once they are damaged. At this point in the audit, you are going to make some difficult decisions about the location of your books and the ease with which you can inspect and care for all of them in the future.

My library is more like a set of lungs than a castle.
It grows and shrinks. It breathes.
—Mike Robinson, booklover, Tacoma, WA

The two most common problems in book maintenance, besides outright abuse by the average human, are accumulated grime and moisture. Accumulated grime can be dealt with by regular cleaning, which means you have to be able to vacuum and dust the books and their immediate environment. Otherwise, dirt, dust, dander, molds, mites, spiders, pollen, and the rest of the living and dead flotsam of the home will work themselves into the pores of your books, speeding their deterioration.

The second problem can be more insidious. One leaky window frame, or an inconspicuous drip from the condensation on a pipe, or a few days of humid weather, can ruin dozens of books. Two days of wet weather can incite a mold uprising. A warm, moist room with one cool wall can generate a cascade of moisture behind a wall of books, which can go undetected for months.

Moisture damage usually occurs in basements and garages, near open windows, near the floor of an outside wall in which there are water pipes, near chimneys, or next to porches and breezeways.

If you have bookcases near floors that are mopped, you risk damaging the books with splashes from sponges, buckets, and mops. This happens even in museums and libraries. Solutions include putting cardboard or plastic over the shelves before you clean the floor and hand-wiping the section of the floor just in front of the shelves. One booklover reports she puts only her expendable magazines on the bottom shelves of her bookcases, so she won't have to worry about books being damaged.

Another booklover told me she had carefully placed attractive copper pans under her plants, so that she would not drip water onto the tops of the bookshelves. One pan leaked invisibly from a crack in the soldering. A steady stream of water over the back of the bookshelf soaked a collection of inexpensive, but irreplaceable, nonfiction paperbacks. By the time the problem was discovered, months of soaking had glued many of the books into a solid mass of pulp.

Most houseplants need regular watering, which increases the possibility of nearby books getting splashed. They can also harbor book-munching bugs. To be on the side of most conservators, plants and books should be segregated.

Basements, garages, and attics should be considered the places you send books to die. Even in dry climates, basements can flood, garages can leak, and attics can soak up the rain from a damaged roof.

4. *Are the books stored so as to minimize structural damage to the book?* There seems to be a consensus regarding the ideal shelving arrangement for a book. What the average person would recognize as an average-sized book should be placed on the shelf straight up and down. In addition, it should be fully supported the entire length and width of the cover on both sides, either by means of another book of similar height and breadth, or the wall at the end of a shelf, or a bookend of similar height. A number of experienced librarians reported that they use height as a criterion for organizing their books in their own home libraries for this very reason. See Chapters VII and XIV for more information about the proper display and storage of books.

The three most common problems to look for are books that lean, books that are supported only up to the lower half or third of the cover, and books that are so tightly packed as to make moving them difficult.

The stress on a book when it leans can cause the spine to crack. The hinges, which are where the cover is attached to the body of the book, can tear, and the covers and pages can crease and bend. In a poorly bound book, this hastens the loosening of pages, particularly where the pages have been glued together at the spine in a solid block, rather than sewn into signatures.

Most of your more expensive books will have sewn pages instead of glued pages. Sewing allows for more "give," but if you took a stressed book apart, you could see where the threads are sawing through the paper from the sideways movement of the parts of the book; it is similar to the stress of tectonic plates, even though the damage is not of earthquake proportions.

Books, particularly taller books that are not well supported over the entire length and width of the cover, will bend and stretch over time. Without support, covers will warp and crack, the part of the cover not supported will separate, and the two halves will splay apart.

Oversized books can be placed on their side, but even then, the sheer weight of a pile of books can cause damage. One author recommends piles of no more than four books.

Packing books too tightly can damage the dust jackets, warp the covers, and stress the spines. Tightly packed shelves encourage the browser to pull the book off the shelf by the *headband*, which is that small woven piece of cloth that sits at the top of most hardbound books. Yes, it does look like a convenient cloth loop for yanking books, but by pulling on it you can rip the spine and cover.

Can you grasp the sides of a book with your index and middle fingers and your thumb, and gently remove it from the shelf without dislodging the books on either side? If there is not enough room to do this, the books are packed too tight. You will have to find a way to loosen up the stacks.

A minor sin is laying a book horizontally across the top of a row of vertically shelved books. The extra weight could eventually hurt the vertically shelved books by putting additional stress on the binding.

5. *Are the books stored so you can examine them and use them?* The books may look fine from the front, but because they are not regularly used, or are in a place that makes their handling inconvenient, they are left to languish for years. You will not be able to tell that mice are nibbling or that insects are excavating the fore-edges.

I have a theory that one of the sins of book storage and display is overt cleverness. You might think that no one else has thought of storing books in the rafters of the attic, or attaching them with metal hook and fishing line to the ceiling of the bathroom, or building shelves over every doorway. I have bad news for you. People have thought about it, and they decided these were REALLY STUPID ideas. The books look great, but it is next to impossible to reach them without anti-gravity boots.

> *My well-brought-up goddaughter has been collecting zillions of books since she was very little (mysteries, cyberpunk). Her mom moved to a new house while she was off at college and so the "helpers" unpacked the book boxes in her new room. When Emily returned, she found all her books totally organized by height! They were sort of doing "the wave" all around the room, totally mixed by author, subject, type of book, et al. After a good laugh, they left them that way, and it has turned out to be rather useful in that when Emily needs a book from there sent to college, her mom is reasonably able to find it by remembering how big it is.*
> —Lisa Kimball, partner, The Meta Network, Arlington, VA

Height is the accessibility issue for most home libraries. You felt righteous when you built those ceiling-high shelves in the spare bedroom, but how often do you drag the high ladder from the garage and pull a book off those shelves? Some books deteriorate into high-priced wallpaper because of their locations. On the other hand, they probably won't drown in the next flood.

This is the time to start taking measurements. You may want to calculate, for example, how many books fit in the accessible space in your house, which you might define as that space you can reach, inspect, and clean without having to use anything higher than a modest footstool. Otherwise, you will have to take an oath to get up on that high ladder, take books off the shelves, and look at the condition of both the books and their physical environment.

6. *Are the books stored and displayed safely?* We may make jokes about death by bookcase, but librarians know this is serious business; making sure shelves and their contents are secure is an important part of maintaining your library's environment.

If I were to go up to every bookcase in your house and shake each one gently, would this cause you to wrestle me to the ground while you screamed in my ear, "Whadareyounuts?" Is it suicide to disturb your bookcases? Are books in tenuously balanced heaps and piles, ready to bean an unsuspecting visitor?

The most dangerous place in my house is the bedroom, where a small shelf over my side of the bed is stacked with current reading. The books are stable, but Gracie and Jeremiah, two agile carnivores who share my home, are not. Both cats enjoy scaling the treacherous row of books. I have narrowly escaped acquiring a black eye, but I have been crowned on several occasions and suffered a bruised cheekbone at least once. Do you have such booby traps in your home? Are you putting guests and family at risk?

It might be messy, but the only ready treatment for dangerous bookshelves is to stack the books in stable piles on the floor until the bookshelves are either repaired or replaced. If this sounds like too much trouble, ask yourself what the cost would be if several hundred books came crashing down in a cloud of splintered wood, torn covers, dust bunnies, broken heads, and lawsuits? This issue is covered in more detail in Chapter VII.

Speaking of torn covers, even if you aren't worried about burying family and friends in avalanches of encyclopedias, what about the health of the books themselves? It would be unthinkable for the collector who is concerned about return on investment to damage valuable books; a good thwack can destroy 95 percent of the value of a collectible.

This is also a good time to look for hidden books that might be dying slow deaths. Books can be crushed between couches and walls and between mattresses and headboards. Books can lie undiscovered for months behind upright pianos, bureaus, china cabinets, and even household appliances.

7. *Are the books stored so that you can change your mind?* Most booklovers share a desire to interact with their collections. And this means physically rearranging the books from time to time.

Is there enough empty space on your shelves to move things around? To gather a set of books for a special project? To create a creative chaos of authors to stimulate your thinking during a time of study? What happens when you bring home a book whose author refers to other books that you own? If there are no empty spots in your library, the difficulty of moving your books around will make your collection less useful.

If your home library is growing, a measure of your success as a book manager is whether you can locate a shelf's worth of empty space. If you do not acquire new books on a regular basis, if you are building a new collection on a particular subject, or if your goals are creating long-term archives of books and information, you might not need to create the slack needed for internal reorganization. Your problem is creating clean, dry, cool, secure, and dimly lit storage. In this case, you can use the audit process to identify physical areas in your display and storage that need upgrading. But even then, you might have to decide between the roles of archivist and librarian.

An archivist will be more likely to keep and store everything, and those items will more likely be arranged according to the function of the time or the date they arrived. Also, archives tend to be more like storage areas, with less active use. Chapter XIV goes into home archival issues in more depth.

A librarian is more likely to choose what is acquired, kept, and discarded. A library is organized by the relationships of the information in the books and documents; in the library universe, these relationships are dictated by formal cataloging systems, which brings me to the next audit question.

8. *Are the books stored so that you can find what you want and so that you know what you have?* Booklovers seem to feel more guilty about their lack of organization than about any other subject. Cobwebs as big as parachutes do not bother them as much as the fact that their libraries have no classification system and no catalog.

One test of how well organized your library is, is whether you can send a stranger into your stacks and tell her where to find a book, without having to take her to the spot yourself. It is perfectly acceptable to rely on clues like the color of the cover and the relationship of the book to the tall black atlas on the left-hand side of the shelf. But if the only information you have is that the book is somewhere in the house, and you think it is maybe a brown paperback, you might need to spend a little more time in organizing your collection. If you can't find a book, you can't read it and enjoy it.

You might have one of those wonderful visual memories that enables you to close your eyes and picture where everything is. For readers blessed with this talent, your shelf list is a mental photo. As you get older (and may you enjoy decades of active, happy bookloving!), those mental photos can get fuzzy.

Scanning your library for patterns of usage might be a way to formulate a classification strategy. After you audit, you can choose to begin organizing those books you use the most. Then, if you don't complete the task (and who ever does finish these big jobs?), you have at least made the active part of your library more useful.

Documentation of the collection is another matter. The most important benefit of maintaining an up-to-date inventory of your home library is having hard data to work with in case of disaster. Without a list of what you have lost, including titles and prices, your insurance company will probably not be able to respond to a claim in a way that will please you.

You don't have to capture all the pertinent data about every book you own right away; choose the books most valuable to you, according to your criteria. See Chapter VIII for more information about classification and cataloging issues.

The End of the Audit

If you did the audit right, you accomplished the following:

1. You rescued some of your favorite books from death or oblivion.

2. You identified some of the worst physical flaws in your current library, including books at risk in damp basements, bright sunlight, and stacks on top of the refrigerator and stove.

3. You cleaned up the worst messes. The desiccated lizard mummy that had been home to a teeming community of unidentified crawlies is history, as are the spilled grape juice and the half-eaten muffin from last Thanksgiving.

4. You have a rough idea of how many linear shelves *of* books you have, versus how many linear shelves *for* books you have, versus how many more shelves your home can contain.

5. You know what you will be doing every weekend for the next year.

6. You are very, very tired and dusty.

7. Your freezer is filled with frozen, rotten books.

What if you did an audit once a month or once a week, instead of waiting for once in your lifetime? What if you started looking at your library as a garden to maintain? It is easier to tweak dead blossoms a few at a time than to accumulate such a huge number of backyard tasks that you risk sunstroke.

Or, what if you viewed your book collection with the same concern you view your car? If you are a devoted booklover, you have probably invested at least as much money in your home library as you have in that sedan parked out front.

One reason it is difficult to pay attention to the problem of book care is that you might think of your books as merely immortal repositories of intellect and spirit. You are one of the dreamers, moving through the physical plane with uncombed hair, an unbalanced checkbook, and a militant disregard for the material side of Western civilization. Since my market research shows that if you are reading this book, you are someone of very high intelligence doing extremely important work with a high degree of competence and focus, it makes sense that you feel you have better things to do than vacuum shelves and check the humidity.

Speaking as a woman who once attended a dinner party wearing a dress that was not only backwards but also inside out, I understand that worrying about the tame niceties is not the most important thing in the world, at least not to some booklovers. But it is not a choice between two extremes. You can balance the concepts of books as containers of wisdom and books as containers. That means taking time to clean your books once in a while, not just stockpiling them against an intellectual Ice Age, with your library serving as mental cordwood.

Pick another periodic activity and tie your library monitoring activity with a particular event. Do something to improve your home library when:

1. You put the new box of baking soda in the freezer.
2. You water the ivy.
3. You add new washer fluid to the car.
4. You comb the cat.
5. You make your bed.
6. You order pizza.
7. The Chicago Cubs lose (good only during the summer months).
8. You clean the kitchen floor.
9. An elected official denounces the First Amendment.
10. Someone sells 5 million copies of a really stupid book.

Deep Audits

Deep audits are for vacations, the first few sweet weeks of retirement, prolonged periods of unemployment, unending struggles with undiagnosed diseases that the doctor prefers you stay home with, the month after your last kid leaves home, and using up sick days.

Tools for a deep audit include: rented dumpster, dropcloths, industrial wet vacuum, forceps, rubber gloves, mask, portable oxygen supply, large hammer, collection of plate glass in a variety of sizes and thicknesses, personal computer with a minimum of 200 megabytes of storage, surgical gurney, bright yellow rain slicker, chilled case of high-caffeine beverages, paper shredder, flamethrower, leeches, scalpel, blender, tanned Nubian goat hides, putty knife, and assorted Wagnerian operas.

An Experiment in Book Cryonics
By Susan Hartman, technical services librarian
Grand Junction, CO

In March 1991, I did some experimenting with the salvage of water-damaged materials. These experiments were the result of a workshop I had taken at the National Archives in San Bruno, California, and I wanted to try what I had learned.

I soaked about fifteen books of various paper types and bindings, and a few catalog cards, in a basin of water for several days. This was easier said than done, since the books kept soaking up the water, and I'd end up with semi-wet books in a dry basin. But eventually they were waterlogged and dripping.

I spent two days salvaging the cards and about a dozen of the books (the *World Almanac* soaked up water like a sponge and took forever to dry). The cotton binding eventually shrank so the almanac has a permanent warp—not much of a success story, but an experience all the same. On the positive side—if you ever spill a gallon of water on the kitchen floor, the almanac would probably work better than a sponge! Paperback books are the easiest to salvage (and the cheapest to replace after a disaster), and those books with really thin pages (like Bibles tend to have) are also easy candidates for salvage. Hardback books are the heaviest to work with as well as the most likely to separate the text block from the cover.

Three volumes are of particular interest: a *National Geographic* magazine with clay-based pages, a ceramic arts magazine with blocks of clay-based pages between pulp-based pages, and an old book (chosen because of its slimy, gelatinous cover that I wasn't about to touch!). These books were put in individual plastic freezer bags (not sealed) and stashed in the freezer above the refrigerator. Although not the recommended method, I had learned that wet books can be dried in a self-defrosting freezer. The results: In May 1995 (yup, four years later) the books were thawed out to determine if they were done. The edges are dry but the centers of the pages are still visibly wet. The pages are separated, even the clay-based pages. The books are basically flat although they tend to take the curl according to how they were stacked in the freezer. Are they done? Maybe in four more years!

Over the holidays we always joke, "I have books in my freezer—don't have room for food! What do you keep in your freezer?"   ❖

General Resources for Getting Your Home Library and Books Into Shape

Home-Cleaning and Fixer-Upper Supply Catalogs

Here are three mail-order catalogs that specialize in home-cleaning supplies, in case you live in a town that has been abandoned by retailers who sell useful products for the home. Products include old-fashioned cleaning tools that have been used for scrubbing dirt since the last century and the very latest in high-technology gadgets to drive critters out of the house for good.

Home Trends. 1450 Lyell Avenue, Rochester, NY 14606-2184; (716) 254-6520; fax (716) 458-9245.

Hundreds of useful home products from Fuller®, Oreck®, Rubbermaid®, and other name-brand companies. Includes brushes and dusters, long-handled mops, mini vacuum attachments, silverfish poison, flypaper, and cedar products.

Improvements™. Hanover, PA 17333-0084; (800) 642-2112; fax (800) 642-2112.

Air cleaners, electronic pest repellents, and products to repair walls, book-shelves, and leaky pipes are among the products in this collection.

Jeff Campbell's Clean Team. 990 South Rogers Circle, #5, Boca Raton, FL 33487; (800) 717-CLEAN; fax (407) 995-6908.

This catalog is part of a commercial empire, based on a successful professional cleaning company, an equally successful book, and dozens of tools and custom cleaning formulas. The most useful products for home librarians include dusting tools and cleaning solutions for shelves.

Product Catalogs for the Home Librarian

These companies are known for their friendly service. Most of their products are meant for circulating collections, which means they are designed to hold together books that suffer from rough wear and have a short lifespan. Demco and Kapco regularly conduct book repair classes in schools and libraries across the country; see if a friend can sneak you in the next time they are in town. Vernon sells a videotape on book repair.

I found all three companies very receptive to working with home librarians, and the staffs are unfailingly polite and eager to please. *The Librarian's Yellow Pages* will provide information about many other companies. Or, ask your local librarian for his or her favorites.

Demco. PO Box 7488, Madison, WI 53707-7488; (800) 356-1200;
fax (800) 245-1329.

Almost 800 pages of library and school supplies, including everything from signs to furniture. Flipping through these pages is like reliving fifth grade, and home librarians with children or large collections will find many tools to make book care easier. Unlike some large, commercial distributors, they do not require a minimum order.

Kapco (aka Kent Adhesive Products Company). Library Products,
PO Box 626, Kent, OH 44240-0011; (800) 791-8965; (330) 678-1626;
fax (800) 451-3724.

Kapco products are for booklovers who need precut, adhesive book covers and reinforcements for their books and magazines. The products are designed to be virtually foolproof; the company will even sell you a simple paper cutter that will trim your efforts with professional ease. If you have lots of beloved paperbacks and magazines to repair and protect, this catalog is for you. Home librarians can also buy a kit, which contains generous quantities of their most popular products at very good prices.

The Librarian's Yellow Pages. PO Box 179, Larchmont, NY 10538;
(914) 834-7070; annual; $9.95/year.

The Librarian's Yellow Pages is the first single-source directory of publications, products, and services for libraries and information centers in the familiar, easy-to-use yellow pages format. The main market is "real" libraries, but much of it is useful to home libraries as well. Please note that this is not a research organization or library; the staff receives too many phone calls from booklovers looking for books.

Vernon Library Supplies. 2851 Cole Court, Norcross, GA 30071;
(800) 878-0253; fax (800) 466-1165; e-mail: vernon@vernlib.com.

A user-friendly catalog with all kinds of serious library goodies, including furniture, book repair products, and practical storage equipment. The people I talked to on the phone were extremely friendly, a good sign for home librarians trying to improve their collections.

❖

The Purge

By R. C. Harvey, cartoonist and freelance critic-historian
of cartooning arts, Champaign, IL

Copyright © 1996, R.C. Harvey

Last spring, Bob launched a major project—purging his library. His library is in his study. Most of it is bookshelves. And until a few years ago, most of the books were the dregs of his career as a teacher of English. For some years after winning his Ph.D. in the state's lotto, Bob refrained from buying books. He had enough, he said.

Then, about five years ago, he started in again. He bought books about cartooning—new books and old, commonplace and rare. Initially, the object was to acquire a few volumes reprinting magazine cartoons from the fifties so he'd have reminders of a youth misspent in browsing through *Colliers* and *The Saturday Evening Post*. But the number of his purchases grew.

When, at last, there was simply no more shelf space in the study, Bob did the logical thing. He bought more bookcases. But that campaign eventually ran aground: no more floor space for bookcases. In fact, there was no more floor space: He'd piled books all over the floor. So he did the next logical thing. Painful as it was, he began disposing of his trove of literature books, books he'd acquired during the years of struggle as a teacher, books he'd taught and was very fond of—yes, books he'd never even read.

He even sold a score of first editions of Bernard Shaw's plays that he'd found during long years of relentless search. He sold them all for a pittance.

("Maybe it was a ha'penny," he said, recalling the occasion with a sob.)

But he didn't sell them all. Just selected volumes. The process of selection took weeks. He could work for only an hour at a time.

"After an hour," he said, "the mind seizes up on you. All those decisions. Keep this one or sell it. After an hour, you're either keeping them all or selling them all. You lose the ability to make finer distinctions."

But slowly, over a period of several months, he sold many boxes of books.

"Look," he announced gleefully at the end of the ordeal, "I've now got 40 empty feet of bookshelves!"

He also had fourteen 6-foot piles on the floor. He spent weeks reorganizing the books on the shelves and then moving the books from the floor to the shelves. Finally, he could see the floor again.

"Aha!" he exclaimed. "I wondered where that Oriental rug was."

Then something went awry. Mostly what happened was, he didn't stop buying books on cartooning. So now the shelves are full again. And the floor has disappeared under new stacks of acquisitions.   ❖

*Gayle and Phil each assumed that her or his
own collection would dominate the
modest cottage they were renting.*
page 80.

Chapter V — Acquisitions

*Being a Discussion of Better Ways to Find
Current Books, Especially the Good Stuff.*

Where Are They Hiding the New Good Stuff?
The Mysteries of Book Publishing

You are improving your home library: throwing out candy bar wrappers, checking the bookcases in the basement for barnacles, and removing dust bunnies by the wheelbarrow. Unless you have infinite resources and infinite time, improving your home library also means thinking before you add another book to your collection. You need to be a book hunter, searching actively for the best.

In this chapter, you will be introduced to some strategies for finding new books. In Chapter VI, you will learn a little bit about the used, rare, and antiquarian market, particularly as it applies to that dread and beloved disease, Book Collecting.

---

*I've made mistakes buying books. Buying what I've
no time to read. Buying what I can't afford. Buying what
I think I should read and have still not read, and trying
to read nonfiction for some reason. Books should be
for joy; school started me on the wrong motive.*
—Patricia Gilson Green, founder, Information Exchange, Key West, FL

As a starting place, here are questions to tattoo on a convenient body part, preferably one of your own. That way, you can refer to them when considering a book purchase.

1. *Do I need this book? This book, right now?*
2. *Is this the best book on the subject?*
3. *Will it make me a better person, a happier person?*
4. *Can I find it in a library?*
5. *Do I already have a copy of this book? Is this copy better?*
6. *Do I have room for this book?*
7. *Do I have money to take care of this book?*
8. *Is this a great book?*

You cannot assume a great new book will automatically find its way into a book review column or be displayed prominently in your favorite bookstore. You cannot assume you will hear about it, and when you do, there are no guarantees that you will be able to find it, let alone buy it.

About 50,000 titles are published in the United States each year. The books that you hear about from the mass media are those published by companies with influence and money, those about controversial subjects, and those by publishers who have learned to play the publicity game via book reviews, radio talk shows, and book signings.

Many big publishers have ties to the movie and television industries; there is a seamless flow of money and ideas among the large publishing houses, the movie studios, and the broadcast and cable television networks. It is easy to assume a well-publicized book is well written and contains important ideas, but its ubiquitous fame might be the result of cross-promotion among different media organizations that are facets of the same large business. Book publishers outside of these loops struggle to get the voices of their authors heard.

I like to buy paperbacks; they are easier to read while lying
flat on one's back, turning pages with the hand that's holding
the book while nibbling crackers or pretzels with the other hand.
—Sarah Stein, librarian and cataloger, Denver, CO

No one can know about all of the books published in America each year, let alone keep up with the more than one million titles that are currently in print. In effect, many people, including public relations consultants, book publisher sales representatives, book wholesalers, book buyers, and bookstore owners, are making your buying decisions for you. You have to hope that everyone in the publishing food chain, from the author and literary agent to the clerk at the store, is making choices based on quality, not just on making a buck.

Going for the Gold

The best friend to have in the book community is a knowledgeable bookseller. Whether they specialize in new or used books, they can steer you to quality titles in every field. The very best ones seem to be able to read the booklover's soul. These anticipate your wishes and suggest books that are perfect for your current needs, even though you could have sworn you never told them that you were studying contemporary European art or building a boat. But what do you do when you favorite store closes?

Booksellers are not the only ones who are trying to maintain the standards in the publishing industry. Hidden away in cubbyholes across the land are intelligent, decent men and women struggling to bring wonderful books into print. If you are a booklover, you should also love the editors and publishers who make a positive difference in the culture. There was a time when names like Knopf and Cerf were known to the reading public in the same way star pitchers are known to baseball fans. The good ones now toil invisible and unheralded.

When you find a book you love, note the publisher. Ask your friendly bookstore staffperson for a look at the catalog from that publishing house. Since it is unlikely that a bookstore will be able to carry everything a particular publisher sells, you might discover great books you would never find on the shelves. Order the books through the bookstore, so they can profit from your interest, and you can reward them for their assistance.

Find out who the individuals are who are responsible for the books you love: the agents who have the guts to stand by the authors; the editors, who champion the books in-house; the publicists, who are able to get the book to the attention of the book reviewers. Write letters, praise them to the skies, keep in touch. Booklovers in the know will track their favorite editors as they move from publishing house to publishing house.

I try not to buy paperbacks if I can help it. They're just no good for the long haul, and I intend to have my books with me through the long haul. (My pre-fall-of-the-Soviet-Union-plan for the day the air raid sirens sounded was my Yeats, a bottle of Chardonnay, and my big green armchair, which is like sitting in a big hug.)
—Kathleen Cain, researcher and writer, Arvada, CO
Kathleen Cain © 1996

Ask the experts where they find the seminal information in their field. Many times, a popular nonfiction book on a subject is a rewrite of a better, more obscure book. I recently read a self-help book on psychology that was based on a model of human behavior that had been developed by another psychologist thirty years before. Although the older model had been publicized in a best-selling book for many years, the new book made no mention of the previous work or its originator. Was it ignorance, neglect, or blatant plagiarism?

Read the bibliographies of your favorite nonfiction books, and note the books that are mentioned frequently.

Contact your local university press and ask for a catalog. Academic presses frequently publish interesting and well-written books on humor, folklore, crafts, ethnic history, nature, cooking, and science fiction, along with weightier tomes about politics, economics, mathematics, and science. Don't worry, you can still find academics publishing books with pretentious vocabulary, bad typesetting, and stilted language.

The smaller presses, at their best, are the wellspring of great publishing. The label "small press" applies to the work of the self-published poet or consultant, the fine art private press, the cutting edge publisher of fine poetry and fiction, or the niche publisher, with a focus on a single author or field of study.

On the other hand, small is not a guarantee of beautiful. The label *vanity press* can refer to printing companies that charge a hefty fee to publish a book, no matter how poorly written. Vanity can also refer to a publisher who publishes her own work and whose ego is much bigger than her talent.

Still, I love the small presses and have been their advocate for twenty-five years. Heck, how can the founder of Terminal Arts Publishing and Eggplant Press behave otherwise? Ask your friends in libraries and bookstores about the best small presses. Find out about your regional publishers, who are likely to focus on issues close to your heart.

Ask the authors of your favorite books for their suggestions. Authors are more accessible than ever because of e-mail and online systems. So long as you don't ask personal questions, expect them to do your homework for you, or ask them questions they have already answered in their books, the majority of authors are gracious. You can also contact them by writing their publishing houses. I have received lovely replies from authors, partly because I wrote them short, interesting letters and asked questions they could answer quickly.

Look with fresh eyes at the bookstores you frequent. Do you need to broaden your horizons? You might dislike the ambience of the superstores, but they often buy "one of everything." I discovered the best collection of art books in my area in a chain bookstore in a mall.

You might ignore the generic paperback exchanges, because you believe they carry only genre fiction in shabby condition. However, in such a store I found a like-new copy of a much-desired, out-of-print philosophy book.

College bookstores are interesting places to browse for unusual books. Savvy professors will have the store stock quality fiction and nonfiction, in addition to textbooks. I also like the bookstores one finds in museums.

A final note on the best books: Don't count on that new book you love staying in print long enough for you to buy a replacement or gift copy. Conventional wisdom gives the average book a life of two years or less. If you find that new book you must have, you may have only a few months to acquire extra copies. The first print run of the average book, which is typically only a few thousand copies, may be the only print run. See the catalog listings at the end of this chapter for examples of mail-order bookstores that rescue and sell fine books that have been orphaned by their publishers.

Many publishers wait a year or more before issuing the paperback version of a book. Others publish cloth and paper editions at the same time. Many serious home librarians reserve their hardbacks for their permanent collections and purchase less expensive paperbacks to lend and give, or in my case, enjoy in the bathtub.

Book Club Fever

I signed up with several national book clubs and used them over several years. My experience was uniformly uneven. Each of these major book clubs mixed up orders, billed me incorrectly, and sent unwanted books, even after I had sent in the "no thank you" postcard in a timely fashion. The biggest disappointment was the missing pages in a poorly bound copy of a nineteenth-century classic. The biggest pleasant surprise was discovering a favorite hardcover book in a very nice paperback edition. Here is a summary of my experiences.

Ten Reasons to Use Book Clubs

1. They do a good job of picking the better books in their field.
2. They can have the exclusive paperback rights to bestsellers.
3. They can be the only source for new editions of out-of-print classics.
4. They keep you in touch with popular contemporary fiction.
5. It can be fun to use the different discount systems.
6. They sometimes distribute books that you can't find anywhere else.
7. They often have cheaper editions of new releases.
8. The catalogs provide great browsing.
9. They are an easy way to buy gifts for friends.
10. "Mail-order" means you can shop for books in the bathtub.

Eleven Reasons Not to Use Book Clubs

1. Book club editions have no value to most collectors.
2. Their picks can be mediocre.
3. Their private-label editions have a reputation for poor construction.
4. Their reprints of public-domain books can be expensive.
5. They can be controlled by certain publishers.
6. They can make or break a book, regardless of quality.
7. The discount systems can hide the true costs of doing business.
8. The shipping costs are high.
9. They can accidentally ship you books you did not order.
10. Your choices are limited to the size of the catalog.
11. You don't necessarily get enough information to make a good decision.

The Prenuptial Book Agreement: A Cautionary Tale

Gayle Pergamit loved Phil Salin, and Phil loved Gayle—two bright and attractive people, falling in love so quickly, engaged only days after their first meeting, and married a few weeks later.

Because each of them had books—lots and lots of books—Gayle and Phil each assumed that her or his own collection would dominate the modest cottage they were renting. Each thought that their newly minted spouse would find extra room somewhere. Gayle recalls that they did shoehorn both home libraries into the new space. Not so bad, she thought.

Then the phone calls started.

"Hi, is Phil there?"

"No," Gayle would reply, and then she would introduce herself.

The caller would explain that, sitting in a garage, basement, or closet, was a box of Phil's books. Now that Phil was married and had his own house, would Phil please take the books back?

The first call didn't bother Gayle very much. After all, she herself had traveled extensively, and it was not unusual to store boxes with friends.

The second call came as a surprise, as did the third, fourth, and fifth.

Phil had lied. He had failed to mention, during the intimate sharing of souls that occurred during their happy, intense courtship, that he had stored boxes of books with friends from one end of California to another. He had failed to mention, when he and Gayle had rented their cute little house, that there was no way all of those books would fit into the new home, let alone leave room for furniture, clothing, food, or Gayle.

The torrent stopped only when Gayle told callers Phil had left the country.

Gayle and Phil had a happy marriage, despite his dishonesty about books. When he died, the bookshelves were stacked with books two and three deep, floor to ceiling. Gayle harbors the suspicion that his death was a successful attempt to get out of moving the collection to their next home.

Out of this experience, Gayle suggests that booklovers in love should jointly require a prenuptial book agreement. The agreement should provide full disclosure, not only of books in the physical possession of the parties involved, but a complete accounting of those books that, upon sealing the sacred vows of matrimony, will come home to roost.

Has your new Significant Other remembered to tell you about the books in storage in the furnace rooms of grandparents in other states? Have you been completely honest in return? What about those cartons you left with your last lover, your parents, your college roommate, your first or second or third spouse, or at the family summer home?

Gayle also recommends that you probe for weird book-related habits, the kind that you don't discover until after the honeymoon. Does the S.O. expect you to organize your library in the same way he or she does? Are you totally controlling about books, or totally indifferent? Is the S.O. a bedtime reader? Are your shelves lined with overdue books? And how will you two divide up the home library if, goodness forbids, the relationship ends?

Phil rests in peace, while Gayle still contends with their collection. Is Heaven big enough to hold all the books Phil didn't tell Gayle about? Does God have a weeding policy? Only time will tell.

I lent a book (War and Remembrance) *to my lover of the moment. At the same time I borrowed from her a poetry handbook. Long after the relationship was ended, I remembered about the dual lending. I had already read the Wouk novel, but was getting a lot of use out of the handbook. A moral dilemma arose. Should I make an effort to return the handbook and retrieve the novel? Or should I keep the book that I now considered more valuable? Well, we all have our vices. I kept the handbook. My only justification is that I don't think my previous paramour ever used the handbook.*
I keep telling myself that, anyway.
—Don McNatt, programmer and poet, Colorado Springs, CO

Resources for Finding Better New Books

Here is help with your hunt for fine reading. I have listed resources here, in Chapter V, which focuses on new books, and in Chapter VI, which is about used, rare, and collectable books.

Some of these resources specialize in rescuing fine-quality "remaindered" books, which are those that publishers dump when sales slow down; they are the books that "remain" when a book is officially out-of-print. Although the book is technically new, it is no longer being actively marketed and can be had for pennies on the dollar.

Fine Book Guides

The Bookworm's Big Apple: *A Guide to Manhattan's Booksellers.*
Susan Paula Barile. *Columbia University Press, $15.95 paper, ISBN 0-231-08495-1.*
Probably the best city on this continent to look for books, with specialized bookstores that probably could not flourish outside the dwarf-star density of Manhattan. The author is an insider who shares her knowledge generously.

81

International Directory of Little Magazines and Small Presses.
Edited by Len Fulton. *Dustbooks, $31.95 paper, ISBN 0-916685-51-1.*
This belongs in the home library of every booklover. Now in its thirty-second edition, it is the 1,000-page bible of the smallest presses. You can find books and journals about everything from taxes and Zen to boating and human rights. Complete political and philosophical spectrums are represented.

Literary Laurels: *A Reader's Guide to Award-Winning Fiction.*
Edited by Laura Carlson, Sean Creighton, and Sheila Cunningham. *Hillyard, $9.95 paper, ISBN 0-9647361-0-1.*
This book lists the winners of all the major literary awards, including the National Book Critics Circle Awards, the Nobel Prize for Literature, the Pulitzer Prize, the Hugo Award, the Edgar Allan Poe Award, and the Western Heritage Award, among others.

The New Book Lover's Guide to ChicagoLand: *Including Southern Wisconsin.* Lane Phalen. *$14.95 paper, ISBN 1-880339-11-0; Brigadoon Bay Books, PO Box 957724, Hoffman Estates, IL 60195-7724; (847) 884-6940.*
There was a time when most of this country's printing was done in the geographical region stretching from Chicago north into the Milwaukee area and beyond. Part of that heritage is a keen local interest in books, libraries, and publishing. This well-annotated guide covers almost 700 stores, including new and used, chain and independent, antiquarian and Christian.

Outposts: *A Catalog of Rare and Disturbing Information.* Russ Kick. *Carroll & Graf, $18.95 paper, ISBN 0-7867-0202-8.*
Our republic has weathered decades of weirdos from the right and left, from deviant sects and strange cults, from people who are vilified for being crazy, dangerous, or ahead of their time. In case you are one of them, or curious about what they believe, here is a polite introduction to some very impolite books.

Reader's Catalog. Second Edition. Edited by Geoffrey O'Brien. *$34.95 paper, ISBN 0-924322-01-2; The Reader's Catalog, 250 West 57th Street, Suite 1330, New York, NY 10107; (800) 733-BOOK; fax (212) 307-1973.*
Impossible. A 1,500-page, annotated compilation of more than 40,000 of the best books in print, in more than 200 categories. With maps, even. With illustrations. Attractively designed. At a price that is in the reach of many booklovers. You can always chip in with a few friends and share. (Sure.) I want one; you will, too. Available after November 1996.

The Reader's Companion: *A Book Lover's Guide to the Most Important Books in Every Field of Knowledge, as Chosen by the Experts.*
Fred Bratman and Scott Lewis. *Hyperion, $9.95 paper, ISBN 0-7868-8095-3.*
The fun is in finding out what books the people you love (and hate) think are the best, and comparing their selections to your own. Although the focus is on nonfiction, there is a small fiction section authored by several household names, such as Marge Piercy and John Updike.

Publishers' Newsletters and Magazines

Major publishers distribute their own magazines and newsletters to entice readers. They include in-house reviews, author interviews, photos, essays on literature, and information for reading groups. Most are available for free through bookstores.

AT RANDOM. Random House. Free subscription available by sending your name and address to *AT RANDOM*, Random House II-I, 201 East 50th Street, New York, NY 10022. Vintage Books, a division of Random House, also produces reading guides, available by calling 800-793-BOOK. Modern Library, another Random House imprint, publishes literary classics; a list of current titles is available from your bookstore. Ballantine Books, yet another imprint, provides several different newsletters and reading guides, including ones that focus on gay, lesbian, and African-American writers.

Classics Chronicle. Penguin USA. Free subscription to newsletter and other information by writing Penguin Classics, Dept. MEC, 375 Hudson Street, New York, NY 10014.

D Magazine. Doubleday, a division of Bantam/Doubleday/Dell Publishing Group. Available at bookstores. Reading group support materials for Doubleday and Anchor Books are available by calling the Doubleday Marketing hotline at (800) 605-3406. Anchor Books are also available by calling (212) 782-8424.

FOCUS. Harvest Books, the trade paperback imprint of Harcourt Brace and Company. Free issues available by calling (800) 543-1918.

Pocket Reader. Pocket Books. For more information, contact Liate Stehlik, Marketing Department, Pocket Books, 1230 Avenue of the Americas, New York, NY 10020.

Fine Book Catalogs

The Bargain Book Warehouse. Soda Creek Press, PO Box 8515, Ukiah, CA 95482-8515; (800) 301-7567; fax (800) 949-4946.

A fast-growing specialist in genre fiction, including science fiction, romance, mystery, adventure, westerns, horror, and crime. People addicted to genre fiction are looked down upon by many booklovers, but I know scholars of note who feast on what some people call "fast-food" books when they can.

Bargain Books. Edward R. Hamilton, Bookseller, Falls Village, CT 06031-5000.

A gloriously illegible catalog, with hundreds of new books at a fraction of their original price. Go blind reading the small print, send in a check plus $3, and receive great values. It is shocking how fast a bestseller loses its peak appeal and ends up being sold through remainder outlets like this one.

A Common Reader. 141 Tomkins, Pleasantville, NY 10570; (800) 832-7323; fax (914) 747-0778.

Those of us who frequent smaller bookstores with skilled and impassioned booklovers as staff know the pleasure of a dialogue with a bookseller who also knows and loves books. Every selection in this catalog is a gem, handpicked for people who read. One nice feature is selections that are parts of series, so that once you get hooked on an author or character, you can easily find the rest.

Daedalus Books. PO Box 9132, Hyattsville, MD 20781-0932; (800) 395-2665, (301) 779-4224; fax (800) 866-5578, (301) 779-1260.

Daedalus combines the quality of *A Common Reader* and the bargains of Edward R. Hamilton and Soda Creek. In addition to new books and remainders, Daedalus sells compact discs of fine classical music, also at very good prices.

The Reader's Catalog. 250 West 57th Street, Suite 1330, New York, NY 10107; (800) 733-BOOK; fax (212) 307-1973.

A free newsletter that provides intelligent, short reviews of what the editors think are the best current books in print, with a handy order form to satisfy book lust. These folks, like any service-conscious bookstore, will also sell you any book in print; all you have to do is call and ask.

After buying three different copies of the same book—
it's missing again!
—Eva Loymendy, booklover, North Fork, CA

84

Specialized Mail-Order New Book Catalogs for BookLovers

These represent a nanosample of what is available to the booklover looking for something special in current books, particularly nonfiction. Some are publisher catalogs, others are compiled by book distributors, and still others are the mail-order catalogs of bookstores and retail businesses. All these companies will deal directly with individuals. Many feature books you won't easily find in your general-interest bookstore. Children's book catalogs are listed in Chapter XIII.

(Editor's note: Many of these organizations were picked for inclusion in this short list because they are small operations. If two phone numbers are listed, the 800 number is usually reserved for paying customers. Please be courteous and patient, and you will be repaid with old-fashioned, personal service.)

B & B Honey Farm. Route 2, PO Box 245, Houston, MN 55943; (504) 896-3955.

Find the books about the business side of keeping bees and buy products to do the job. They provide craft supplies and honey-based products, and you can order Italian queens and Nucs. If you have to ask, you shouldn't own one.

Books of Scotland. 50 West Hunter Avenue, Maywood, NJ 07607; (201) 291-9621; fax (201) 843-0057.

Two dozen Scottish publishers have ganged together to sell their wares. The catalog is organized by subject and is worth the couple of dollars to cover mailing.

Bowling's™ Bookstore. Tech Ed Publishing Co., PO Box 4, Deerfield, IL 60015; (800) 521-BOWL.

Books, videos, and posters about bowling. My favorite jillion-square-feet bookstores do not have a bowling section, so what do you do when you must have a book on the mental game of bowling? Now I know.

Dog and Cat Book Catalog. Direct Book Service, PO Box 2778, Wenatchee, WA 98807-2778; (800) 776-2665.

More than 2,000 titles are represented, many of which I have not seen outside of large, specialty pet stores, pet shows, and conferences.

Firefighters Bookstore™. 18281 Gothard, #105, Huntington Beach, CA 92648-1205; (800) 727-3327, (714) 375-4888; fax (800) 848-4566, (714) 848-4566.

Fire department personnel in small towns must find this catalog a blessing, but it is also useful to people contemplating a career switch, or whose jobs require knowledge about the firefighting field.

Gambler's Book Shop. Gambler's Book Club/GBC Press, 630 South 11th Street, Las Vegas, NV 89101; (800) 522-1777; fax (702) 382-7594.

In case you can't make it to Las Vegas to pick up books on betting on jai alai, hockey, video machines, bingo, or mah-jongg, this catalog has what you need. One section is devoted to cheating; one hopes so this is that you will learn how to keep from being ripped off, rather than as a way to promote illegal behavior.

Gemstone Press. PO Box 237, Woodstock, VT 05091; (800) 962-4544, (802) 457-4000; fax (802) 457-4004.

Reference books for dealers, serious hobbyists, collectors, and wishful thinkers. Like the subject matter, many of the books are not inexpensive.

The Herpetocultural Library Series. Published by Advanced Vivarium Systems, 10728 Prospect Avenue, Suite G, Santee, CA 92071; (619) 258-2629; fax (619) 258-7262.

Absolutely beautiful and totally cool books on every aspect of the care and enjoyment of reptiles. For those of you who were concerned you wouldn't find good books about the breeding of corn snakes or the general care of bearded dragons, your worries are over.

International Marine®. The McGraw Hill Companies, Columbus, OH 43004; (800) 822-8158; fax (614) 759-3644; e-mail: 70007.1531@compuserve.com.

Since boat lovers are notorious for spending money, bookloving boat folk must be doubly broke! This is a nice mix of technical manuals, kids' books, fiction, and reference material.

Invisible Ink™. Books on Ghosts and Hauntings, 1811 Stonewood Drive, Beavercreek, OH 45432-4002; (800) 31-GHOST, (513) 426-5110; fax (513) 320-1832.

Are your favorite ghosts Japanese, English, or Bermudan? Are you hunting ghosts in Kentucky, Virginia, or Hawaii? This is a veritable travel directory of books on hauntings and the mysterious. The editors have thoughtfully marked the "frankly fiction" with an *f* so as not to confuse gullible readers.

Island Press. Order Department, PO Box 7, Covelo, CA 95428; (800) 828-1302, (707) 983-6432; fax (707) 983-6414.

High-quality, high-minded books on conservation and environmental issues, for serious students and activists.

Charles H. Kerr Publishing Company. 1740 West Greenleaf Avenue, Chicago, IL 60626; catalog $2.

Since 1886, Kerr has been publishing and distributing books about the labor movement, socialism, communism, and Marxism. If you are tracking down radicals of different flavors, this publisher is at the other end of the spectrum from Laissez Faire Books, listed below, except, of course, where the *most* radical folk from each collection of philosophies converge.

Laissez Faire Books. 938 Howard, Suite 202, San Francisco, CA 94103; (800) 326-0996; fax (415) 541-0597; e-mail: oders@lfb.org.

My favorite source for books from the libertarian corner of the political spectrum, which includes radical individualists, conservative economists, and a few mainstream authors who advocate personal and economic freedom. They often have remaindered books squirreled away when other outlets have run dry.

Lion House Distributors. PO Box 91283, Pittsburgh, PA 15221; (800) 786-6235.

A nice collection of regional and specialty cookbooks. The books seem to focus on food, rather than culinary art. Perfect for the New England chowder lover who lives in the Southwest.

Lonely Planet. 155 Filbert Street, Suite 251, Oakland, CA 94607; (800) 275-8555; fax (510) 893-8563; e-mail: info@lonelyplanet.com.

The well-respected, offbeat travel guide publisher. Each book features insider information about customs, fees, special deals, and cultural barriers. Many readers say this is the best source if you want to be more than a tourist in the countries you visit. Some of the truths are unpleasant, but they make for compelling reading, even if you never leave the comfort of your armchair.

Loompanics Unlimited. PO Box 1197, Port Townsend, WA 98368; (360) 385-7471.

My best-loved catalog of weird books. Sex, drugs, criminal behavior, fringe political beliefs, etc. You will find a rabid adherence to belief in the rights of the individual and some interesting books on history, politics, ethics, and the law.

Mountain Press Publishing Company. PO Box 2399, Missoula, MT 59806; (800) 234-5308; fax (406) 728-1635; e-mail: mtnpress@montana.com.

A REAL western publisher, with books about cowboys, rodeo skills, horses and ranching, and also western natural history, fishing, and children's books with western themes.

Peanut Books. PO Box 331934, Coconut Grove, FL 33233-1934; (305) 666-4082; fax (305) 666-4697.

Dime novels are back, reincarnated in these postcard-size novellas. The topics are cheap barbershop fun, from fantasy to military action. They have a great gimmick. Each small book can be part of a series, so you get hooked. A great gift for the book-liker who needs a quick fix while waiting for the doctor.

Penguin USA. Consumer Sales, PO Box 999, Dept. 17109, Bergenfield, NJ 07621; (800) 253-6476; catalogs issued 3x/year.

Like Dover Publications, (see Chapter II), Penguin does a great job of keeping classics in print. I included them in this listing because of the importance of their backlist and their positive attitude toward individuals who want to buy direct, an attitude not shared by all large publishers. A typical catalog has hundreds of listings sans descriptions, so you need to know what you want.

Radio Bookstore. PO Box 209, Rindge, NH 03461-0209; (800) 457-7373; fax (603) 899-6826.

It is easy to forget that ham radio operators were the original techies and nerds, and that radio is still the best form of communication in many parts of the globe. If you are overwhelmed by fancy computer talk, learn about technology firsthand by buying a book about building a crystal set.

Small Press Distribution. 1814 San Pablo Avenue, Berkeley, CA 94702-1624; (510) 549-3336; fax (510) 549-2201.

SPD is a nonprofit membership organization devoted to promoting the literary arts. Their catalog features the fine fiction, poetry, and cross-cultural literature of dozens of small presses, such as Lynx House, Yellow Moon, Left Hand Books, and Konch. A standard $40 membership provides a 10 percent discount.

Special Needs Project. World Wide Disability Information Resources, 3463 State Street, Suite 282, Santa Barbara, CA 93105; (805) 683-9633; fax (805) 683-2341; e-mail: snpbooks@eworld.com; catalog $2.

You request a simple form, on which you check off from dozens of categories, ranging from Accessible Design to Young Adults and Teens. Then you receive custom information about books, videotapes, periodicals, and product information in those topic areas. The $2 is credited to the first order. The range of topics is extraordinary, on the challenges and triumphs of the human condition: adoption, autism, cancer, fathering, heart disease, sign language, and violence.

Vintage '45 Press. Selected Booklist, PO Box 266, Orinda, CA 94563.

I am old enough so that Mom is looking more like a contemporary. If you are a woman growing older, or if you know women who are growing older, this modest catalog will make a welcome gift. It contains a bookshelf full of hand-picked titles that deal with women, aging, and family.

The Whole Work Catalog™. The New Careers Center, 1515 23rd Street, PO Box 339-CT, Boulder, CO 80306; (303) 447-1087; fax (303) 447-8684.

To avoid the tragedy of losing your job and consequently having to cut back on your book buying, you need help with life planning. These books, representing many publishers and authors, focus on everything but the conventional resumé and career track.

Publishers' Resources: The Inside Story

Is your favorite publisher about to go under? (Better make sure you have the books you want from that publisher, before they become hard to find.) Is your favorite obscure author about to launch a new series of books with a small press? (Better notify your bookstore to order them for you, before the print run is sold out.) Are publishers coming up with new sales strategies? (Better know how these will affect your pocketbook.)

Advanced bookloving requires access to professional-level gossip about the publishing industry. You can use the knowledge of how the publishing and book-selling industry works to improve your home library, because you will be able to understand and anticipate trends in publishing.

The Biggest New Book Bookselling Organizations

These two organizations do not accept average readers as members (you have to own a store or be part of the industry), but they do offer information about locating stores. Their conferences are not open to the general public. But, if you are at the stage of your bibliotosis that you are seriously thinking about opening a bookstore, both offer classes and all kinds of support. See Chapters II, VI, and XII for information on organizations related to rare and collectable books.

American Booksellers Association (ABA). 828 South Broadway, Tarrytown, NY 10591; (800) 637-0037, (914) 591-2665; fax (814) 591-2720.

Your favorite bookstore probably belongs to this organization. As of the end of 1996, it is going through some drastic changes, including the shedding of its hallmark annual conference, now to be called BookExpo America and run by Reed Exhibition Companies.

Christian Booksellers Association (CBA). PO Box 200, Colorado Springs, CO 80901-0200.

Another organization for professionals only, but the place to go if you decide that you want to locate, sell to, or work for a Christian bookseller.

Publisher Groups and Magazines That Inform BookLovers

Some of the secrets of the book publishing world are easily learned by joining marketing and educational organizations that focus on the writing and publishing communities, or by subscribing to key magazines.

Poets & Writers Magazine. 72 Spring Street, New York, NY 10012; (212) 226-3586; fax (212) 226-3963; e-mail: pwsubs@aol.com; 6x/year; $18/year.

Poets, editors, writers, and novelists worry out loud about the future of their professions and debate concerns such as copyrights, freedom of speech, contracts, and the electronic book. Booklovers will also enjoy the interviews.

Publishers Marketing Association (PMA). 2401 Pacific Coast Highway, Suite 102, Hermosa Beach, CA 90254; (310) 372-2732; fax (310) 374-3342; e-mail: pmaonline@aol.com. $125/year.

The largest national organization that supports the marketing efforts of smaller publishers; it has affiliated regional groups all over the country. The newsletter is packed with choice wisdom about publishing, ranging from writing contracts to the choice of a cover. The staff bends over backward to help publishers.

Publishers Weekly®. Subscriptions Services, PO Box 6457, Torrance, CA 90504; (800) 278-2991; weekly; $149/year.

Booksellers and publishers devour each issue, which is packed with reviews of upcoming books (months before they arrive in stores), profiles of publishers and authors, essays on the publishing industry, and the latest hoo-haw about "the end of publishing as we know it."

Sisters in Crime™. PO Box 442124, Lawrence, KS 66044-8933; $25/year.

An international membership organization for booksellers, writers, publishers, and fans "to combat discrimination against women in the mystery field, educate publishers and the general public as to the inequalities in the treatment of female authors, and raise the level of awareness of their contribution to the field." This translates into a really cool newsletter about the mystery writing biz, with insider information about conferences, new books, awards, and publishing advice. Regional chapters offer local support.

Small Press: *The Magazine of Independent Publishing.* Jenkins Group,
121 East Front Street, 4th Floor, Traverse City, MI 49684; (616) 933-0445;
fax (616) 933-0445; e-mail: jenkins.group@smallpress.com; bimonthly; $34/year.

Many good books that don't get reviewed elsewhere will get reviewed here.
This is an industry trade publication, which means you also get the behind-the
scenes stories about how the smaller presses are doing.

Small Press Review (SPR). Dustbooks, PO Box 100, Paradise, CA 95967;
(916) 877-6110; fax (916) 877-0222; e-mail: len@dustbooks.com or
dustbooks@tells.org; monthly; $25/year.

The best place to learn about the small press world from the point of view of the
militantly noncommercial writers and publishers, through letters, reviews, essays,
ads, and piquant gossip.

Small Publishers Association of North America (SPAN). PO Box 1306, Buena
Vista, CO 81211; (719) 395-4790; fax (719) 395-8374; $75/year.

A newly formed organization started by two of the leading supporters of
small presses, Tom and Marilyn Ross. Besides assisting the small presses, SPAN
also helps authors who have to step in and help promote their books.

Women Writing the West. PO Box 12, Boulder, CO 80306-0012; $35/year.

An association of writers and other professionals promoting the women's
West. Membership includes agents, librarians, published writers, and fans. A
quarterly newsletter details the group's marketing efforts and provides readers
with names of new books. It also offers an intriguing look into the challenges facing smaller publishers and lesser-known authors. A very direct way to support
quality in publishing, at least in one genre.

❖

*So, you want to become a book collector
in order to make big money?
page 94.*

Chapter VI — Collecting Books

Being a Chapter About the Economics, Secret Handshakes, Diseases, and Joys Associated With the Conscious Collecting of the Book, and Sources for Used, Rare, and Antiquarian Books.

Where Are They Hiding the Old Good Stuff?
The Book Collecting Game

Some booklovers stalk their prey in used bookstores because, they claim, the old books are the best books. Some search for out-of-print reference books and inexpensive multiple copies of old favorites. But many play a game called Collecting Books. You can play the game any way you want. Just remember that most of the people who win make their money selling the rule books and sponsoring the tournaments. Here are some current rules of the book collecting game.

The Fun Rule

If you want to collect books, do it because it is fun and gives you pleasure. This is the first consideration. Don't let anyone admonish you because what you collect is not important enough, fine enough, or expensive enough.

The Serious Rule

If you want to collect books in order to build a collection that has historical or artistic significance, get serious. Get educated about book collecting.

> *I've been buying books for better than thirty-five years and keep fairly good records on each book. I didn't start out to be a collector and even now reject that label. About ten years ago, I started paying attention to first editions and when I realized what I was doing I quickly stopped. Only after I decide to buy a book because I want or need it, do I then look to see first edition status. With rare exceptions, all the books in "the library" are hardbound. Most have dust jackets encased in plastic covers. Almost never do I lend books to others and people seldom ask. The arrangement, condition, etc. of the books clearly indicate to any perceptive person that the books aren't just a collection of odd volumes stuffed in a bookcase.*
> —Thomas C. Dall, retired landscape architect
> who works in a bookstore, Littleton, CO

It is necessary to attend conferences, read, take classes, and find several mentors to help you make the best decisions because there are few shortcuts, unless you have enough money to buy yourself a significant library. Assume that you will serve an informal apprenticeship for many years.

You also need to educate yourself about your field of interest.

The "Brain Trust" Rule

The biggest danger for the neophyte collector is to pay attention to the advice of only one person, or to consort only with experts from one field. You will inherit all the biases and blind spots of that person, or that group of experts, unless you are willing to seek out many different points of view.

Say you have decided to start a collection of business books published before World War I. The book dealer who cares about the subject could have a different idea about what is valuable or important than does the reference librarian at a business school or a government archivist. As an example, this business book collector should have a network of experts that includes:

1. An experienced book collector in a related field, such as economics.
2. A used book dealer with experience in fine books of all kinds.
3. A business or business history librarian.
4. Someone who knows how to clean and repair fine books.
5. A business historian who does not necessarily know about books.

Many professional associations have their own archives or libraries for the use of their memberships, which is a reason in itself to join.

The Money Rule

So, you want to become a book collector in order to make big money? Sigh. If you talk to financial wizards who consistently make big money for themselves and their clients over many decades, they will tell you that they are very leery of collectibles as investments, such as stamps, coins, paintings, furniture, lunchboxes, and books. They will encourage you to put the bulk of your money in financial instruments such as stocks and bonds, and to devote only a small part of your extra income to collecting anything as an investment. They will advise you that, to compete with a mutual fund with average risks and rewards, a book purchased for investment purposes should increase in value by 12 to 15 percent a year. (That figure needs to increase if the current low rate of inflation increases.)

Do you think that everyone will spend huge amounts of money on a particular book, just because you did? Ethical book collectors and book dealers cringe at this attitude and do their best to dissuade people who are buying and stashing away books as if they were certificates of deposit with government guarantees.

> *Personal libraries function as self-portraits. Most people who
> collect books that mean something serious to them like the
> feeling of having them around, as if these books somehow
> define the character or belonging of the person to whom they
> are connected. They are a security blanket. They are family.
> They comfort with the familiarity of home turf.*
> —Al Lehmann, booklover, Terrace, British Columbia, Canada

Here are the basics of book collecting for money, which I will convey to you only with your promise that you will not spend the dog food money on any deal to "double your money in two weeks."

1. *If you are collecting books for profit, be prepared to invest in ensuring that the books are kept in absolutely pristine condition.* The slightest damage to a book jacket, cover, or contents can immediately reduce the resale value of the book. These are books to keep and sell, not to read and enjoy. Think of your investment collection as a farm where it is not smart to make friends with the lambs.

2. *Buy the best copy you can, and keep trading up.* You always want to own the best edition of a particular book; use the discards to finance new purchases.

3. *Buy what you think people will want, not just what you love.* How do you find out what people want? There is the rub. What you read in the books and magazines on book collecting are only best guesses, based on today's fashions.

An example is the current craze for first editions of twentieth-century books in virgin condition, specifically what are commonly referred to as *modern first editions*. What started as the booklover's desire to acquire the finest copies of favorite current authors has evolved into an institution as ruthless as a feedlot. Any and every author's books—even the lousy ones—are now purchased and held, on the theory that most of them will increase in value. And they do, at least in the short run, because there are enough people around with the same belief to buy them.

The book collectors who collect only to maximize the resale value of their acquisitions will end up owning books they know nothing about, do not respect, and will never open, let alone read.

4. *Be aware of the most common myths.* Old does not equal valuable. Rare does not equal valuable. Libraries, museums, government archives, and historical societies rarely have money to buy books at a price that would please an investor. The result is that the very nice nineteenth-century novel, which has been in the family for generations, will probably not bring in five figures, no matter what Aunt Amy told you.

5. *Any trend can reverse itself; any fad can fail.* Just because there has been a constant market for a particular author's work for forty years does not guarantee that market will continue.

The overwhelming number of book dealers are honest. The caveats in this chapter are meant to impress you with the subjectiveness of choice in the marketplace, and with the dangers of assuming that what happens to the price of something in the future can be predicted accurately and consistently based on what has happened in the past. The past can give you clues, but no guarantees.

One of the saddest aspects of the book world is that most books lose most of their value within a few months or years after they are sold. It is heartbreaking to see the endless stream of individuals who come into a used bookstore toting books that cost them hundreds of dollars, but that are now worthless. It is especially sad when those individuals are down on their luck, hoping to pay the rent or buy food with a pile of ancient textbooks or well-worn bestsellers.

Knowing a little about economic theory should not take away from the joy you derive from collecting books you love. It might protect you from the bitterness of disappointment, if you know when promises about profits are made that cannot be kept. This kind of knowledge can improve your ability to invest in books and other collectibles because it can give you a sense of perspective that can lead to better decisions.

How Is the Price of a Used Book Determined?

Selling books to dealers, who maintain inventories and sell their wares at their stores, at book fairs, and through catalogs, or to book scouts, who buy and sell books for specific clients and usually do not maintain inventories, is different from selling to another collector. In order to make a profit, the dealer or scout might only pay you 25 to 50 percent of the retail price, but there are no fixed rules, only conventions that experienced book dealers and scouts tend to follow. That margin covers overhead, which can include the book sitting on a shelf for months, or the risk involved in case the buyer guesses wrong and pays too much.

But no matter whom you sell to, the money you will receive for a book is based on what the buyer thinks it is worth, not on what you think it is worth. It is the buyer's ability and willingness to part with the cash that determines the selling price of the book; everything else is smoke and mirrors. An offer to sell and a bid to buy are hopeful guesses; a completed transaction becomes a historical fact that has emotional impact on future guesses. That is why the books that list recent sale prices are so valuable; these dollar amounts provide guideposts in what is otherwise a ferocious and disorienting wilderness.

The value of a book to a potential buyer, and his or her willingness to pay that price, are not based on objective criteria. There is a consensual mythology in book collecting that pretends that a book has value because of, among other factors, its age, its association with someone famous by means of ownership or autograph, its historical value, its condition, the amount of time it took to construct it, the price someone paid for it originally, the price someone paid for it yesterday, the cost of the materials that went into its design, the number of copies printed, its rarity, etc.

I may hunger for books until my teeth bleed, always full of suspicion that the one book with all the answers still eludes me but will one day turn up. But I have not killed for mere print.
—Gregory McNamee, author of 12 books, Tucson, AZ
including *A Desert Bestiary* (Johnson Books) and
The Sierra Club Desert Reader (Sierra Club Books).
Gregory McNamee ©1996

These factors will influence someone's decision, but the final decision will be based on what one school of economics calls "counterfactual information." This is information that is not necessarily rational or useful. It is the Big Unknown in how people make decisions. It is the reason people tell market researchers that they want purple velvet pants in spring and then buy blue denim skirts. It is the reason that 80 percent of new product introductions fail, even after millions of dollars of research. It is the reason that perfectly good solutions to problems languish and stupid expensive solutions prosper. The reason is: There is no rational reason. The rules of the game are made up, and then the reasons are rationalized.

The next time the rare unethical bookseller tells you that a particular book is guaranteed to go up in price, tell him that you will take him up on that guarantee. Tell him your lawyer would be happy to draw up a contract stating that after a certain period of time, the dealer will buy the book back at an agreed-upon price that reflects the increase. (If you ever find dealers who take you up on that offer, please give me their names and phone numbers!) This is a different situation from that of ethical dealers offering to buy books back at the price you paid.

The Book Market

It is in the best interest of everyone in a collectibles market to keep the prices of books up by means of boosterism and active recruitment. The more people buy, the more money flows into the collectibles market, and the more money for the people selling.

Is this unethical or illegal? Nope, it is just a truth about human behavior. Knowing that humans behave this way, however, might keep you from being swept away by statistics of growth and profit that can change overnight. Just because a knowledgeable dealer is excited about book collecting today is not enough to ensure that you will make a profit twenty years from now.

It is in the best interest of established collectors to keep the prices down on desirable items they themselves wish to purchase. An unethical dealer will disparage an author, publisher, or particular book, hoping that a lack of interest will lower the price.

An influential person writing an article in a newsletter or being quoted at an important conference can start a buying trend. The important question is whether this influential person is the sole owner of a stash of these books. It is considered good form for a book dealer who is promoting a particular investment to let the chumps—excuse me, the customers—know if that dealer has a stake in that investment. That does not make the investment suspect, by the way, but knowing that the person promoting the investment will benefit personally if you buy is useful information. Sometimes it is difficult to differentiate between an honestly exciting and healthy collectibles market and one that is fueled by lies.

Markets collapse when people stop buying. Cornering the market does not work well with collectibles. Discouraged buyers find something else to pique their interest, and the person with the world's largest and only collection of twelfth-century Irish salmon cooking manuscripts will need to find another obsessive-compulsive with the same obsession and lots of money.

A healthy market means that there are many sources of both buyers and sellers, a wide variety of products, continuing innovation (new products, new discoveries, new scholarship), and a widespread interest in the products, both inside and outside of the market.

The average person can enter a healthy collectibles market with a modest sum of money and, on the other hand, wealthy people see it as worth their while to participate as well. A healthy collectibles market is somewhat chaotic as a result, with many sources of information.

Is Profit Evil?

Are you corrupting the book community by becoming someone who makes money from your love for books? Are booksellers, particularly those who deal in used, rare, and antiquarian books, bad people?

Booklovers who consider books and libraries as sacred trusts where Truth and Beauty reside may feel uncomfortable with the thought that books can ever be bought and sold. They prefer to focus on books as art and icon. Scholarly librarians and archivists might operate under rules that actually prevent the institutions they work for from ever selling books; even in a cash crunch, they must donate those books to another nonprofit institution.

The people who work for the private presses, which produce the best examples of fine printing and writing; for the nonprofit presses, which tout unpopular political positions, and for those bookstores that are fortunate enough to be subsidized by low rent and an owner with a day job: Those people will tend to denounce anyone who they think "profits" from books. Also, there is a battle raging in the public library community about "fees for services." Libraries ought to be free, say the members of one camp, and supply everything for everybody with no upfront charges; taxes and donations should pay the bills. Librarians in the other camp think libraries should charge for everything from renting computers to conducting computer searches.

People who create books, from the writers and editors to the folks who resell used paperbacks by the pound, are a notoriously underpaid lot. (I average about 20 hours each month as a book industry "volunteer," in addition to what I am paid to do.) And some of these folks, as a result, develop a misplaced pride in being broke. It is as if being part of the marketplace, if you are a booklover, is acceptable only if you aren't financially successful.

When I was a bookseller and small press publisher, I would have loved to have gotten rich off of my books. But, I was not smart or experienced enough to know how. I admire prosperous booksellers and publishers, because I believe that making money off of books fuels individuals to write, print, and distribute books, as much as the love of art and culture does. Used book dealers, in their quest for profits, rescue many precious books from oblivion. My experience has been that many of the people who have disdain for profitable enterprise in the book community rely on someone else or something else to pay their rent.

One of the glorious triumphs in the book world is to make lots of money because customers are voting with their pocketbooks to tell you they are happy with what you are creating and selling. This is true whether you are a best-selling author or a rare book dealer.

On the other hand, I have seen greed and carelessness hurt both publishers and booksellers. Greed from publishers of all sizes who cynically produce books that they cheerfully admit are ugly and worthless, just to make a very quick dollar. Carelessness from booksellers who think they never have to become competent at customer service, marketing, and financial management. As a consequence, the book industry has a crisis about once an hour these days, fueled in part by the response of bookloving customers to prices that do not reflect value, or to indifferent booksellers. But, we don't need a Ministry of Social Equity in Books to mandate the price of books.

Deciphering the Language of the Collector

In order to collect books, you need to understand the basic terminology. There is an art to describing the condition of a book in used book catalogs. The basic bibliographic data, such as author, publisher, date of publication, city of publication, and, of course, the asking price, are easy to decipher. But what about the other information? There is no uniform model of what constitutes "good" versus "very good." The gray areas are what dealers and disgruntled customers contest. The other problem is the inconsistent use of vocabulary. One book dealer told me that it is popular among some U.S. dealers to adopt British book collecting terms, partly because the vocabulary adds panache to their catalogs. The result is minor border skirmishes among the intelligentsia of the book business about what is the *right* word and what a word *really* means.

A book can be described several ways:

The features of the book, from the luster of the leather to tantalizing gossip about the publisher, are what will make you salivate. Boy, are you easy. This is the sales pitch.

Serious book collectors pay more attention to the physical condition of the books. Most dealers use a scale of "fine" through "poor" to approximate how the book stacks up relative to a generally agreed-upon range of defects. Here is one version of a list of those basic descriptors. Don't blame me if you think these terms are vague; many experts would agree with you. And ten different book collectors would provide you with ten different lists.

As New: Perfect. *Mint,* which is often used instead, is a term that some book dealers would prefer be reserved for coins. The book looks like it did the day it came out of the bindery.

Fine: Not as crisp and squeaky-clean as *as new,* but no defects.

Very good: Few small defects, like a bumped corner, but no tears.

Good: This book has been read and loved, and it shows. It may suffer some tears in its pages or covers, and the dirt stains are obvious, but nothing is missing.

Fair: The contents are intact, but some extraneous pieces, like an endsheet, may be missing. The cover or dust jacket shows real wear.

Poor: This is the "reading copy," where the defects exceed the room to describe them. My reading copy of a favorite out-of-print science fiction novel smells of mold, lacks a front cover, and the first half of the book looks like it was dipped in strong tea. And I don't care.

Ex-Lib: Refers to books that were once part of a "real" library. The book is covered with rubber-stamped information, written dates, etc. Many collectors abhor such books, but one of the nineteenth-century treasures I bought while researching this book was discarded by a public library in Alabama.

Book club: The pariahs of book collecting, unless this is what you collect. Considered a defect that must be noted.

Another way to describe a book is by enumerating those defects in detail, which might include torn pages or dust jackets, missing illustrations or pages, faded cloth covers, stained pages, bumped corners, musty odor, worn spine, soiled covers, library and remainder markings, bookplates and labels, wrinkled pages, pencil and pen notations, and damaged hinges.

There are always people who like to read. Their shelves are stuffed with aging paperbacks and things picked up from the thrift store. Reader's Digest Condensed Books *and dog-eared, bulging, mass-market thrillers. Let us gently but firmly close the door on their enucleative labors. Reading is better than not reading, but these people are not necessarily booklovers.*
—Philip Normand, graphic designer and illustrator, Denver, CO
Philip Normand © 1996

It is considered a sin to not note defects, and a conscientious dealer will record them in detail, since those details do affect the perceived value of the book. But the amount of detail varies from dealer to dealer. A dealer selling the content of the book is less interested in every nick and scratch. Dealers who rebind books in fancy editions will go into lengthy rhapsodies about the color of the leather and the amount of gold leaf on the cover, but might omit details such as size.

Dealing in used, rare, and antiquarian books is still a game based on mutual trust. Electronic communication has accelerated the gossip about untrustworthy souls, but it is good to start learning about book catalogs and book collecting from someone who is geographically near you, if for no other reason than you can go to her in person and complain when things go wrong. Then as your experience increases, you can work with people farther away.

The consensus is that almost all of your book buying and selling experiences will be positive. The ones that are not are part of the price you pay for your education as a book collector.

The Used Bookstore Relationship to Book Collecting

The best place in the world is a used bookstore. There is the heady perfume of the books themselves that permeates most bookstores and is part of their romance; it is the sweet smell of leaves underfoot in an autumn forest. There is an incredible richness, as Jo March recognized in *Little Women*. Here, for small change, are wisdom and fun, honor and horror, sex and death, and a flock of different ways to make chicken with garlic.

I love a used bookstore because I feel safe there. Any questions I have can be answered, and the answers have been in the books on the shelves for many years.

Plus, there is the pleasure of exploring the universe through the eccentric vision of the owner of the store. Because, profit aside (and I have met only one used bookstore owner out of hundreds who seems to be in it just for the money), there is the aesthetic and theological issue of bibliographical free will. The thousands of volumes in the average used bookstore are usually there because of the decisions of one person.

The public or academic librarian must acquire books according to guidelines dictated by community standards, committee members, and 1,000 scholarly articles in 100 professional journals. By comparison, the owner of a used bookstore is a free spirit. A used bookstore owner can choose what to keep and what to discard, what to sell and what to buy, what to put on the free shelf in front and what needs to be keep in cold storage, away from oily fingers.

If her store only accepts paperback romance novels, that is her choice, not a policy set down by a library board or city council. On the other hand, if the owner develops a fondness for French cookbooks or Civil War battlefield guides or first editions of Catholic American novels, no one can stop her from filling her shelves; it is not a public decision, except that the individual members of her public can protest by not buying anything from those shelves.

This is the poorly kept secret of the used book industry. Used bookstores, from the paperback exchanges to the rare press monasteries, are often the public extension of the owner's personal library. It is book idiosyncrasy in a storefront. The genesis of the store was probably that last argument with the nonbookloving members of the family, or the retiring booklover's dream come true. Or perhaps, it was the booklover selling a few books to a favorite dealer, and the dealer casually remarking, "You know, you have good taste. Have you ever thought of selling books for a living?" The earth moved, and Dorothy Sayer's angels sang on the other side.

Of course, some bookstore owners have a small problem with actually parting with any of their treasures. Here are the warning signs that the owner of the store would just prefer that you go away and leave him in peace: stores whose friendly clutter has evolved into a hazardous waste dump, making browsing and buying difficult; surly staff; no lights in the stacks; no shelf signs; no organization; the shop is never open; no one has change for anything larger than a $1 bill; the shop is run by the owner's ten-year-old daughter; the owner tries to talk you out of buying a book.

What About Book Fairs?

Book fairs are as much about meeting book dealers and fellow booklovers as they are about buying books. They are true free markets, with an honorable history going back centuries. Hold onto your pocketbook, because the combination of fresh air and dozens of booksellers offering thousands of books is dangerously intoxicating for people like you and me.

The experts say you have a better chance of negotiating with a book dealer if you don't have an audience. Wait for a lull in the business if you want to haggle. Also, look for the odd book that does not seem to fit in with the rest of the books displayed; the dealer might want to get rid of it.

Another version of the book fair is the book mall. The one near my house is like a permanent fair, with bookshelves filled with the wares of dozens of dealers, each of whom has a different focus. I mention this only because, as a booklover, you might consider getting together with a group of book-savvy friends, renting an inexpensive storefront in a bookloving neighborhood, and financing your home library out of the proceeds. You will make a lot of money with no effort. Just make sure you sell your best books real cheap. And send me your address.

If you are serious about your book collecting, you need to talk to a tax adviser, whether you think you operate as a business or as a hobby. The Internal Revenue Service has its own tests for deciding which category you fall into, and your good intentions will not impress them.

But don't rely on the not-so-expert opinions of friends or even other book collectors. Find a qualified tax consultant who has experience with collectibles, and who keeps up on the latest in the federal and state regulations.

What About Library Sales?

Since the groups that put on the sales usually give first dibs to their members, this should be an impetus to join the local Friends of the Library organization, so that you can take advantage of this perk. More and more libraries have ongoing sales, where "weeds" are displayed at all times. The prices are ridiculously cheap, often less than 10 cents on the dollar.

The collector who looks for signed first editions will shun a circulating library edition, with all of its disfiguring stamps. However, many of the books at a library sale have never been part of the library circulating collection, but rather are gifts to help raise money. Collectors who are looking for antiquarian books or out-of-print editions to complete a set can find books and manuscripts to die for.

You will have to arrive early to find the good stuff, if you live in a town where library sales are already popular and serious dealers show up at first light.

The Deadly Sin of the Book Collecting Community

Too many collectors and dealers horrify the rest of the book world by using lighter fluid, spray-on tile cleaner, rubber cement, rubber cement thinner, paint solvents, and a host of over-the-counter chemicals to clean books. They will tell you that it is no big deal, the chemicals work fine, and they are still alive, ha, ha.

Book conservation experts report lasting stains and damage from the casual use of hardware store chemicals. One reason is that there are many different kinds of chemicals in the over-the-counter formulas, including dyes, preservatives, and stuff to make them taste bad to kids and dogs. The extra chemicals, which have nothing to do with the stated purpose of the product, can leave residues that might not appear for months, but might linger for years.

A professional book conservator uses chemicals that are formulated for expert use. These chemicals are not for lighting cigarettes or removing paint from your kitchen table; they are manufactured for a very specific conservation purpose. They are subjected to tests that the over-the-counter chemicals are not. How often do the people who make lighter fluid, for example, run tests to determine how well their product removes labels from the back of fine books?

Rubber cement migrates through paper creating a wonderful
red/brown color, and it is almost impossible to remove the stains.
—Douglas Stone, paper conservator, Milwaukee, WI

Also, unlike the special cleaning formulas for books, the commercial brands can and do change their recipes without telling the customer. So, even if you find that perfect mix of varnish thinner, windshield washer fluid, and model plane glue, you do not know if the next batch you mix will contain the same chemicals.

Finally, the physical side effects of many chemicals do not show up for years. Why expose your family to the volatile fumes in these products?

This is where I side with the experts. If you have a valuable book that needs cleaning, take it to a book conservator whose job it is to preserve and repair fine books. Or, learn how to do it the right way, and order the right product to handle the job from one of the catalogs listed in this book.

If you are running out of space for bookcases to store your valuable books, consider using archival-quality boxes that exactly fit the book. Experts who design storage facilities estimate that up to 70 per cent of the space in ordinary shelves and boxes is wasted, usually because there is so much unused space behind and above the books. ❖

Resources for Book Collectors

Where to Start

Antiquarian Booksellers Association of America (ABAA).
50 Rockefeller Plaza, Lobby, New York, NY 10020; (212) 757-9395;
fax (212) 459-0307; e-mail: abba@panix.com.

The premier organization in the country for the rare, used, and antiquarian bookseller. Members of the ABAA engage in the sale, purchase, and appraisal of antiquarian books and manuscripts. The ABAA headquarters is available to provide directories and information about member booksellers, and to handle questions or complaints related to the association.

ABAA members can provide valuations of antiquarian material within their fields of specialty for estate, insurance, tax, or sales purposes. The appraisal of books and manuscripts is a professional service for which a fee will be charged. The bookseller can waive the fee if he is able to purchase the material, or if it has little or no value.

Please see Chapter VIII for more information about appraisals and appraisal organizations.

Antiquarian, Specialty, and Used Book Sellers 1996–97: *A Subject Guide and Directory.* Edited by James M. Ethridge and Karen Ethridge. *$85.00 cloth, ISBN 0-7808-0024-9; Omnigraphics, Inc., Penobscot Building, Detroit, MI 48226; (800) 234-1340; fax (800) 875-1340.*

The hardest part of doing this book came when I started to collect the names of used, rare, and antiquarian bookstores and book dealers. As I gathered more and more responses from reputable dealers from all over the world, I knew I could not do them justice in the limited space in this book.

At the last minute, I have been rescued by the kindness of a stranger, who forwarded me pages from this 700-page directory. This is the answer. Buy this book, and you will have comprehensive indexes of more than 5,000 dealers, cross-referenced by 2,000 topics and subtopics, alphabetized by store name, organized by state and city, and supplemented with an owner and manager listing.

Celebration Books. Lois J. Harvey, 3617 Meade Street, Denver, CO 80211; (303) 480-5193.

A mail-order source that focuses on books related to book collecting, plus provides information on book collecting in general. Harvey is an experienced bookseller and collector who also teaches classes on book collecting and book dealing at conferences around the country.

Books for Book Collectors

There are books about book collecting as sport, illness, dangerous adventure, and pleasure. There are narratives that describe book collecting and provide advice on locating, buying, caring for, and selling books. They also explain the archaic vocabulary of the book collector. There are references that list books with recent sale prices and provide the identification and history of particular books.

The books in this list are either widely available, reasonably priced, or specifically recommended by experienced used book dealers or collectors, but this list is by no means inclusive. **Gale Research, Inc.,** (800) 877-GALE, and **Spoon River Press,** (888) 730-2665, are two sources of price indexes and other books for the serious collector.

American Book Prices Current. *Edited by Katherine K. Leab. Bancroft-Parkman, $140.00 cloth, ISBN 0-914022-30-X.*
One of the standard price listings for serious collectors and dealers.

Book Collecting: *A Comprehensive Guide.* 1995 Edition.
Allen and Patricia Ahearn. *Putnam, $35.00 cloth, ISBN 0-399-14049-2.*
Mostly reference lists and some narrative.

Book Finds: *How to Find, Buy, and Sell Used and Rare Books.* Ian C. Ellis. *Perigee, $13.00 paper, ISBN 0-399-51978-5.*
Mostly narrative, with a list of popular collectable authors and information on identifying first editions.

Book Hunter Press. David S. and Susan Siegel. PO Box 193,
Yorktown Heights, NY 10598; (914) 245-6608. Send SASE for a current brochure.
Book Hunter Press provides geographical guides to used, rare, and antiquarian book dealers. Each guide is organized by region, and the entries are based on personal visits. (And they make a living doing this!) For those who have been known to plan vacations around buying rare books.

Booking Pleasures. Jack Matthews. *Ohio University Press, $24.95 cloth, ISBN 0-8214-1129-2.*
Inspirational and entertaining stories from a book collector.

Books: *Identification and Price Guide.* Nancy Wright. *Avon, $15.00 paper, ISBN 0-380-76941-7.*
Part of The Confident Collector™ series. Mostly price lists of specific sales.

Collecting: *An Unruly Passion: Psychological Perspectives.*
Werner Muensterberger. *Harvest/Harcourt Brace, $13.00 paper,*
ISBN 0-15-600253-1.
The author does not just pick on book collectors. He also offers disturbing insights into all kinds of collecting manias, including the folks who break legal and moral codes in the quest for that one special item.

The Collector's Bookshelf: *A Comprehensive Listing of Authors,*
Their Pseudonyms, and Their Books. Joseph Raymond Lefontaine.
Prometheus Books, $75.95 cloth, ISBN 0-87975-491-5.
A listing of hundreds of authors and all the different names under which they published, plus a list of their books.

First Editions: *A Guide to Identification.* Edited by Edward N. Zempel and Linda A. Verkler. *Spoon River, $35.00 cloth, ISBN 0-930358-13-9.*
Information from hundreds of publishers about the codes and marks they use to indicate first editions.

A Gentle Madness: *Bibliophiles, Bibliomanes, and the Eternal Passion for*
Books. Nicholas A. Basbanes. *Henry Holt, $35.00 cloth, ISBN 0-8050-3653-9.*
A rogue's gallery of collectors, dealers, home librarians, and book criminals through the ages. A contemporary classic.

Maloney's Antiques and Collectibles Resource Directory. Third Edition.
David J. Maloney, Jr. *Antique Trader Books, $24.95 paper. ISBN 0-930625-40-4.*
Hundreds of resources for collectors of all kinds of goodies, including books, magazines, paper, and art, with a special index of appraisers.

Miller's Collecting Books. Catherine Porter. *Reed International, $30.00 cloth,*
ISBN 1-85732-766-7.
A history of books from the collector's viewpoint, with full-color pictures.

Modern Book Collecting. Robert A. Wilson. *Lyons & Burford, $16.95 paper,*
ISBN 1-55821-179-9.
Introduction to book collecting, with narrative and author bibliographies. Focus is on modern literature with some general information.

Official Price Guide to Old Books. Marie Tedford and Pat Goudey.
House of Collectibles, $15.00 paper, ISBN 0-8763-7915-3.
Thousands of recent sale prices and a dictionary of terms.

Over My Dead Body: *The Sensational Age of the American Paperback.*
Lee Server. *Chronicle Books, $16.95 paper, ISBN 0-8118-0550-6.*
Amusing account of genre pulp fiction from the years after World War II.
Plenty of photographs and cover art.

A Pocket Guide to the Identification of First Editions. Fifth Edition.
Compiled by Bill McBride. *McBride/Publisher, $9.95 paper, ISBN 0-9917969-3-4;
585 Prospect Avenue, West Hartford, CT 06105; (203) 523-1622.*
The indispensable shirt-pocket listing of hundreds of identifying codes used
by publishers to indicate first editions.

Understanding Book-Collecting. Grant Uden. *Antique Collectors Club,
$29.50 cloth, ISBN 0-907462-13-8.*
A narrative about the history, philosophy, and myths of book collecting, with
many black-and-white photos.

General Mail-Order Catalogs on Books and Related Collectibles

Antique Trader Publications. PO Box 1050, Dubuque, IA 52001;
(800) 334-7165; fax (800) 531-0880.
Price guides, manuals, and narratives on all kinds of collectibles.

Art Books Services. PO Box 360, Hughsonville, NY 12537; (800) 247-9955.
Distributes books on every aspect of collecting art, including books on
books, prints, postcards, and illustrated books.

Collector Books. PO Box 3009, Paducah, KY 42002-3009; (800) 626-5420.
Books on paper, books, prints, and comic books.

Magazines for Book Collectors and Book Dealers

AB Bookman's Weekly. PO Box AB, Clifton, NJ 07015; (201) 772-0020;
fax (201) 772-9281; weekly; $125/year (first-class delivery).

Biblio: *The Magazine for Collectors of Books, Manuscripts, and Ephemera.*
845 Willamette Street, Eugene, OR 97401; (541) 345-3800;
fax (541) 302-9872; monthly; $34.95/year.

Book Source Monthly. PO Box 567, Cazenovia, NY 13035-0567;
phone/fax (315) 655-8499; monthly; $15/year.

BookQuote. 2319-C West Rohmann Avenue, Peoria, IL 61604; (309) 672-2665; fax (309) 672-7853; e-mail: srppress@aol.com; biweekly; $32/year.

Firsts: *The Book Collector's Magazine.* PO Box 65166, Tucson, AZ 85728; (520) 529-1355; fax (520) 529-5847; 11x/year; $40/year.

❖

If your collection is growing, and you don't
weed at the same rate at which you
acquire books, and you don't build
more shelves, you will run
out of space.
page 120.

Chapter VII — Display and Storage

Being Suggestions on Managing and Manipulating
the Physical Environment of Your Home Library, With Information
on Critters Who Like to Homestead in Your Books.

Bibliophysics: Books, Space, Infinity. Your Bookshelves

Why don't more booklovers have attractive, safe, clean, and well-designed home libraries?

1. *The Handy Factor.* Booklovers read, and, therefore, think they know everything. They think they can milk cows, fly planes, grow orchids, and build sturdy, beautiful, inexpensive bookcases, relying only on the information they find in a book. If this were true, booklovers would be the richest, most physically attractive, longest-lived, and most influential group of people on the planet.

2. *The Cost Factor.* People with books spend their money on books. Most home librarians never stop and say, "If I buy this complete set of Sherlock Holmes, I will not have the money to build sturdy, chemically inert shelving."

I've found that lining the walls of our 1884 vintage brick
house with bookcases packed with the 1,700+ volumes of
my library has made a significant difference in keeping
the old place warm in winter and cool in summer.
—Ron Chidester, artist, Denver, CO

---

3. *The Rot Factor.* Too many booklovers assume that a book is a physically stable object and needs no more care than a hunk of rock. Wrong again. Books interact with their surroundings; like deep-sea creatures, they constantly adjust to a deadly environment and are at risk of being destroyed by predators, water, and gravity.

4. *The Clueless Factor.* The folks who write the books on building shelves and remodeling homes are not necessarily experts on book care or library design. Here are four examples of potentially fatal problems I found in the popular literature.

    a. How-to articles give excellent information about using preparations to stain and seal bookshelves, but say little about how those chemicals might migrate into the fore-edge of a paperback or interact with a leather cover.

    b. You will be told to build bookshelves next to windows, without any warning about how a driving rain can leak through caulk.

c. Information in the popular press about the stress put on a wall or floor by the weight of a large collection of hardbacks is virtually nonexistent.

d. Suggestions about lighting emphasize aesthetics; the cumulative damage light does to the exposed spines is rarely mentioned.

Here are tips on improving your home library, gathered from people who know both books and carpentry.

1. If you are building shelves in your home, you risk generating a veil of sawdust throughout your library. If you must do the carpentry in the same room as the books, cover your collection carefully beforehand and vacuum even more carefully afterward. Remember to vacuum the top shelves! Remember to vacuum the corners!

2. If you are building the shelves elsewhere, make sure you both dust the shelves with a dry duster and wipe the shelves with a slightly damp cloth before you move them into your home. Let the shelves dry thoroughly. This will reduce the amount of sawdust you move into your home.

3. If the wood for the shelves is bowed or curved, place the shelf so the curve looks like an upside-down U. Otherwise, the weight of the books can make the curve worse. A slightly bowed piece of wood is not a problem.

4. If the weather is humid and hot, any paint or stain you use on wood shelves could take forever to dry. If you have any doubt that the shelves are ready to use, put a sheet of inert material like Tyvek or 100 percent rag content, acid-free mat board between the books and the shelf for a few days. That way, if there is damage from sticky chemicals, the barrier should protect the books.

Question: *Couldn't that hurt the bookshelf?*

Answer: *Better that you risk damage to the bookshelf than to the books.*

5. As you put books into a new bookcase, fill the shelves from the bottom up. Test for stability by trying to gently rock the bookcase as each shelf is filled. If your bookcase is too wobbly or too fragile to stand such treatment, it is probably too wobbly or fragile. Remember that a bookcase that is stable on a flat wooden floor might be less stable on a carpeted surface or uneven, dirt basement floor.

If a bookcase needs a small shim or piece of wood or cardboard underneath one of its corners to keep it stable, you can bet the bookcase will crash some day. If you are concerned about wobbly bookcases, you have several options. You can reinforce existing shelving by using L-shaped metal braces screwed into the corners. You can anchor the bookshelf to the wall, making sure that you have attached it to a solid part of the frame of the house. You can attach the shelf to the floor and ceiling. You can remove the heavier books from the top shelves, or even completely remove all books. You can also replace the shelves with ones that don't wobble, which are built and installed correctly in the first place.

6. Insects and other invertebrates lay their eggs in tiny crevices. Those great used bookcases you bought at the rummage sale can harbor a nursery of destruction. Examine your new purchase very carefully for slumbering hitchhikers before you bring it into the house.

Depending on the type of bookcase and the type and value of its finish, a thorough cleaning—top, bottom, back, and sides—is in order. Turn the bookcase upside-down, and clean the undersides of the shelves as well as you do the tops. Unless it is a museum piece, all but the most tender of antiques can benefit from cleansing with a mild vegetable-oil wood soap like Murphy's Oil Soap™.

7. The confederation of materials that constitute a building form an imperfect union of wood, plaster, steel, plastic, glass, and goodness-knows-what-else. In dry climates wood can shrink, glue can dry up, and nails can work themselves loose. This is most noticeable in fine pieces of furniture that have spent their lives in moist regions and then move with their families to places like New Mexico. You might not be aware of it, but the building that houses your library also shifts, as wood swells and shrinks and the ground below moves. If your built-in bookcases are not built to shift, stress cracks can appear.

The Chinese scholar Achiles Fang had the shelves of his Boston apartment built with planks broad enough to house books two deep. This sounds like a practical remedy, but a friend told me a couple years ago that even Fang had run out of space.
Again, the problem has no solution.
—Karl Young, poet and publisher, Kenosha, WI

---

8. Keep a list of the measurements of your rooms on a card in your wallet; you will always be ready to shop for new or used ready-made bookshelves.

9. If you live in earthquake country, find out what you can do to make your bookshelves more secure. Some people put strips of wood in front of their bookshelves as railings to keep books from sliding off during a tremor. Experienced home librarians in earthquake-sensitive zones never store books higher than chest-tall.

10. If you have a large collection of valuable, oversized art books, consider buying one of those multidrawer cases used to store large sheets of paper in art supply stores, graphic studios, etc.

11. So-called legal bookcases, which have glass doors that swing out of the way, are one way to store books in dusty environments. I have noticed that the prices of these shelves are coming down, and they can often be purchased at reasonable prices in big-city stores that specialize in oak furniture.

Do You Know How Much Your Home Library Weighs?

The biggest mistake the home librarian makes when building or acquiring new bookcases is underestimating the sums of the sizes, weights, and numbers of books that need to go into a specific space.

Size

The size of a book was once determined by the choices the printer could offer a book publisher (the two were often the same person). Paper came in standard sizes, and for the sake of economy a few formats emerged that took best advantage of the number of pages that could be printed on a sheet, with as little waste as possible. Also, the mechanics of printing, with its metal and wooden type clasped in a frame called a *chase*, limited the size of the printing area.

Those limitations became tradition, and, as the printing industry became more automated, the tradition translated into specifications based on technology no longer in use.

For example, the word *folio* refers to a sheet of paper that is folded once to produce a signature, and thus used to define the size of a book. *Quarto, octavo, duodecimo*, etc., refer to books made from folios folded additional times, producing books that were subsequently smaller and had more pages per signature. The terms are used by rare book dealers and archivists who want to be precise and whose books are from an era when printing was mostly done by hand. The use of these terms in modern book printing is at best a quaint anachronism and at worst a way some people in the book community like to make the rest of us feel stupid.

How do these traditions affect the book industry?

As printing technology has become more advanced, book publishers have been offered more choices. This is very evident if you compare the books on your shelves printed in the last three years to those of twenty or more years ago. Although most paperback publishers still speak of mass market versus trade size (about 4-1/4 inches wide by 7 inches high versus 5 inches wide by 8 inches high), one trend seems to be toward books that are larger and come in many different ratios of the rectangle. The two shelves of mass market–size books in my library are almost entirely from the fifties and sixties. A shelf of recent paperbacks on the same topics from the same publishers are at least an inch taller.

The only 7-inch-high new paperbacks on the shelves in our house are popular genre fiction: science fiction, mystery, fantasy, horror, westerns, and romance.

On the other hand, the latest version of a book that has been popular and has gone through several editions and several publishers is likely to be smaller and cheaper than earlier versions. Some of the book publishers who specialize in reprinting classics on inexpensive paper use the smaller formats. And the dime novel format is coming back, as mentioned in Chapter V. But, except for these three examples, larger formats in both hardbacks and paperbacks seem to be more common.

This is why those lovely bookshelves you built for the den in the sixties don't work anymore. If you built the shelves just to clear the tops of the mass market westerns you used to read, your new books won't fit. The solution is to either build every bookcase with adjustable shelves, or build your shelves to fit the books you are going to buy ten years from now. Assume there will be even more variety than there is now, and that if you can't install adjustable shelves, add at least an inch to your calculations of how high the new shelves should be.

Another size issue is the amount of space you need between the top of the book and the bottom of the next-higher shelf. If you try to save space by allowing only the smallest interval of space, you are sure to damage your books when you move them on and off a shelf.

The correct way to pull a book from a shelf is to grasp it gently by its sides using your index and middle fingers and your thumb and pull it off the shelf slowly. This method works only if the books are stacked on the shelf with enough "give" on the sides and top, because when you pull the book out, you will cause the books on either side to shift. Without room at the top, all three books could be creased, the spines could be bent, or the book jackets torn.

In addition, books need to breathe. The slow decomposition of the materials in books produces chemical gases that need to dissipate, and the exchange of moisture between the books and the atmosphere is an ongoing process. Without room to inhale and exhale, books can age faster. Air needs to circulate throughout your shelves.

What about the biggest books? Because of the stress on the spine of the book, many experts prefer that you pile up your largest books so that they lie flat. However, this is not an excuse for building skyscrapers. I witnessed a disastrous situation at a large public library recently, where the oversized books had been placed in tall piles on tables. The piles were shifting, and conscientious patrons were struggling to rearrange the books to prevent serious crashes. They were not successful. It was not a pretty sight.

Finally, size also has to do with the depth of the shelves. A 12-inch-deep shelf is probably the minimum you can get away with, if you have a growing collection. Books also need to have space between themselves and the back of the bookshelf. This is especially true if the shelves are built against a wall, where condensation, debris from the wall, or old paint can damage the backside of the books without your knowing it, until it is too late.

Weight

Do you know how much your collection weighs? Do you know how much the walls and floor of your home can hold? Are you building bookshelves into load-bearing walls or into a marshmallow puff of plaster, paint, and detritus?

Experts warn against formulas because every library is different, so the only way to accurately estimate the weight is to do some calculations based on samples of your own books.

A tape measure and a scale that can accurately weigh half-ounce increments are necessary to complete this research. An electronic postage scale is ideal, and if you are on good terms with the staff of your local post office, small business, or hardware store, they might be willing to weigh a few samples for you.

Imagine a bookcase with four shelves of books that weighs a total of 200 pounds. If the bookcase is 4 feet wide and 1 foot deep, this bookcase would have a footprint of 4 square feet. Two hundred pounds spread over 4 square feet gives a weight of 50 pounds per square foot of stack space. (See the figure below.)

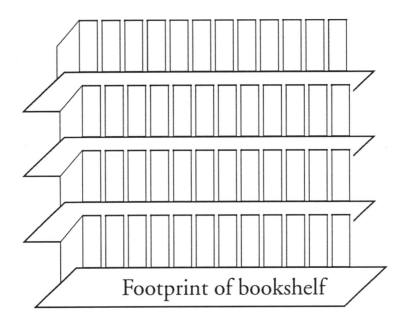

Footprint of bookshelf

One hundred fifty to 175 pounds per square foot of stack space is one number used by the professional library community to determine the weight load that the physical foundation of a library building can bear. This is the number you can use as a benchmark when figuring the weight of your library.

It never occurred to me that the thousands of pounds of books on my shelves might collapse the floor of the house until a library building consultant warned me of the dangers. In fact, she said, the anxiety about what could happen, given the numbers of books and the age of our seventy-year-old bungalow, woke her up in a sweat in the middle of the night.

Also, it never occurred to the person who built the first of my custom bookcases that the wood he used was not thick enough to sustain the weight of hundreds of hardback books. I lived with bowed bookshelves until a sympathetic and more experienced carpenter built new supports.

Since most of us build our bookshelves against the outer walls of our homes, the danger of collapse is reduced. But when was the last time you crawled into the basement of your house and checked the supporting beams for stress? If you live in an apartment above the first floor, are there signs of stress in the ceiling of the apartment below you? And what would be the consequences if you started to build large, freestanding shelves in the middle of a room?

Measuring Your Library

If math is not your forte, you might be tempted to skip the next few paragraphs. But this is not like cramming to pass an algebra exam. The point is to collect some data and make educated guesses about how your library might be impacting your home, so that you can learn if you are harboring the bibliophile's equivalent of the San Andreas Fault.

In my home library, which contains a mix of paperbacks and hardbacks of all sizes, the number of books in a linear foot of shelving ranges from eight to twenty-seven. Most of them are between 1/2 and 1 inch wide.

An 800-page, mass market paperback with a spine 1-1/4 inches wide and a height of 6-3/4 inches weighs 14 ounces.

An 8-inch-high trade paperback of 300 pages with a spine about 7/8 inch thick also weighs about 14 ounces. However, a 1-inch-thick hardback with 400 pages that is 9-1/2 inches tall weighs more than 2 pounds.

If my library is mostly trade paperbacks at least 8 inches tall, a weight of 16 ounces or 1 pound per linear inch is not out of line.

Mass market paperbacks can average 11 ounces per inch, and hardbacks can weigh 50 percent more than a trade paperback, which means up to 1-1/2 pounds per book.

What increases the weight of a book over these averages is the kind of paper used to manufacture the book. The weighty 2-pound hardback book is printed on the kind of shiny paper that takes photos and illustrations well, and the clay in the paper adds to the weight. If you have many art and photography books, your library will weigh more than average, too. (That is why moving a collection of *National Geographic* magazines is such an ordeal.)

Short of weighing every single book, I gathered enough information to make some estimates by taking samples from several shelves in several different rooms. Using the simple formula presented below, I calculated that the weight of a specific 30 feet of shelving is 400 pounds, based on the shelves containing about 10 percent hardbacks. The footprint of the 400-pound bookshelf is about 3-1/3 square feet. The weight of the books alone is about 120 pounds per square foot, not counting the lumber.

I was amazed to come out so close to the 150 pounds suggested by an American Library Association publication.

Here is the formula I used:

Number of feet of shelving: 30
Number of inches in 30 feet: 360
Number of pounds based on trade paperback weight: 360
Add 10 percent to total based on percentage of hardback books: 396
Footprint of one shelf: 5 feet by 8 inches equals 3.3 square feet
396 pounds, divided by 3.3 square feet, equals 120 pounds per square foot.

You will probably find that you need to use a different formula, based on the kinds of books you have on your shelves. Some general categories by size in inches include:

1. Mass market paperbacks (4" x 7").

2. Trade paperbacks (5" x 8", 6" x 9", etc.).

3. Workbooks (8-1/2" x 11" or larger).

4. Dictionaries, almanacs, etc., are often printed on a very thin and lightweight book paper that is both opaque and dense (8" x 10", 14-1/2" x 11", etc.).

5. Children's picture books that have few pages and sturdy coated covers (9" x 12", 12" x 12", etc.).

6. Popular hardbacks (6-1/4" x 9-1/4", 6-1/4" x 9-1/2").

7. College textbooks, manuals, and hardback reference books (similar to hardbacks and manuals).

8. Oversized art, photography, and travel books, commonly called "coffee-table books" (assume at least one dimension is greater than 14 inches).

The weight of your book collection should be of concern to you if you are living in an older home, if you have trouble with unstable foundations, if you live in earthquake country, if you live in a mobile home, or if you live in an apartment building or other multistory structure. (The weight of the libraries of other booklovers can also be a potential hazard; find an excuse to visit the people in the apartment above yours and examine the locations of their overloaded bookcases.)

It might also be useful information if you plan to do heavy remodeling, such as removing interior walls. But most important, you need to estimate the weight if you are building shelves to make sure you use the correct building materials and hardware.

Number of Books

The growth of a book collection is the issue that challenges all but the most disciplined booklovers. Need I rub it in? Sure, you claim that you acquire books out of love and necessity, but you would not acquire the sheer numbers you do if you did not suffer from overwhelming denial. You refuse to admit that you buy more books than you can manage, and when you do build new shelves, you base your measurements on the present, rather than the future.

You might have heard the rule of thumb about bookshelves: that you need to leave 10 percent of the space empty for future growth. So, you build 11 feet of shelving to display 10 feet of books, and you pride yourself on your foresight.

My wife says there are no books in the bathroom because she has become "upwardly mobile."
—Anonymous (by request)

Your mistake is in leaving out a key component of the 10 percent formula: the formula actually calls for *10 percent per year* growth. If you want your bookshelves to serve you for five years, according to this formula, you need to leave 5 feet of the shelves empty for each 10 feet you have already filled. And if you want to build shelves to last you a decade, you need 10 feet empty for each 10 feet you have already filled.

Impossible, you say? This is where the soft rubber wheels of your book-addicted, denial-ridden fantasy hit the hard road of pine board reality.

You visit three used bookstores, two garage sales, the superstore at the mall, the fundraiser at the humane shelter, and your favorite college bookstore. Also you celebrate a birthday, and you are the kind of person to whom everybody gives books. But you have nowhere to put these new acquisitions, because when you built the bookshelves, you pretended you would never get another book so long as you live. You lied to yourself.

Of course, 10 percent a year is a guess, but it is probably a better guess than the ones you make now. It comes down to this:

If your collection is growing, and you don't weed at the same rate at which you acquire books, and you don't build more shelves, you will run out of space.
The issue of change is also discussed in Chapter IV and is part of the basic audit of the health of your library. A living library needs the ability to grow, and it needs to be able to change. It is very difficult to rearrange a library when the books are packed solid. You end up removing half the books off the shelves and leaving them on the floor. There is no room to add a book without taking another from the same location. It is like one of those puzzles where you must put all the sliding pieces in order. If there is room to move only one piece at a time, you end up moving every piece to get to the one you want.

Slack is room to breathe. Slack is shelves perfectly packed, which means just tight enough for all the books to be standing (unless the book is oversized and lying on its side), with their sides supported by the other books. Slack is books packed just loose enough so that you can easily grasp a book by its sides by gently moving the books on either side of it, without damaging any of the books. It is the way your library is supposed to be.

Slack is having books fit on the shelves like you fit into your favorite pair of comfortable pants, but this perfect balance of support and comfortable "give" offends some booklovers. They squeeze themselves into clothing a size too small, just so that they can brag about how much weight they have allegedly lost. In their libraries, they pride themselves on the ability to jam one more book on the shelf so they can boast about the room they save.

Allow these folks the benefit of the doubt and assume they do not know the damage they do to the books, all for the sake of the weird status of squeezing more sheets of dry wood pulp into a space than the next person.

Even the experts can go to extremes. Buried in the literature about conserving space in public and academic libraries are gruesome stories about the edges of books being chopped off in order to make room in storage areas.

One of the ways people deal with the space issue is to store books in dangerous places. If you insist on storing books in basements, attics, porches, and garages, at least give them extra protection from water by lining shelves and boxes with plastic. Avoid polyvinyl chloride (PVC). When it breaks down, it can release hydrochloric acid. Instead, use an inert polyester plastic such as Mylar. Any plastic that smells like plastic should be avoided.

Coffee-table books stacked on tables can be damaged, because the temptation is to use them as portable desks. Dust jackets and covers are embossed, punctured, and stained with alarming frequency, and there is little a book conservator can do to fix the damage. Avoid using books as writing surfaces (or even—horrors—as coasters at your next cocktail party).

Electronic gadgets, such as stereos, televisions, VCRs, computers, etc., are giant dust magnets. If you keep them on the same shelves as your books, they can increase the flow of dirt and dust onto the shelves, as well as provide breeding grounds for some of the bugs that attack your books. And, as mentioned in Chapter IV, living plants in a library need to keep their distance from the books, since plants provide convenient tract housing for bugs that commute to your book collection every day.

Air cleaners that use ion generators can create a dust problem for your library. The negative ions attract the positively charged dust particles and cause them to clump and fall to the ground. Some households discover an increased quantity of dust and dirt on furniture, lamps, and books. So the air might seem cleaner, but you will need to dust and vacuum more often.

What About the Fancy Stuff?

Open bookcases are not the best place to store books; they are a compromise between convenience of easy access and cost of bookshelves with doors. If you have books that are of value, or if you live in a climate that is antibook (moist, coastal environments come to mind), caring for your books and displaying your books are incompatible goals. You have several choices:

1. Turn your entire home into an archival tomb, with dim lights, purified air, and a constant 60-degree temperature and 50-percent relative humidity.

2. Pick one small room, such as a closet, and make it perfect. Put the best books in there.

3. Store individual books in archival storage boxes that are made of materials that will protect the book from deterioration. The mail-order catalogs listed in Chapter XIV specialize in boxes, folders, envelopes, etc., to protect the best of your collection.

My ideal way of housing my books would be specific enclosures for each genre. A trunk with traveling stickers could hold my books dealing with explorations. I'd need an interesting-shaped end table in a deep, rich wood tone with some offset shelves for Marge Piercy, Maya Angelou, and Clarissa Pinkola Estés. My books on clowning, movement, and theater would be perfect in an old, freestanding wardrobe along with my costumes, props, and makeup. My collection of erotica, which is my latest passion, needs a cherrywood case within reach of an upholstered chaise. My poetry might like a wicker stand or a Victorian trunk.
—Jean Mavromatis, artist in the classroom, Lakewood, CO

The Health of Books and Humans

People are more important than books, and sometimes the needs of people and the needs of the books you are managing collide.

Library Ergonomics

Most home librarians do not have the budget, the room, or the leisure to acquire furniture that is just for their libraries. You make do with kitchen chairs, plastic lounges from the backyard, the couch in the den, and the dining room table. But no matter what your budget, you need to take note of one serious defect in almost every library: Human bodies were not designed to read books.

A booklover spends long, happy hours reading a book that is laid in a cozy lap, cradled in loving hands, or propped up on a table. These positions tend to push the booklover's head forward on the neck. This forward motion puts strain on the complicated matrix of bone and sinew that holds the head erect over the spinal column, where it gets the most support. Booklovers morph into long-necked, hunchbacked headache sufferers. A group of us resembles a flock of storybook cranes. Or, a booklover will slump for hours in a squishy chair, oblivious to the fact that bad posture is cutting off the blood supply to the spinal region and putting tremendous pressure on discs and ligaments.

Even the most ardent booklover needs to get up and walk around at least once an hour, even when sitting in the best ergonomic chair. A little stretching wouldn't hurt, either. Nothing keeps the body healthier than movement.

Booklovers need to invest in healthy furnishings.

1. Footrests can elevate the legs and improve circulation.
2. Pillows can support the small of the back and the neck.
3. Bookrests can bring books to eye level and lessen the strain on the neck. Be sure to get the kind that supports the book cover and spine fully and does not require the book to lie open perfectly flat.
4. Good lighting can reduce squinting.

Cleaning

If you are serious about maintaining your library in the best condition, you should wipe and vacuum your shelves before they look dusty. However, if you are human, or if you don't have a crackerjack cleaning staff to clean at the still invisible stage of dirt, you will probably wait until a sufficient interval, such as a presidential term, has gone by.

Home libraries must contend with pets, children, baths and showers, slow-simmering pot roasts, burnt pot roasts, dryers, indoor plants, carpets, upholstered furniture, science projects gone awry, fireplaces, and other sources of airborne contamination usually not found in public institutions.

The preferred liquid cleaner around books is plain water, unless you have the kind of greasy dirt that comes from cooking fumes and steel mills. Plain water is least likely to damage your books. However, I have lived in neighborhoods where particles of gray grease floated in the air like small jellyfish; these particles laugh—ha!—at water like the gypsy hero in a light opera. So what do you use?

The neighborhood hardware store displays a plethora of space-age cleaning fluids: Avoid most of them and use the mildest and simplest products, like the mild vegetable-oil soaps. You neither want to poison yourself nor leave a residue that will seep into your books.

If you live in a high-grime area, metal bookshelves are less likely than wooden shelves to suck in dirt from the air and transfer it to your books. Also, in high critter-density climates, metal shelves are less likely to harbor animal life.

Lighting

Before I was chastised by my favorite bookbinder, I loved the glow of the early morning sun on my bookcases. It was responsible for accelerating the fading the same way that the tennis star with the heavy tan ends up looking years older than the couch potato who rarely sees the light of day.

There are three major considerations for lighting your home library.

1. The *healthy vision approach*, which should be the most important consideration, focuses on having enough light fall on the printed page so you can read comfortably without squinting. Some people seem to frown when they read; the frown can indicate they are trying to overcome a poor eyeglass prescription or a poor light source. Instead, you should be able to read your book with facial muscles relaxed, unless you are really angry at the author.

The light source itself should not shine directly into your eyes, and there should be no interfering glare from windows or mirrors.

Think of the light reflecting off the page as delivering the information to your eyes effortlessly, and this should give you the intuitive information you need. As we get older, we might need better lighting, which does not necessarily mean that we will buy new lamps. It might mean we position existing light sources so that they illuminate the page more fully, or we use more than one light source in a room at one time.

Some people suffer physically because they are saving pennies each month by using low-wattage bulbs. Clip a few breakfast cereal coupons, and use the extra money to keep on a few more and brighter lights.

2. The *book conservator approach* is the vampire approach: Light kills. While you want plenty of nonglaring light by which to read, you want your books to be kept in the dark as much as possible. Direct sunlight is the worst threat, but even artificial light can damage books over long periods of time.

The problem is that the effect light has is cumulative, and the breakdown continues even after the light source is blocked or turned off. Museums keep the lights dim and forbid the use of flashbulbs to lower that cumulative damage. What efforts you make will depend on the value of your collection.

Overexposure to light and heat can cause a book to appear to "age" faster. In fact, a good way to make a document look older is to subject it to the light of the direct sun or put it in the oven at 250 degrees and cook until toasted a tasty chestnut brown.

3. The *display approach* is the decorator approach. You want your collection to look good, and you want the interplay of color and shape to make an emotional statement about your inherent sense of taste and your bank balance. You want track lighting so that you can create a subliminal dialogue with the viewer about the importance you place on specific parts of the collection. You want light that is part of the negative space that surrounds the bookshelves and becomes that which is not book, but is nonbook. You want Tiffany shades and a voice-activated control center that allows you to turn the lights on by saying, "Illuminate me, James." You want to impress your in-laws.

The decorator and healthy vision approaches to lighting your library contradict the book conservator approach. This is a conflict that haunts most libraries with important collections. One librarian described it as the War of the Drapes. For instance, an architect builds a beautiful library building with high ceilings and huge windows that would do a cathedral proud. Drapes are installed to protect the books from light damage, but the marble floors are not conducive to retrofitting with electrical outlets, and the fire code forbids extension cords. (It is still in the living memory of many librarians that putting electrical outlets in every room of the library was considered advanced thinking.)

Consequently, the rooms in these libraries have two modes. Either they are drowning in bright sunlight or they are dreary as tombs. Opening the drapes a crack subjects only a vertical sliver of books instead of the whole stack to irreversible damage. This is still unacceptable to the book conservators, who are constantly closing the drapes; the readers and librarians are constantly opening them. Civil war breaks out.

If you do have lights near your books, you should be able to turn them on and off easily, so that you can find what you want in bright light, and then turn the lights off. The lesson is that the lack of controllable lighting is a major design flaw in an otherwise excellent home library. Make sure you are also on the building committee of your local library so that you can make a speech about drape wars and adequate wiring.

The one exception to the conflict between book health and book beauty in your home library is the children's library. You want to make books irresistible to kids; the spines should glow like apples in October. There should be plenty of light to browse and read, with the illumination extending to the floor. Some people actually set lights close to the ground to accommodate short folk. You should be able to get down with the short folk and read with the book spread out on the floor.

If you have valuable children's books that you want to protect, keep them in a cool, dark place and take them out for special occasions. But keep the cheap copies in the light, easy to find for reading every day.

Allergies

Can you be allergic to books? More likely you are allergic to the leavings of the creatures who inhabit your house. These leavings (use your imagination) settle in and around your library. Books tend to be depositories of the airborne filth of the household, be it the feces of mites, the dander of pets, or the pollen and spores from household plants and their soil.

If you are allergic to dust, books will be a problem unless you are an exceptionally careful housekeeper. If you have strong allergies to mold and live in a hothouse climate, it will be very difficult to maintain a home library without central air-conditioning and filtering systems.

Here are a few suggestions for managing allergies.

1. Keep your library out of your bedroom. This will minimize your exposure to the dust, etc., during the hours you sleep and relax.

2. Maintain your books in a room with a door and its own filtering system. This, again, will isolate and control the amount of dust.

3. Consult with an allergist about the various products that can be used to kill dust mites or remove the allergens they produce. These are not to be used with your rare volumes, and I assume that you will risk permanently staining covers and pages. On the other hand, I would rather you deface a few common books than forego the pleasures of a home library completely.

4. Keep books you use infrequently in dustproof storage.

If you have a contact allergy problem, which means that you break out in a rash if you touch a book, you might be allergic to the chemicals used to clean the covers in the book's past. Put books that seem to give you a problem into Mylar jackets. Also, several of the catalogs of book repair products listed in Chapters III, IV, IX, and XIV carry disposable and washable gloves.

If you need medical advice about managing allergies, you can call the LUNG LINE Information Service in Denver, Colorado, at 800-222-LUNG, for free information about lung and immunologic diseases. This is a free service sponsored by the National Jewish Center for Immunology and Respiratory Medicine.

The service is available weekdays. They also have a nationally known medical library, which has pioneered many collaborative projects in the medical library community.

The Challenges of Disease, Injury, and Age

The Gutenberg-era book satisfies me, but I can see, hear, walk, talk, and hold a book with little need for help, except a pair of glasses. But what about the person with limited or fading vision, or one who spends most of her life in a wheelchair or hospital bed? What about those with wasting diseases that pull an otherwise bright mind out of the mainstream of life, so that even reading a book becomes a major physical effort? What about the accident that temporarily keeps someone homebound? How do you win the relentless war between a healthy body and the aging process?

Technology is a blessing to the reader. It expands the concept of accessing and interacting with physical memory to the borders of science. The most extraordinary book I ever saw was a moving, mechanical gloved hand hooked up to a keyboard. It was designed to allow communication between a person who can see and hear, but who does not know the finger alphabet used by the physically challenged, and a person who knows the alphabet but cannot speak, see, or hear.

I am sure the participants in the demonstration did not think of this technology as a book, but I thought of the hand, being programmed to read to people who could not use a Braille text or hear an audiotape, as a book.

There are times when I simply sit and look at the books,
remembering not so much their content as how they made
me feel, and the times, people, and places in my life
that I associate with them.
—Scott VanGerpen, inveterate reader, Auburn, WA

If there is someone in your household with physical limitations, assume that the technology needed to provide them with better access to information is available. Maybe it is a matter of listening to audiotapes instead of reading, or getting an eyeglass prescription checked. Your public library will be able to put you in touch with all kinds of resources.

Although I preach ruthless weeding of library collections throughout this book, here is an exception. There may come a time in my life when all I can do is hold a book and remember what I loved about it. If that time comes, I think I will want to see my books, whether or not I can use them. There are books that I have read so often that the title is enough to trigger a stream of words and images in my mind and heart. I would want those books here, by me, even though a helpful relative or friend would urge me to discard them or give them away. Let that be my choice, and let me do it in my own time. I think you will feel the same way if and when some of your physical abilities start to fail.

Death by the Book

Famous books that have started wars, including religious texts such as the Bible and the Koran, are often cited as being books that have killed. *Uncle Tom's Cabin*, the Victorian melodrama that sparked a nation's conscience against slavery, claims a dubious title as the most deadly book ever published on this continent, if you count the lives lost in the American Civil War. However, I could only find four categories of death by the physical book.

1. *Death by fire.* Before the advent of electricity, many libraries were only open from dawn until dusk. Students who had access to the great research libraries could be required to sign a contract promising never to light a lamp or candle. Fire is an ever-present danger for the contemporary home library, but not merely because books burn well. Do you have smoke detectors throughout your library? Do you have a sprinkler system specifically designed for your library, so that it will put out the fire without drowning your books? Do you periodically check the wiring in the walls behind your library's shelves?

2. *Death by poison.* Most of the worst offending chemicals are now either banned or under strict control. It is still possible to receive an ugly dose of some liver-destroying toxin, particularly if you insist on licking your naked finger to turn the page of a rare manuscript; you never know what was used to treat the pages. Home librarians should leave the use of toxic cleaning fluids to the well-insured and well-trained expert.

3. *Death by mold.* I know booklovers who have no books in their house, since the exposure to mold can kick off a deadly asthma attack. If you live in a humid climate and have breathing difficulties, please check with your medical professional about the danger of a mold explosion in your home collection. Remember that such a mold invasion can be generated by as little as forty-eight hours of humid weather, which means it is a constant threat in certain climates.

4. *Death by book avalanche.* As explained in numbing detail in this chapter, books are heavy, and I don't mean philosophically. Bookcases do tip over, and

people do get hurt. If you live in earthquake country, which is most of the land surface of the planet, don't sleep under a loaded shelf.

Transporting Books

Shipping and Mailing

When you ship or mail a book, you need to create layers that provide different types of protection to ward off the several ways a book can be damaged. This may sound like a lot of work, but the cost is usually less than a dollar per book. I buy my supplies from a wholesale paper warehouse or from one of the large office supply superstores that can be found in most cities. If you use a mail-order source for shipping supplies, prepare to pay as much as twice the going rate, which is still a bargain per book. If the book you are shipping is rare or very valuable, it is worth investing in archival-quality packing materials.

A Nebraska bookman told me he chips away at a wall of books 4 feet high and 6 feet long near his bed. "It hasn't fallen over yet," he says, in defense of the arrangement that annoys his wife.
—Bernadine Clark, author and writer, Winter Park, FL

First, to prevent losing the book in the mail, place a piece of paper in with the book, with your name, address, and phone number. Use indelible ink or pencil, so that it will not stain the book if it gets wet. Some experts suggest that you write the information on a piece of acid-free paper, fold the paper so that the writing is on the inside, and put the folded sheet in the package.

Wrap or secure the book in such a way as to ensure it will not open inside the package. One preferred method is to bind the book with woven cloth strips, which should be soft and wide enough not to damage the cover. A device called a Pink Pull Fastener, which looks like a pink shoelace, can be purchased for this purpose. Both ends are threaded through a small, plastic ring; books are held together inside the loop. They can be ordered through book supply catalogs or purchased directly from GripTites, 67 Country Place Lane, Rochester, New York 14612-1445, or you can call them at (617) 392-8637.

Another method is to wrap the entire book with brown or white wrapping paper (no color dyes, please) and secure the paper with adhesive tape; it should look like a wrapped gift.

The least recommended method, which should not be used on anything but throwaway books, is to use string or large rubber bands. This method leaves marks on the edges of the cover. Also, the sulfur content in rubber bands is a conservator's nightmare. If the book is accidentally left with the rubber bands on in a hot, moist environment, damage is almost inevitable.

Next, you need to protect the book from moisture and dirt with some kind of waterproof layer. Environmentally conscious readers might shun plastic, but, frankly, I am tired of receiving damaged books in the mail. Most damaged books arrive wrapped in disintegrating paper bags and brown mailing envelopes that have been reused twenty times. When I managed a bookstore, at least 10 percent of the books I received from small presses and individuals were damaged in the mail because of poor packaging.

I put a valuable book, after it has been secured as just described, into a waterproof cover, such as a large, resealable plastic bag. My theory is that the book will be protected against water damage even if the outer layers of the wrappings are punctured.

The next layer protects against bumps and bruises. I prefer the mailing bags that have brown paper on the outside and plastic bubble wrap on the inside; mailing bags filled with recycled paper fluff are not as good. When I open a mailing bag that uses recycled paper fluff instead of plastic, I end up with fluff over everything, including the books.

Many publishers and book clubs encase the book in rigid corrugated cardboard. However, using only the rigid cardboard wrap will not protect the book from water or punctures. A rigid box is a necessity for more valuable books.

I carry two purses, one of which always contains several books in three languages. One never knows when the bus will be hijacked, and I will not be stranded without reading material.
—Barbara Ayanian, quiltmaker, Mission Viejo, CA

Are you still with me? The outer layer should be indestructible. Some people will nest a valuable book in successively larger boxes, with each box packed with some kind of buffering material. The outside box should be sealed with filament tape. If you are using envelopes or a small box, the Tyvek bags available at the post office are wonderful as an indestructible final layer—and they are free! They are not marked for cheaper rates, but you can get plain Tyvek bags at a stationery store in several sizes.

The final step is shipping insurance. No matter which carrier you use, accidents happen.

If you are sending an inexpensive book through the mail and do not want to treat it like the Hope Diamond, I recommend putting the book in a mailing envelope lined in bubble wrap, and then slipping that into a larger Tyvek envelope. Even though these envelopes come with self-sealing flaps, I suggest securing them with a piece of filament tape.

I once tortured a package of valuable documents by sending them overnight mail with no protection other than the cardboard envelope provided by the carrier. I naively thought that paying for the fast service would signal the delivery person not to leave the unprotected envelope outside in the middle of a blizzard in Anchorage, Alaska. The recipient rescued the contents only after it had endured several hours under wet, heavy snow. By that time the cardboard envelope had dissolved, but the laser-printed information survived.

Moving

Moving books is the worst part of having a home library. It is not just the logistics, the dirt, and the sheer weight. It is the lack of preparation. The way most people move books goes something like this.

1. Give yourself one day to pack the books.

2. Go to the liquor store and get some empty boxes from the huge pile next to the loading dock.

3. Take the boxes home. Start piling books into the boxes. Stop when you realize that you do not have enough boxes.

4. Take all the books out of the boxes and repack everything, with the idea of stuffing as many books into each box as possible.

5. Try to lift one of the boxes. Quickly put it down before you do permanent damage to your back.

Burn your library and move the ashes.
—Harold Wagner, pathologist,
somewhere in Library Heaven

---

6. Realize that you will need more boxes and return to the liquor store. The Evil Box Goblin has removed all the empty boxes from the loading dock.

7. Return home. Start shoveling books into your car until you cannot see out the back window. Stuff the remaining books into any available container, including snow boots, paper bags, and the dishwasher.

8. Make eight trips to your new home this way.

9. On the last trip, discover the 163 boxes of unpacked books you have stored in the garage since the last move. Pay for an extra day to use the rental truck and cough up an extra day's rent for your old landlord.

10. Your new home is filled with piles of books and piles of boxes filled with books. Suddenly, you notice that everything is covered with years of dirt and grime. Unless it is snowing or raining, you take everything out and put it in the

front yard to air out. If it is raining, the books remain where they were dumped, often until the next move.

11. Over the next several months, you unload, clean, and reshelve your library. The books you did not unpack from the last three moves are sent to their new home in the basement, in the same boxes they have inhabited for the last five years.

12. Notice that several of your favorite books are missing.

13. Repeat the procedure the next time you move.

This method, which I have practiced several times, is common among book-lovers who suffer from Moving Amnesia. This disease causes otherwise intelligent people to keep repeating the same dumb mistakes.

Remember several truths about moving libraries.

1. *The Dirt Truth.* Even if you are a good housekeeper, moving your books will stir up a ton of dust. Vacuum the books while they are still on the shelves, or vacuum them as you pack them up. If you dust, use one of several types of anti-static cloths that pick up and hold dust. Despite these precautions, you still need to be prepared for a dusty arrival at the new residence. Vacuum as you put the books back on the shelves.

2. *The Size Truth.* If you have been using the information in this book, you have some idea of how much your library weighs, the range of sizes among your books, how many linear feet of bookshelves you have, and how many linear feet of shelves you need. You have measured the space in the new house and have made some drawings to show where your library will fit. You have weeded your collection ruthlessly before the move. You have driven everyone around you raving mad with your superhuman efficiency, and you have very few friends left to help you move.

But seriously, a little space planning can save you a lot of problems later. It can also help the move go faster if the master plan is written down in such a way as to provide useful directions to people trying to figure out where, exactly, you want the collection of eighteenth-century medical textbooks. If you keep the plan in your head, which is the same as having no plan, you force everyone to come to you for advice. Then you can complain about how you can't get anything done, because everyone keeps coming to you for advice. As my mom would say, "Are you complaining, or are you bragging?"

3. *The Weight Truth.* Books are heavy. A bathroom scale can help you decide how much to put in the boxes or bags, so that you and your helpers do not hurt yourselves. The trick is to know your comfort limit, which is different than your "I can do this and not rupture a disc" limit. Since my back surgery, I can carry 15 pounds comfortably. If I were to move my library and I had to do much of the work myself, I would be packing the boxes based on that modest parameter. I

would also use ramps, carts, and dollies with wheels—the way the real librarians do.

One subjective truth about gravity is that 15 pounds of books can feel like 60 pounds by the end of a long day. One popular moving strategy would have you move one giant container of books rather than fifty reasonably sized boxes. Tired people tend to drop boxes and make mistakes, however.

Cherish, use, accept potential loss.
—Carol Kimball, artist and
puppetmaker, Denver, CO

---

4. *The Damage Truth.* Books get hurt during moves. They rattle around in boxes and bruise. Covers are bent. They fly open and fall, face down, in the only puddle in sight. Boxes are dropped, and the books inside recoil at the impact. The boxes themselves fall apart during the move, spilling the contents on the highway from the back of your pickup.

Books get lost, sometimes forever.

If you care about your books, invest in their protection. Your valuable books need to be wrapped individually, protected from moisture and dirt, and buffered against bumps. Anything that you really cherish should be treated like good china. Your less valuable books can be packed in boxes and buffered by crumpled, clean paper. (Old, crumpled newspaper can mark your books with ink during a move, particularly if the day is humid and the books are tightly packed.)

If it is raining the day you move, waterproof protection is a must. A box can look perfectly dry on the outside, but the books on the inside can still absorb water through cracks and folds.

If you have hired movers or are shipping your library a long distance, you cannot count on your books being treated with the consideration that is their due. Your budget will dictate your investment in bubble wrap, foam peanuts, hand-wrapping, and labeling.

Assign one trustworthy person to do nothing but see to the care of your books when you move. This person will not only know which boxes hold what, but will also have it all written down and have multiple identical copies of the list in places known to several people. People who keep important information in their heads are often targeted for abduction by aliens at crucial times during a move.

Since damage and loss happens, get insurance. Find out from your insurance agent what kind of coverage you can get through your personal policy, and how it compares with what is offered by the moving company, if you are using one. Most book experts insure everything during a move. Make sure that the insurance covers the full replacement cost of your library. Please see Chapter VIII for more information on insurance and appraisals.

5. *The Archeology Truth.* If you are carting around unopened boxes of books from one home to another, and the boxes remain unopened for years at a time, it is time to let go. If you don't care about the books enough to use them, have them on display, or store them under archival conditions, you are relegating them to a slow death. Open up those boxes and make some decisions, Bucko.

Taking Books for a Ride

Automobiles are book tombs. Books fade and turn to brown cracker crumbs when left on sunny dashboards, even in winter. They suffer from chemical contamination when left unprotected in trunks. The heavy oils used in cars migrate easily into porous pages. Who has a perfectly clean car? When tossed onto the backseat, books inevitably end up on the floor, where they are crushed underfoot or marked with muddy footprints.

Do you leave your books in cars? Keep them in an inert, plastic-lined banker box while you transport them. These are inexpensive cardboard boxes, which come with covers and handles, that you can buy at most office supply stores. A banker box will not protect them from being baked after months of neglect, however.

Bookends and Book Supports

The first purpose of a bookend or book support is to protect books from damage. Aesthetics should be a distant second. If you have pretty bookends you want to show off, treat them as artwork and limit their contact with your more valuable books.

A book support that allows a book to be displayed open should support the covers of the book and the spine so that the open book does not lie flat; this can cause the spine to crack, hinges to tear, and the sewed binding to rip. It should be made of some inert material, and if the book is valuable, the entire book should be displayed in some kind of case to protect it from dirt, etc.

Those inexpensive metal bookends from office supply stores can damage your books in several ways. The sharp metal uprights can impress themselves on the cover of your book, particularly if you tend to pack your shelves too tightly, and the tongue, which is the part on which the books sit, can rip a fragile cover.

The perfect bookend is easy to clean, so that it does not become home to dust and denizens, which can then migrate to your books. It is smooth and flat where it touches the book, and it is made of an inert material that will not interact with the materials in the cover. Also, because it has a smooth, flat face, there is no danger of it accidentally embossing the cover or dust jacket. It does not have any sharp edges, which could slice fingers or paper.

The perfect bookend does not have any extending pieces that slip under the book. It needs to be big enough to support the entire surface of the cover of the book. The short bookend next to the stiff, tall cover might look nice, but if it is left in place long enough, the cover of the book will splay like a flower opening up to the sun.

The perfect bookend is another book the same size as the book that needs support, but wide enough and heavy enough to stay upright on its own and support the other books on the shelf.

You can gut dead books and create excellent bookends from the skeletons of old hardbacks. Replace the pages with a sanded and finished block of wood (unfinished wood is likely to shed sawdust and splinters), and glue one or more of the altered books together as a block. Be careful not to get any glue on the covers, where it might touch one of the books that it supports.

Insects and Vermin

There are creatures that view your books as the Promised Land, where they can fall in love, marry, raise families, build homes, feed their friends, and die in comfort. Some species will merely vacation in your library, gorging on rich food and dating indiscriminately, before moving on. They like storage areas because they can pursue their small happiness undisturbed.

Why did I not include pictures of book bugs in this book? Because I don't care. Frequent cleaning and the judicious use of certain organic controls do not require memorizing Latin insect names.

You can protect books to some extent with chemical and physical barriers, but the horror stories of infestations despite poisons and plastic seals are legion. If you have no choice but to keep the books in a storage area attractive to insects and rodents, keep the area clean, dry, and cool. Most bugs like it warm and damp. But without the kind of specialized equipment found in a well-financed museum, you can't put your books away and assume they will be okay. It is sort of like forgetting to feed the goldfish for a month or six.

Check your books in storage at seasonal intervals (at the very least). Inspect the books, especially those at the bottom of dark boxes. Insect and rodent traps can help protect items locked away, but traps are more useful as collection devices for taking a census of the local "thing" population than as a way to halt destruction. Do what the experts do: Write down the date you checked the box on the box itself.

Mothballs are a popular anticritter device in home libraries. However, the fumes can irritate eyes and skin, and they must be disposed of carefully. Cedar-based products, which have been used to protect libraries since biblical times, and herbal-based products are preferred. Cedar oil sprays should be used only where the wood does not touch the books and with the books covered or removed during treatment. Herbal-based repellents can be purchased in small tea bags, which solves the problem of how to scatter dead plant matter artfully throughout your library.

Two additional products for pest control that are rated as being both safe and effective are boric acid and diatomaceous earth. Both can be purchased from the garden catalogs listed at the end of this chapter.

Boric acid is available in powder and liquid form and is most effective against cockroaches and ants. However, it can be toxic in large quantities, so don't squirt it around your shelves and forget about it, particularly if you have pets and children.

Diatomaceous earth is composed of the fossilized remains of one-celled plants called diatoms. It kills all kinds of insects, slugs, bugs, and critters by destroying the outsides of soft bugs and the insides of hard bugs. More, you don't want to know. Diatomaceous earth is safe enough to eat, if you are into that kind of thing. I personally would not inhale the stuff or sprinkle it into my eyes. It is useful against silverfish, cockroaches, and bedbugs.

In your war against book bugs, don't forget the various species of fly. They won't munch on your books, but they can speckle the covers and fore-edges with brown spots, a sure way to destroy the value of your modern first edition collection. Fly specks can be lifted from the surface of a page, cover, or dust jacket with the edge of a surgical knife, without disturbing the fibers. Keeping the flies away in the first place versus picking off fly specks—it's a choice.

Several new pest control products look promising, including a variation on old, reliable flypaper. This product uses orange-colored glue, which imitates the color of rotting food (yum!), and silhouettes of landed flies (ducks don't work) to act as lures. A new inside zapper glows with light in a range that many insects will find appealing. The advantage to both of these methods is that there are no chemicals to poison the air in your home.

I realize that some of you live in places where the exterminators drive Porsches and you plan your vacations for those times when you can make the semi-annual appointment to debug your house. I was able to find little that addressed the hazards of using heavy-duty chemicals in the home to rid your personal book collections of bugs, so I am playing it careful for the time being, and I hope you do, too. Even some museum conservators are rethinking their "nuke them into atomic dust" policy toward pests.

Resources for BookLovers on Display and Storage

Books on Building Shelves

Standard bookshelf design and construction manuals have all the information you need to build decent shelves. Just remember that your books can be as fragile as a living thing and need the same considerations.

Bookshelves and Cabinets: *Design Ideas, Building Techniques, Step-by Step Projects.* The Editors of Sunset Books. *Sunset Books, $8.99 paper, ISBN 0-376-01086-X.*

The Complete Home Organizer: *A Guide to Functional Storage Space for All the Rooms in Your Home.* Maxine Ordesky. *Grove Press, $22.00 paper, ISBN 0-8021-3340-1.*

How to Plan and Build Bookcases, Cabinets and Shelves. The Staff of Ortho Books. *Ortho Books, $9.95 paper, ISBN 0-89721-088-3.*

Books on Organizing the Rest of Your Life

Clutter Control: *Putting Your Home on a Diet.* Jeff Campbell. Illustrated by Axelle Fortier. *Dell, $7.99 paper, ISBN 0-440-50339-6.*

Ready, Set, Organize: *Get Your Stuff Together.* Pipi Campbell Peterson. Illustrated by Bruce Berrigan. *Park Avenue, $12.95 paper, ISBN 1-57112-072-6.*

Library Ergonomics

The Computer User's Survival Guide. Joan Stigliani. *O'Reilly and Associates, $21.95 paper, ISBN 1-56592-030-9; 103 Morris Street, Suite A, Sebastopol, CA 95472; inquiries (800) 998-9938, orders (800) 889-8969.*

There is very little written about ergonomics for home librarians. The best sources of information about how to prevent back strain and eye strain can be found in books for office workers, particularly those who work with computers. Many of the issues are the same. This book details the damage that people who sit too long and read too long can do to their bodies and what to do instead.

If you are planning to sell your home in the near future, check with a real estate agent before you build custom bookcases. In some markets, built-in furniture is not considered an asset. ❖

Lighting Resources

American Lighting Association (ALA). PO Box 580168, Dallas, TX 753421; (800) 274-4484.

They can direct you to local ALA showrooms throughout North America. Three consumer brochures are available at $2 each: *Lighting Your Life, Light Up Your Landscape,* and *Light Up Your Kitchen and Bath.*

Real Goods®. 555 Leslie Street, Ukiah, CA 95482-5507; (800) 762-7325; fax (707) 468-9486.

Cool household products for aging hippies, such as your humble editor, and people who wish they were. Several pages feature interesting lamps and lighting accessories for the home, including many of the long-life bulbs that use less electricity.

NiteOwl™ Book Light. Lumatec® Industries, 500 Shady Lane, Austin, TX 78702; (800) 586-2832 (for local dealers); fax (512) 389-0808 (for orders).

A portable light specifically designed for booklovers. Instead of clipping onto one page, the stem of this lightweight lamp slips into the pages like a giant bookmark. This useful product is carried by many bookstores. The suggested retail price is $25; a deluxe gift set, which includes an AC adapter and a spare lamp, costs $40. Shipping and handling are extra.

Pest Control Resources

Gardener's Supply Company. 128 Intervale Road, Burlington, VT 05401-2804; (802) 863-1700; fax (802) 660-4600.

Gardens Alive!® 5100 Schenley Place, Lawrenceburg, IN 47025; (812) 537-8650; fax (812) 537-5108.

I have ordered many products from both these companies over several years and have found them to have high quality and more sensible prices than many of the newer garden supply companies. Both stock a number of products for controlling all kinds of insects and vermin; many of these products are designed to be used around children and pets.

Least Toxic Home Pest Control. Second Edition. Dan Stein.
The Book Publishing Company, $8.95 paper, ISBN 0-913990-07-8.

A friendly handbook for learning how to outsmart everything from ants to wasps, including some of the worst home library pests, such as silverfish, mice, and cockroaches. The author warns that you will have to coordinate your efforts with your neighbors if you live in an apartment house or condominium.

Mail-Order Bookshelf Catalogs

Some of the best shelves I have found are sold through mail-order catalogs. I like them because they are made from solid wood or sturdy composite material, are designed to fold up for moving, and are modular units.

However, shipped goods are sometimes damaged goods. (I have also found damage in folding bookcases sold through discount stores.) The bookcases are stored, moved, and displayed in sealed boxes, so it makes it difficult for even a conscientious person to check for chips and dents.

These shelves are not archival for your rare books, but are fine for the home librarian who is looking for mail-order storage furniture that looks good at an affordable price.

Barnes & Noble. Books by Mail, 126 Fifth Avenue, New York NY 10011; (800) 242-6657; fax (201) 767-9169.

Book giant Barnes & Noble offers booklovers the convenience of buying bookcases at the same time you order your books. They are solid wood, and they stack and fold. The unfinished three-shelf cases cost about $55.

Crate and Barrel. PO Box 9059, Wheeling, IL 60090-9059; (800) 323-5461; fax (847) 215-0482.

The metal and wood cases assemble without tools. Crate and Barrel is one of the few catalogs to carry attractive bookcarts for the home. Bookcarts are one of the most useful tools for real libraries, and one that more home librarians should use.

The Crate Shoppe. PO Box 154, Kipton, OH 44049; fax (216) 985-2008.

These clever people took a practical item everyone loved and used for decades, and made it better. A wooden crate is a practical bookshelf module, but how about these made of solid oak? Or stained pine? Both apple and orange crate designs are available for the connoisseur.

Hold Everything®. Mail-Order Department, PO 7807, San Francisco, CA 94120-7807; (800) 421-2285 (customer service); fax (415) 421-5153.

These are not archival storage products, but the average home librarian will find lots of nifty ideas for storing and displaying books, including shelving, bags, boxes, drawers, and various stacking units. The products I have purchased have been uniformly excellent.

L.L. Bean. Freeport, ME 04033; (800) 221-4221; fax (207) 552-3080.

No, your books don't need hiking boots. L.L. Bean sells Mission furniture, which is that geometric and elegant style of wood design from the early part of the century. Lovely stuff that you aren't going to find in the average store.

Pottery Barn. Mail-Order Department, PO Box 7044, San Francisco, CA 94120-7044; (800) 922-5507; fax (415) 421-5153.

Another division of the same company that owns Hold Everything. If you like the new "minimalist nature" look in home furnishings, you will like Pottery Barn's bookshelves and end tables, which feature clean designs in wood and metal. I like this much better than the Danish Modern designs of my childhood. The prices are very sensible for such attractive pieces.

Reliable Home Office. PO Box 1501, Ottawa, IL 61350-9916; (800) 869-6000; fax (800) 326-3233.

If you don't live near one of the new mega-office supply stores, this is the next best thing. Lots of bookcases, desks, drawers, and storage cases for books and personal archives.

Bread Boxes for Cookbook Lovers

Colorado writer and columnist Ed Quillen suggests a bread box as a place to store books in the kitchen.

Miles Kimball. 41 West Eighth Avenue, Oshkosh, WI 54906; (414) 231-4886.

Amidst the lace tablecloths and totebags are two clear plastic bread and bakery boxes. One design has a clear, rolltop cover and comes in two sizes, 7-1/2 x 11-1/4 x 6-1/2 and 9 x 15 x 7 inches. The other is composed of two plastic sections that expand and contract around a standard-size loaf.

The Vermont Country Store®. Mail-Order Office, PO Box 3000, Manchester Center, VT 05255-3000; (802) 362-2400; fax (802) 362-0285.

This venerable company sells a white metal bread box, 17" x 10" x 11", for around $40.

❖

The real world is not limited
to one viewpoint.
page 146.

Chapter VIII — Classification and Cataloging

Being an Orderly Collection of Stories and Admonitions Concerning the Classification and Cataloging of Your Home Library, With Musings on Insurance, Appraisals, and the History of the Bookmark.

How to Organize Your Library the Right Way, and Why the Wrong Way Is Just Fine and Better Than the Best Way, Which Does Not Exist

Classification refers to the system you use to organize your books and their contents; *cataloging* is the location of the book in the system. This location is indicated by: 1. the physical position of the book in the book stacks in relationship to the other books; 2. a sequential identification code; and 3. a description of the book, its history, and its contents. For the home librarian, classification is your grand scheme, and cataloging is the description and location of each piece in the scheme.

Your personal information classification and cataloging systems are unlikely to be identical to those of the experts, who make their livings organizing the world's knowledge. Your systems are formed by your experience, values, education, and the practical considerations of your life. The experts' official systems are formed by extensive research, a complete familiarity with all the data in the universe, and hours spent arguing in hotel lobbies during cataloging conferences.

I categorize my personal library into two gross divisions—
whether I have already read the book or not.
—Laurie Wermter, reference librarian, Madison, WI

The main difference between a home library and a publicly accessible library is not just the difference between a personal and a professional classification system. The main difference is that your library must please only you, while public and academic libraries must please everybody. The "real" librarian needs a classification system that can be linked to the classification systems of other libraries, so that a person walking into a library in Alaska has a chance of knowing where things are, even though they just moved there from Florida. Real librarians must spend a lot of time negotiating with each other about the way things are ordered and labeled.

What Is the Right Way?

I began the serious research on the subject of books and home libraries in our excellent public library in Denver. Because books regarding books are scattered throughout the Dewey universe, I careened from one floor to another, lugging books with me to protect them from overzealous shelvers. Not until I had visited *General Knowledge, Philosophy, Religion, Social Sciences, Language, Technology, Literature, History,* and *Reference* did I have enough information to begin to contrast and compare. In my personal library, all of these books now coexist in the same bookcase, cheek to jowl, regardless of their call numbers.

Some of the better books I needed were sequestered, like errant children at a holiday dinner, in their own *YA (Young Adult)* or *J (Juvenile)* section. In my home library, a book is a book, whether it was written for a ten-year-old or for her father. (See Chapter XIII for a description of one public library that does it differently.)

Even a small library will stick to the official systems, although some maverick librarians will create special "interdisciplinary collections." This allows the librarians to raid every category to create a usable body of work on a topic like "How to Manage a Home Library." What is considered radical in a public or academic library is customary in the home library.

Bookstores Versus Libraries: Which Does It Best?

When I visited local bookstores, the situation was the same. In the basement of one large bookstore were children's books on books, books on children's literature, books on organizing home offices, and technical books on databases. On the first floor were books on the history of different civilizations (and how they handled books) and gifts for booklovers, including kits for the construction of handmade books and blank journals.

On the second floor I found decorative bookends, postcards with booklovers' themes, and bargain books on collecting, repairing, and displaying books; each kind of book was in its own section of the store. The third floor had new books on the history of books, book arts, collecting books, book repair, displaying books, starting book reading groups, papermaking, typography, and the critical enjoyment of books. Each category of new book was also in a separate section.

(I eavesdrop on librarians and booksellers. When they discuss the relative merits of the ways libraries and bookstores are organized, professionals from each group proclaim that they could do a much better job than their counterparts. Librarians think that bookstores should follow library classification systems, and bookstore owners are for "Keep It Intuitive, Stupid.")

The exceptions? The experts would request that if you have valuable books and papers, you ask for assistance when organizing them, particularly if you plan to donate them to an archive, museum, or library. This will make it easier on the people who accept your gift, because some of their work will have already been done. Also, as explained in Chapter XIV, archivists and historians deal with documents created within the context of an organization or a period of time, rather than books that happen to share a similar topic. They prefer that information be kept in chronological order, and that copious notes be provided about each piece of paper.

There are several major classification systems used in formal libraries, but the two best known are the Library of Congress and the Dewey decimal.

The Library of Congress Classification System

Most academic and research libraries use the Library of Congress system. One librarian told me that a new employee at her academic library, fresh from a public library, demanded that someone tell him how the $^&$ library was organized; the new employee had never seen the Library of Congress system.

The major classes or categories of the system are:

A	General works, such as almanacs, encyclopedias, and collections too diverse or general to fit anywhere else
B	Religion, philosophy, psychology
C	Auxiliary sciences of history, which include biography and archaeology
D	General history, except for the Americas
E	United States history
F	History of the Americas and local United States history
G	Geography, anthropology, folklore, dance
H	Social sciences, such as economics, sociology, and labor
J	Political sciences
K	Law
L	Education
M	Music
N	Fine arts, including architecture and crafts
P	Language and literature
Q	Science
R	Medicine
S	Agriculture
T	Technology, including engineering and other applied sciences
U	Military sciences
V	Naval science
Z	History of books, bibliography, and library science

The Dewey Decimal Classification System

This is probably the first library classification system you learned at your school library or local public library. It has some similarities to the Library of Congress classification (they were developed about the same time) and, like the LC system, is constantly growing and changing. Historians have written that when Melvil Dewey, the author of the system, was still alive, many of his colleagues were so angry at him for various reasons, from his arrogant personality to his alleged anti-Semitism, that they refused on principle to adopt his classification system, and therefore created their own.

The main classes or categories of the system are:

000	Generalities, which includes a catchall of computer manuals, book-related information, encyclopedias, and journalism
100	Philosophy, psychology, and mysticism
200	Religion
300	Social sciences, including education, law, culture, economics, and politics
400	Languages
500	Pure science
600	Technology, including engineering and other applied sciences
700	The arts, including architecture, music, and dance
800	Literature
900	General history, biography, and geography

It is likely that your local library is operating under different versions of either system. Every few years, new subclasses are added, and adjustments are made to old ones. In theory, a library should update its cataloging every time there is a new release of the classification system. This means changing records, changing the identification codes on the books, and changing their location. Many libraries do not have the budget or inclination to do so. Also, library staff have been known to "tweak" the official Dewey decimal and Library of Congress systems in order to meet the needs of their patrons (or satisfy the megalomania of the person on the staff who thinks he or she can do it better). You may discover that your local college or public library has been operating under *"Fred and Fanny's Friendly Factfinder Filing Forum,"* much to the horror of visiting library officials.

My advice for your home library, which is echoed by most of the "real" catalogers I interviewed, is to learn more about the conventional classification systems and apply their wisdom in your home library. But appreciate the freedom you have to make a system that works for you.

I don't want to be ruled by a system that takes up my time.
My advice to anyone organizing a home collection is:
"Let it reflect your own personality."
—Gay Ellen Roesch, librarian and booklover, Golden, CO

Both major systems suffer several limitations that you can overcome in your homegrown, customized system.

1. The real world does not obey the dictates of the curriculum committee. Major library classification systems have been designed by individuals who have been brainwashed by the university-bred attitude that packs up the known universe into neat shoeboxes.

For example, in the real world, an experienced professional writer knows many ways to communicate information. Is it a newspaper opinion piece or a sales brochure, a television documentary or a work of fiction, a book or an audiotape? Does it require photographs, fine art illustrations, or interactive multimedia? The successful writer needs to be fluent in a dozen different voices, from the stripped-to-the-bone, rapid fire of the radio news anchor to the rich fugue of the essayist, and needs to know many different tools, from a typewriter to computer-generated animation workstations (or at least know how to work with the people who do know).

But in the typical university, the writer's toolbox is spread across a dozen different departments with autonomous faculty, independent curricula, and an Italian city-state attitude toward their neighbors. The journalists learn their trade in the mass communication department, and the advertising copywriters scribble away in the business and marketing departments. The essayists pontificate in the creative nonfiction department, and the interactive media nerds reside in the computer department. Interdisciplinary programs, which allow a would-be writer to learn all the nuances of human communication under the tutelage of one integrated collegial program, are almost always the exception and can evoke feelings of suspicion from cloistered professors.

The genesis of classification systems occurs in this highly structured environment. Individuals who inhabit academe can forget the lesson every explorer, trader, and military commander has learned the hard way: A map is not the same as the terrain it documents. Expert mapping systems of human knowledge are not the same as knowledge.

You can create a library that is a map of your world. All of your beloved books on France, from political histories to cookbooks, can be together if it makes sense to you. You can put the applied and pure science books together, the math and science books together, or the books on journalism, creative writing, computer graphics, and advertising on one shelf.

2. The real world is not sequential. Both major library classification systems suffer from being designed during the ancient days of information (circa the late 1800s), when data management systems were bound by the same factors that still limit the Gutenberg-era book. Information was stored in gross physical objects, fixed in time and space, with little ability to move and change. A book that was on the third shelf of the fourth bookcase on the fifth floor—well, that's where it is, right? A book can't be in two places, can it? Also, when the book was cataloged, it was assigned one code number, which was not changed unless the High Priestess of Cataloging said so.

Technology has addressed that limitation. Entire books are stored on computers and can be accessed, for practical purposes, by unlimited numbers of people at the same time, who can store the location of the book as a nonsequential number. (See Chapter XII for sources of the virtual book.)

In the old days, a book would be tracked down by title, author, or subject, which required a piece of paper with the pertinent data to be filed in different file cabinets. Today, books can be found by searching through key words that describe the contents, even if these words are not located in either the text or bibliographic information.

At home, you can use your computer to create a classification system that defies conventional logic, but which allows you to describe the true, chaotic state of the information on your shelves. You can assign as many codes and key words as you like. The book can be located in any number of places in your system and can be assigned any number of code numbers.

Home librarians have been known to do something else that accurately resembles the amorphous nature of the world. It is, to the best of my knowledge, almost totally unknown in the world of the real library. Home librarians acquire more than one copy of a book, and then *put the different copies in different places!* What a concept! In my home library, there are drowned-rat copies of favorite fiction in the bathroom, sturdy reading copies of the same books next to my bed, and clean, well-tended, and protected hardback versions on the upper shelves in my office. I also have different editions and versions of the same book, which serve my purposes as a researcher.

3. The real world is not limited to one viewpoint. Both major classification systems are a product of the world view of late nineteenth-century, college-educated North Americans. Their inventors shared a Victorian cultural belief in an orderly world, that is, a world ordered in the one right way—theirs. Like fish in water, it was difficult for them to describe water, or to understand that other

beings might breathe air through lungs, not gills. Flight is incomprehensible to a fish, as are beings that fly.

The individuals who design formal classification systems have to make decisions about the relative importance of particular information. For example, look at the number of major classes within the Library of Congress system that have to do with history. History? Excuse me? The major classifications in my home library, in order of the number of volumes on a subject and the relative importance to my universe, would include books on economics and philosophy (in my home library these go together); how-to books on dozens of subjects; the novels of science fiction author Poul Anderson; interdisciplinary books on conflict management; what I like to call my "hypochondria" books on medicine, health, and healing; classic children's literature; and biography. The only history books I own are history club books I inherited from my father, but I never read them. They sit on a shelf overlooking the living room; seeing them every day makes me happy.

I can describe my book collection as the product of many, many years of Liberal Education including the four-year program at St. John's College, which is based on the Great Books of Western Civilization. My books number around 5,000, and I thought, being classically trained, I would arrange them by the Trivium-Quadrivium (Trivium = Grammar, Logic, Rhetoric; Quadrivium = Arithmetic, Astronomy, Geometry, Music). Then I applied my standard litmus test: Where would I place Jane Austen? So, back to square one. I had some very disturbing days when I thought I would cave in to accession of my collection by color: red, orange, yellow, green, blue, indigo, violet. However, here, too, my litmus test failed. I almost wished I had stopped reading anything written after 405 B.C. And, Martianus Capella's De Nuptilis Philologae et Mercurii *was no bloody help at all. I arrived at Seven Zones, each to be presided over by one or more Muse. Here is the plan: Zone 1: Thalia & Melopomene: Drama and Commentaries; Zone 2: Polyhymniea: Philosophy, Logic, Rhetoric, Metaphysics, and Religion; Zone 3: Urania & Auadrivium: Arithmetic, Geometry, Pure & Applied Sciences; Zone 4: Trivium: Grammar, Languages, Dictionaries; Zone 5: Cleo: History & Biography; Zone 6: Calliope & Erato: Literature (Enfin! Jane Austen) & Poetry; Zone; 7: Euterpe: Music ...*
—Diane H. Kaferly, senior member of technical staff, USWest Technologies, Denver, CO

My friend Lee's home library has one major class: cookbooks. My friend Chip's is 99 percent engineering texts. Would the Library of Congress emphasis on history serve you?

It is a serious issue among real librarians that many people believe books no longer have to be organized according to a generally accepted classification system. Outside the boundaries of libraries that obey the official rules, information is being produced and made available by people who don't care. The Internet, for example, has been described as a library without a classification system or a card catalog. While those arguments are important, booklovers can listen, learn, and then go home and have fun organizing their own collections any way they want.

4. The real world changes, often in ways that are unexpected. Recently, a popular author proclaimed that we have come to the end of significant scientific discovery. Sound familiar? Every few years, a fish proclaims there is nothing left to learn in the bowl.

People who design classification systems probably wish the world *was* a closed and static system. Dang those inventors! Dang those artists! Dang those explorers! Dang those citizens who insist on writing new books, voting new people into office, breeding new species of flowers, building new cities, waging new wars, and discovering that what we believed was dogma yesterday is heresy tomorrow. (Or is it the other way around?)

As mentioned before, the changes in the world require constant updates to the existing classification systems, and this is an expensive and time-consuming process for a publicly accessible library.

It is an issue for home librarians only if you insist on creating a steel-plated, sunk-in-concrete-pilings, frozen-in-time system for your books. In the next section, you will learn how to create a flexible library classification system that can deal with, among other things, space aliens landing in your backyard, new species of tulips, and the shifting of political boundaries.

But more important to you are the changes in your life. Right now, on the corner of a shelf, is a single book on music, or religion, or the ocean, representing your idle curiosity about the topic. Nothing serious, you say. But if I visited your library in a few years and noticed a wall of books on the piano, or on the concept of redemption or seashells, would you remember when your interests shifted, and the very first book you acquired on the topic? And could your classification system cope with the change?

Booklovers who use their libraries as tools often will rearrange their collections after a major research project to accommodate new insights. When I look at my bookcases during these turbulent moments, my current classification system crumbles. I sigh, because I know it will be weeks before I create a satisfactory new order and have my books snug in their new locations.

Confessions of a Former BookLover
By Susan A. Benjamin, catalog librarian, Denver, CO
Susan A. Benjamin © 1996

I used to hoard, accumulate, and amass books. Floor to ceiling, double-stacked, even up in the space above my kitchen cupboards. Books, books, everywhere, and all required dusting. I never lent my books, after all they were mine, all mine. I coveted, treasured, lusted after the next Dick Francis, P. D. James, Robert B. Parker. Books threatened to take over my apartment. Eyeing each departing guest's handbag with suspicion, my sanity was in question. All this was abetted by my job as a catalog librarian at a large California university. Heaven, you'd think, to be surrounded by books, but alas, none were fit to read. That is to say, not a mystery novel in sight amongst dry tomes on superconductors, photovoltaic cells, and the aeronautical implications of sky camps. Life, but was it worth reading?

Change came as a result of a new job. Still a catalog librarian, but for the first time in over fifteen years, not in an academic setting. The Denver Public Library welcomed me to the world of John Q. Public and a stunning array of reading, listening, viewing tapes, and fiction. Glorious murder mysteries reached out as I passed on my way to the shelf list, the phone, the bathroom. There was no avoiding them. I put holds on all the newest titles, tens of new authors. And a curious thing happened. I no longer needed to own books. The fact that they were there whenever I wanted them, delivered to my desk, freed me from the tyranny of owning, arranging, dusting books.

My books used to be carefully arranged in alphabetical order by author and then by title in order by date of publication. After all, it would never do to read a mystery series out of order. Now that my collection is reduced in size (moving halfway across the country will do that) and I have antique mahogany cases to display my books in, I am considering reorganizing them by size and color. ❖

How to Organize Your Home Library

Hire an Expert

What if you hire someone to come to your home and do the work for you? A classification system for a library is always someone's interpretation of how the world is organized. So long as your brain works the way the designer's brain works, you will think the system is wonderful.

However, I have heard too many reports from booklovers who had professional librarians organize and catalog their collections, but who found themselves as disorganized as ever a year later.

Here are two common scenarios. In one, the professional designed a complex system that would be appropriate for a well-financed private research library with a well-paid and well-trained staff, but which made no sense at all for the average booklover with limited resources. In the other scenario, the professional religiously cataloged the library according to an existing system, which did not reflect the way the booklover used the library. In either case, as the booklovers brought new books into their collections, the time it would take to decide the right place for the book and the appropriate notations in the recordkeeping system became an overwhelming barrier to keeping the system current and correct.

I don't catalog my books. After one semester of cataloging
at the University of Denver's School of Librarianship, I
decided I would much rather read than catalog.
—Elizabeth Gardener, water conservation officer, Lakewood, CO

The intention to keep up the cataloging was there, but the reality translated into piles of books waiting for the perfect and unobtainable moment when the booklover had the time to catch up. Eventually, the books did get shelved, but the frustrated booklover shoved the books into empty spots on the shelves during random bursts of inspiration. Cataloging deteriorates, and anarchy returns.

One home librarian, a college professor, used the services of a librarian who spent six month organizing and documenting the professor's extensive home library. It was a gift from a loving daughter. Two years later, the library is again a mess. The professor is embarrassed and does not want her daughter to know.

Hire an expert if you have a stable collection, if you really are the kind of person who will keep it up when the expert has done her job, and if you have to put your collection in formal order for some greater purpose, such as opening your own, private library. See Chapter XI and XIV for more information.

Don't wait for the perfect person to put your library in order.

Buy Fancy Tools (i.e., a Computer)

Complicated and expensive is better only if complicated and expensive fits your needs, and you have the resources to support complicated and expensive.

You don't need a computer. I say this as a computer-loving booklover, with a really cool, to-die-for computer system on my desk. But for many of the sorting tasks that I deal with on a daily basis, I use paper, colored pens, and whiteboards to keep track of my life. I use tools; they don't rule me.

You probably already have the physical tools around your house to create a catalog of your library: an old tin recipe book with colored file cards; a three-ring binder with clean, lined notepaper; a bulletin board with places to pin information; a clipboard hanging from a nail, holding a list of your books; small pieces of paper attached to shelves, indicating the general topic of the books at that location. Don't wait for the perfect tool to put your library in order.

The Perfect System

Once upon a time, I was part of a team of people creating a computer system for one of the largest educational systems in the Rocky Mountain region. It was to be a combination database and registration system, with the ability to keep track of hundreds of classes and thousands of students through a school year that could have as many as six semesters.

It was an organization that I knew well as a student, teacher, and board member. I had participated in many registrations and knew the problems. Over the course of weeks, the team asked detailed questions and passed the information on to the system designer, who made many visits to the site.

The big day arrived. The computer system was set up, the staff was poised at the terminals, and the students started arriving to register. The system designer had shown up to troubleshoot, but everything was going very smoothly. And then the head of registration tapped me on the shoulder.

"I forgot to tell you," she began.

She forgot to tell us about the exceptions to the normal routine. She had forgotten to tell us that classes were added and cancelled at the last minute. She had forgotten to tell us about the special discounts for registering early and for taking more than four classes. She had forgotten to tell us that the director had decided that none of the staff needed training on the system, so that everyone was entering the information according to their own whim.

She forgot. And you will, too.

There are many theories about how to create an information system. One theory says do nothing and hope that order will be created naturally, sort of like the perfectly balanced ecology of a summer meadow drenched in wildflowers. People who adhere to this theory forget about how an invasive weed can destroy the beauty of that meadow in a season. In the book world, this attitude is most common among home librarians who pride themselves on the disorder of their collections, which is sort of a "don't you miss the fun we had cleaning up after the flood" mentality.

Another theory says that you can anticipate every single detail of a system and create the perfect system. These are the fish-in-the-bowl folks, who think life can be engineered by really smart people. These are people who have never raised children or tried to keep order in a fast-moving knot of puppies or kittens.

Elaborate home library systems can have a flash point. One day it becomes too much, and the system, and booklover, collapse. After The Fall, there is no system, which is a shame.

My method is a balance between the two extremes. Better that you start a simple system you can maintain without heartbreak or theological tragedy.

What rescued the day for our computer team, when the head of registration told us she had forgotten key information, is that the system designer had created a system that could change and grow very easily. Even under the pressure of a line of students in front of him, he sat down and made the system do what it needed to do in a few minutes. He had created the registration system on the assumption that there would be unexpected changes from the beginning. By being flexible, his system was bulletproof.

Your system for organizing your library should allow you to change your mind frequently. Whether it be a computer program or pieces of paper in a file folder, you should choose tools that allow you to expand your ideas about your books.

There will be times, for example, when your interest in the history of books requires that you keep track of detailed information about the lineage of ownership, the typefaces, and the current location of the same edition in other collections. You might want to have a place to graph the sale price of the book at various auctions. As you become more educated about your books, it is likely you will want to keep track of more information. You will probably invent new ways of organizing your information as new areas of interest are introduced into your collection.

Another approach, which I promote for those who have a mostly modest collection of disposal paperbacks and cheap hardbacks, is to reserve the cataloging of your books to the few that are worth something, or to develop a system that keeps minimal records on most of the books and "deep" catalogs of only the most precious.

What information do you need to capture in your cataloging system?

The basic bibliographic information includes title, author or editor, publisher, and the year the current edition was published or copyrighted. Home librarians often like to keep track of when and where they acquired a book, the price, and a personal annotation, which could include their opinions of the book or of the person who gave it to them.

A few years ago I discovered a charming economics book, which I wanted to share with several friends. I ordered several copies from the author, a Canadian businessman. Several months later, when I decided to order more copies, I discovered I had failed to keep his address. I could not locate the author, but a local bookstore tracked down a distributor. By the time my order was placed, the distributor was out of business and the book was out of print. Now I am careful to save the ordering information about books from smaller presses.

Our personal libraries do not obey the rules of the Dewey decimal system; they obey the rules of the heart.
—Jonathan Zimmerman, architect, San Francisco, CA

Various experts in the book community have complicated cataloging codes, with their own jargon and abbreviations. Collectors will make note of the condition of the book and the sales history, including the flaws and the salable points, as touched on in Chapter VI. Researchers might write a brief biography of the author and note the relationship of the book to others of its ilk, and the importance of the book in relationship to the discipline. A real cataloger will include the codes, or call numbers, that position the book in the classification system of the library and, depending on the kind of library or archive, the value of the item and a detailed technical description of the book.

If you look at the copyright page in contemporary books, you will almost always find the cataloging data used by the Library of Congress; the page will also include the actual Library of Congress and Dewey decimal call numbers. Some home librarians photocopy that information and create a catalog card directly from the image.

A librarian might include the physical location of the book in the shelves of his or her library, and refer to other categories where similar books might be found. An archivist might have descriptive information about the sequence of the item in time, so that it is positioned with all the other information created on July 3, 1917. A book artist will want to record the details of the creation of the book, including the kind of leather, paper, and construction methods.

In any formal classification system, the most important category is the one marked "Other." This is where you put your ambiguities, your one-of-a-kind items, your leftovers, and your painfully new ideas. Then, as you play with the data in this category, you will discover new relationships among the pieces of information, and if you don't find an established category to put them in, you will create a new one.

The Basic Elements of a Computer Database System

If you have trouble understanding how a computer database works, please check out some of the resources in Chapter XII. Also, if you are working with computer friends who speak in computer spy code, insist that they draw pictures and use everyday language to explain what is going on. If they can't, find someone who can. Every organization on the planet, from senior centers to university graduate schools, is offering classes in practical computer science, and many of them are very good.

I list my Southwest collection on the computer. Each line is a mini catalog card, and I can print out the collection according to Dewey or author. I now must carry this weighty printout whenever I shop for books, because the collection has over 1,500 books, and I cannot remember all the titles.
—Kathleen L. Keffer, 36 years with libraries,
as a trustee, volunteer, or employee, Littleton, CO
Kathleen L. Keffer © 1996

The names of the various parts of a computer database will differ, depending on the software. Some companies delight in coming up with their own darling and obscure nomenclature. This vocabulary is what I learned in 1977, and most computer people will understand what you mean, or at least be able to translate these words into comparable terms for their computer systems.

A *file* is a collection of information that has similar characteristics, such as a file cabinet of folders that holds the same kind of information for different people in a personnel department. A file in your computer system would be all the books in your library.

A *record* is one file folder in that file. All the information about a single book would be put into one record.

The individual characteristics, which are often called *fields*, might include everything from the name of the book, to the number of pages, to the date you acquired the book.

Some fields may contain more than one piece of data. A book can have more than one author, or you might have a field that lists different key words that can be used to catalog the book. Those pieces of data are called *values*.

In some computer databases a field that can handle more than one value is called a *multivalued* field. If, for example, each chapter in a book has a field to keep track of its information, and each page has a value, it would be possible to catalog multiple pieces of data on each page in a multivalued field.

Appraisals and Insurance:
Do You Know How Much Your Library Is Worth?

There are many reasons to classify and catalog your library. The least important reason is to be able to find what you want. If you have so many books that you can't find them without a system, and you choose not to have a system because you don't have the time to deal with so many books, and you don't get to enjoy the books you have because you can't find them or have forgotten what you have, I have nothing to say, except "Brush after meals and look both ways before crossing the street."

The most important reason to organize and document your library is to protect against loss. Appraisals and insurance are why you need to know what you have and where it all is.

The Appraisal Process

All appraisal processes face one test: Can you find someone who will give you your price when you want it? If you damage or lose a book through theft, fire, flood, etc., will the insurance company go along with the appraiser's figures and provide you with the sum you need to repair or replace the book?

Book prices, for the most part, do not move all that fast, compared to the volatility of penny stock prices, but the value of books can rise and fall dramatically in response to what people like to call *market conditions*. Market conditions is a way of saying "the collective and individual opinions of people who are willing to back those opinions with cash." Nothing else really counts when it comes to the price the seller puts on something.

A real appraisal means hiring a certified and bonded professional, who is recognized as an expert not only by the book community but also by the legal and financial communities, to provide you with an accurate estimate of today's value, based on current market conditions, of your books. You are paying for objective truth, not to hear what you want to hear, or to be quoted a price that will personally benefit the appraiser. What keeps an appraiser honest is her own sense of honor, the ethics of the profession, the constant scrutiny of her peers, and her desire to maintain her reputation in the book community.

The appraisal process might seem coldhearted and unfair, particularly when you realize that the thousands of dollars you paid for those books over a lifetime might not be recovered by selling them.

The best time to have your library appraised is before there is a financial and personal crisis. Appraisers cannot tell you what a library is going to cost to replace when there are no records or inventory, and the only thing they have to go by is your faulty memory and a pile of fluffy ashes.

It is also too late when you are facing a financial disaster and have been counting on the sale of Uncle Sven's Bible to pay off the mortgage, but have never bothered to find out what value the market puts on the Bible.

Appraisals are not just for rich people and collectors of rare and expensive books. Appraisals are necessary if you want to provide your insurance company with accurate information in case of disaster. Appraisals are also important for the peace of mind of your family. If you had invested the time and money in the services of a professional appraiser a few years ago, you would have discovered that the Bible was not worth the thousands that Uncle Sven had stated in his will. You might also have discovered that those first editions you have been buying and stashing away like U.S. Savings Bonds have not evolved into the gold mine the friendly dealer led you to believe would happen.

Set up someone with a limited power of attorney
for disposal of your home library, in the event no
heir wants it nor has the knowledge or interest to
evaluate the collection, sell it, and/or find
a good home for the items.
Barbara Wagner, librarian, Lakewood, CO

If you do not have the inclination to keep track of every single item, you can at least inventory the books that you would be most anxious to replace and have those appraised. You might make this decision based on both financial and emotional considerations.

Whether or not you use the services of an appraiser, you need to educate yourself about the book market. You can't rely on one source for advice, and you can't check the prices and trends in the market once every five years and expect to have accurate information. Part of the investment you make in your books is talking to book dealers, librarians, and archivists; reading the magazines of the book industry; perusing catalogs for current prices; and attending book fairs and conferences. You will still make mistakes, but they will tend to be smaller mistakes. Chapter VI lists some of the resources you need.

If you are worried about the dollar value of your library, keep it in excellent physical shape. Is dirt sifting into those pristine first editions you have on the top shelf of your closet? A Mylar book jacket is not going to protect the fore-edges of the books, which can absorb filth like a sponge. Do any of your older books need the services of a conservator who knows how to repair a book without diminishing its value? That is one factor the appraiser will use when judging your books.

To keep your collection in top condition, you need to keep replacing books of lesser value with those of greater value, as mentioned in Chapter VI. Collectors who focus on increasing the financial value of their book portfolios advocate using less valuable books to finance new acquisitions. Just indiscriminately keeping everything will not ensure a more valuable library. Also, books wear out. You need to know enough about the availability of the books in your collection to be able to track down replacement copies of cheap beloved books as well as the valuable collectibles.

Part of the value of your library is the relationship of the individual volumes to each other. A complete collection of an author's works, or all the publications of a single book arts press, are worth more than the combined value of the individual volumes. Can you get accurate appraisals without paying a fortune? After you educate yourself, you might take a couple of your most valuable books to several rare book dealers and see what they offer you. Sometimes they will waive the appraisal fee if it is an area in which they are personally interested, or if they intend to buy the book. As mentioned before, their offers might be less than what you might get from an individual collector, because the dealer must figure in the cost of selling the book and the profit she hopes to make after deciding what to pay you. Ideally, you will find more than one serious collector in your area who specializes in your kinds of books. You might be able to get an idea based on what they are willing to offer.

However, if you abuse the generosity of the local dealers by expecting free appraisals as the rule rather than the exception, word will get out and you will get a chilly reception. If you don't want to take the time to educate yourself about the value of your library, you will have to pay for the information. And if you have valuable and rare books to protect, the insurance company will demand credible information about their value.

Geography can create problems for all collectibles, in that prices tend to be specific to an area. This can be due to regional historical interest in certain types of books, the location of a significant collector or dealer in a field, a density of collectors in one city, or the magnet of a major library or book arts community. Your books might have a much higher value outside your area, but you must take into account the cost of finding paying customers at a distance.

Book dealers circulate printed catalogs and post notices in newsletters to reach the out-of-town markets. (See Chapter VI for more information about finding out-of-state book dealers.) They have also created a number of computerized services; the idea is to use the power of the computer to lower the cost of locating books. (See Chapter XII for some of these services.) These national and international services are creating a more responsive world market for books, where barriers, such as the time it takes to find out about a book, are dissolving.

How and When to Insure Books

Next to keeping your books clean and dry, the best investment in time and money for your library is insurance. Here are some guidelines to ensure your policies are up to snuff. Because each state has a different set of laws and there are hundreds of available policies, you need to work with local insurance companies.

If your current company can't help you, look around. Not every insurance company insures books, but you can find someone to help you, depending on how much you are willing to pay. I found that having an independent agent who represented dozens of different companies and who had experience with the unusual liability problems of small businesses was the best solution for understanding our home library insurance needs.

Find out what your current insurance covers. If you are a homeowner, your insurance policy probably includes household goods. Without a documented inventory, you won't know if the check the insurance company hands you after a fire or theft will actually cover the cost of repairing or replacing beloved volumes. Most people underestimate how much it costs to replace furniture, clothing, appliances, etc., let alone a 5,000-volume home library.

Most insurance policies exclude flood and water damage, which are among the leading causes of book death in the home. As of this writing, you must buy flood insurance through the federal government, and there is a thirty-day period between the time you buy the insurance and the time it goes into effect. Also, federal flood insurance will not cover the flood damage to books stored in a basement. If you open your window right now, you will hear the collective gasp of thousands of fellow booklovers who have just read this last paragraph and the calliope of thousands of fingers thumping phone buttons, as booklovers call their insurance agents and ask if I am telling the truth.

For more information about federal flood insurance, call your insurance agent or the National Flood Insurance Program direct at (800) 611-6123.

If you are a condominium owner, you might see "insurance" listed on your monthly and annual reports, and therefore assume that the fees you pay cover your household goods. Wrong. As one insurance expert put it, condominium insurance usually stops at the edge of the paint job on your walls. The insurance you pay in your monthly condominium fees is for the buildings and grounds, not for your sofa and books.

If you are a renter, the same holds true. You need your own insurance policy to cover the cost of replacing your library in case of theft, fire, or flood; your landlord's insurance policy will cover only her losses.

Do you use your books for your business? Do you have a business in your home? Your insurance agent can explain to you how to make sure you have covered your business property. Otherwise, you might find your business library is excluded as part of your household goods.

Once you know what you have, you can make some decisions. Do you move your books from your home and transport them to other places, for book fairs or for repair? If so, you can choose to get insurance that covers your books wherever they are.

Do you want to insure your library based on the full replacement value or on its depreciated value? This is a trick question. If you choose to insure your library on its depreciated value, expect to get a check for the cost of carting the ashes to the dump. Some people think that they save money if they do not insure the full replacement value, until a crisis occurs. Discuss this with your insurance agent.

> *My current favorites sit next to my stuffed bird where*
> *he can keep an eye out for predators (namely my husband,*
> *who hates "Bird" and avoids all contact with it).*
> —Carol Olsen, Medical Librarian Technician II,
> Englewood, CO

Is there anything in your collection that is very valuable or very hard to replace or repair? Tell your insurance agent so you can decide how to protect these items. Some people hesitate to tell an insurance company if they have something valuable, in the same way that some people prefer to keep their money stuffed in their mattress. Some people think buying insurance is tempting the fates. I think insurance is a way to protect yourself financially and soothe some of the heartache of loss.

Insurance can buy the tools you need to fix damaged property. Insurance also can cover reconstructing valuable papers and recapturing the data you lost when someone pulled the plug on your computer at the wrong moment.

How can you lower the cost of insuring your home library? Some insurance companies give discounts for home alarm systems. The best discounts I have discovered come from special policies that combine several types of insurance, such as home and auto, into one policy. Also, a written appraisal and documented inventory ensure that you will be paying the right amount. Finally, get two or three bids in writing from different companies, if your agent represents only one insurance company. I saved hundreds of dollars by shopping around.

What about the recordkeeping? Whether or not you use an appraiser, you need to maintain an up-to-date inventory of your collection. It should include the purchase price and current replacement cost of the book. With this information, your insurance company can respond much more quickly to a claim.

Whatever system you use to keep your insurance records, follow two rules:

1. *The records should be current.* Simple systems, as I have said before, are easier to maintain than complicated systems. The world's perfect, but complex inventory system for home libraries is in danger of never being current because it takes too much trouble to update the information.

2. *Copies of the inventories, insurance contracts, and appraisal records should be kept in places you can easily reach, and that are secure from harm.* Yes, it is nice to have your cataloging system near your bookshelves, but it is not useful if your home just burned down. Some people choose to have one copy in their safe deposit box, which works well so long as you can plan your crises so they do not happen on weekends and national holidays. (Also, you might want to keep your safe deposit key on you at all times, just in case.)

Another strategy is to keep one copy with your lawyer. The simplest strategy is to keep at least one copy of important records with a friend who lives near you.

Organizing the Internal Book, and Some Bothersome Copyright Issues

One of the more interesting cataloging issues has to do with organizing the information within certain books in relationship to information in other books. For example, if you have 500 Gutenberg-era books about horses, and you want to catalog the information each book contains about colic, horseshoes, or training a horse to harness, you have few satisfactory choices.

You could use bookmarks; see the end of this chapter for examples of current bookmark art.

You can create a system that documents the location of the important information in each book. I saw such a system at a think tank in California. It had file folders, each about a different topic, with pieces of paper that described the location and contents of books and magazines that refer to the topic. The file system took up the wall of a large room.

A computer version of that system could let you create a customized printout of where each piece of information about treatments for colic or horseshoes resides. This would be like your own *Readers' Guide to Periodical Literature,* which was originally the bright idea of legendary librarian William Frederick Poole.

Some booklovers advocate building a personal library by copying other people's work from publicly accessible libraries and creating compilations, without asking permission or paying any fees. In this way, they explain, they can pick the best from many books and create documents containing the relevant information from dozens of sources. (This is in contrast to people who copy out of books they already own, and who use the copies for personal use.)

I have an elaborate system of marks indicating a hierarchy of importance, with underlining for things that interest me most. I also make notes in margins when I want to remember my response to a point made in a book. I also turn down the corners of pages: top corner for important, bottom corner for essential.
—Suzanne M. Spencer-Wood, Ph.D., Associate, Peabody Museum, Harvard University, Cambridge, MA

Booklovers who advocate copying from other libraries are usually academics who have used this method for creating custom textbooks for their classrooms. They have done so under the banner of *fair use*, which is supposed to promote the dissemination of information to educational audiences, specifically classrooms in public and private institutions of learning. Implicit is the idea that the audience is limited in size, the person providing the information is not making money off it, and the audience will be stimulated to go out and seek more information, ideally for money.

Recently, I read a book on economics by a former professor, who claimed "fair use" for the right to print material from many copyrighted sources without permission. He will, I am sure, be highly indignant when the authors whose work he borrowed choose to complain, and will claim a high moral ground for what the authors consider as theft.

I have a problem with the attitude that copyright only counts if you get caught. One of the principles underlying copyright law is that of acknowledging the origin of goods. Reward creators, so that they can keep creating.

If you were hungry and passed by a peach tree on a hot day, you might pick a peach. If the tree looked thirsty, you would water the tree as a way of saying thanks, even if the law did not require it. If you think of authors and publishers as peach trees that need watering, you might be less likely to violate copyright. Ignoring the origins of the books can result in dead peach trees, that is, publishers who cease to exist because they are not paid.

Right now, copyright law and practice are in turmoil because of the impact of electronic media. If you own a book and want to make a copy of a chapter for your own files, I doubt you need to tie up phone lines and court systems by asking. But if you plan to make multiple copies for distribution, or you don't own the book, my advice is to err on the side of the angels and ask.

In my experience, living authors are easy to deal with. Also, it could be the beginning of a beautiful friendship with a favorite author or writer. The people who watch over the estates of the dead are usually more interested in collecting fees.

The Bookmark
By F. X. Roberts, Ph.D., Professor of Librarianship
Greeley, CO

Bookmarks in one form or another have been in existence as long as the book; but they came into their own, so to speak, about the fourth century A.D. when the codex or "leaf-book" replaced the "roll book" as the principal method of preserving and storing the written word. St. Augustine, in about A.D. 386, recorded in Book 8, Chapter 12, of his *Confessions* his use of a bookmark in a manuscript book containing St. Paul's Epistles to the Romans; and bookmarks have been found in manuscripts from as far back as the seventh century. From the introduction of the printed book (about 1450) up to the present time, readers have continued to use these handy locational devices as an aide-mémoire.

Generally speaking, three types of locational bookmarks came into use with the ascendancy of the codex book:

1. "Fore-edge" bookmarks, such as tabs, tags, or loops of parchment, leather, string, thread, paper, silk, or bead attached in various ways to the fore-edge of the pages of early books. Fore-edge bookmarks were used to mark parts of a book because pagination, tables of contents, indexes, and alphabetical arrangement were normally not available.

2. "Register" bookmarks, such as bookmarks made of lengths of parchment (vellum), string, leather, cotton, or silk sewn or knotted into the headband or spine of medieval manuscripts or early printed books, long enough to reach beyond the bottom of each page in a book.

Certain medieval register bookmarks have attached parchment or vellum discs, which rotate or revolve to reveal, through a small hole, numbers indicating columns or lines on a page.

3. "Loose" or "portable" bookmarks. These are the kinds of bookmarks we all are familiar with. Such bookmarks were very popular in the Victorian and Edwardian periods, and have made a real comeback since the end of World War II.

Some bookmarks are not really suitable for placing between the pages of books that have any value at all. The true lover and wise user of books will try to form the habit of using bookmarks made from thin, pliable, chemically stable, and acid-free materials, and not use as bookmarks items that could tear, scratch, or mar the pages or do damage to the binding of a book.   ❖

Resources to Classify, Catalog, Insure, and Appraise Your Library
Contemporary Bookmarks

What do booklovers leave in their books as bookmarks? Librarians report: money; plane tickets; valuable documents such as contracts, wills, and concert tickets; and even passports. Wily entrepreneurs sometimes leave their business cards in selected books in public libraries on purpose, as a way of advertising their services.

As Dr. Roberts and other experts have pointed out to me, most bookmarks eventually damage the books they inhabit. Even if you use the most pristine, acid-free paper as a bookmark, interleaving your book with multiple bookmarks can put pressure on the spine and cover of the book.

The booklover can buy a wide variety of clever devices for keeping track of what he is reading. These bookmarks are for the circulating books in your library, and even if a devout preservationist would never use them, they are a way of expressing affection for the booklover and the book. Some are ornamental and serve as a kind of "bibliojewelry." Others are practical devices that help booklovers organize their reading.

I rejected several bookmarks because they caused too much damage; the worst were made of heavy elastic that buckled the cover of the paperback on which I tested them. One had a spring clamp that immediately tore the page of the book.

Although I like these bookmarks as objects of art and ingenuity, I must regretfully ask you to keep them away from the valuable books in your home library. In those cases, if you need to remember a page number, write it down on a piece of paper. In pencil, of course.

The following bookmarks can be ordered through your favorite bookstore.

David Howell and Company in Bedford Hills, New York, offers a huge selection of all-metal, fine art bookmarks that slide onto the top of a page. Their **Museum Bookmark**® line incorporates historical, mythical, and artistic images in lacy metal creations, usually about 1 inch in diameter. They also do custom work, so that your favorite library, bookstore, or museum can have its preferred images reproduced. Royalties are paid to the design source, and the bookmarks start at about $6. The company is very conscientious about doing business in the United States and using methods that do not pollute.

Debry-Pexton of Bountiful, Utah, produces a series of elegant and useful bookmarks. Each combines a ribbon body attached to a pewter talisman, and the bookmark comes wrapped with a card that contains lines of poetry or quotes from books. The ones I tried ranged from about $5 to $7 retail.

The Elegant Bookworm™ is basically a bean bag for booklovers. The hefty, palm-sized "worm" is made of attractive fabric filled with what feels like sand and is capped with a handy metal ring and frilly tassel. Placed across an open page, it is designed to keep a book open while you read and/or work. A smart idea for cooks, and other readers who need both hands free while they read. It is also useful for booklovers without the ability to hold a book open on their own because of disability or disease. It retails at about $11.

The Handi-Lens Magnifier Bookmark incorporates a ruler into a 6-inch-long, 2-inch-wide plastic bookmark, for about $2. It is thin and light enough to be used around most books, and is a godsend for people who need help with small type. I was pleasantly surprised at the clarity and resolution of the viewing area. A perfect gift for the booklover who enjoys reading detailed maps.

Hold the Line™ and **Reflections and More™** are examples of a Korean-produced paper bookmark that gently marks the correct page in a magnetic grasp. It comes in many designs, and is lightweight enough to avoid damaging all but the thinnest of pages. This bookmark solves the problem of bookmarks that fall out of the book too easily.

Notewell's Book Darts are lightweight, bronze pointers, which delicately clamp the page and can be used to indicate a particular line or column. A package of twelve costs about $2.50. They can be reused or become a permanent part of the page. The Hood River, Oregon, inventor claims that they cannot hurt pages, since the metal is inert and the bookmark itself is so delicate, but I don't know that he counted on clumsy people like me. This is my favorite bookmark among the many kinds I tested, and it was the only one recommended by other booklovers by name.

Seagull™ Pewter Bookmarks are lovely creations from Pugwash, Nova Scotia. They consist of a thin piece of metal, which slides over the page, and are topped by a substantial chunk of pewter ornamentation. The one I purchased had a rendering of the familiar masks of Comedy and Tragedy. The ornamentation is perhaps too heavy for thin pages, but it is a nice gift for show at about $6.

The Silver String Bookmark™, hand-strung by artisans in Dixon, New Mexico, is constructed of silverplate tubes, silver beads, chips of Chinese turquoise, and pewter feather fetishes. It is a silver string about 11 inches long, with the silver and turquoise beads and decoration at each end. It costs about $8 retail.

Books Related to Cataloging and Classification

Introduction to Cataloging and Classification. Bohdan S. Wynar. Eighth edition by Arlene G. Taylor. *Libraries Unlimited, $37.50 paper,* *ISBN 0-87287-967-4.*

If you want to know how the experts approach the problems of cataloging and classifying collections, this is the best introductory text.

Library Research Models: *A Guide to Classification, Cataloging, and* *Computers.* Thomas Mann. *Oxford University Press, $14.95 paper,* *ISBN 0-19-509395-X.*

This book is about being a researcher and using libraries to the best advantage and how skilled researchers prefer to organize their own resources.

Organizations for Orderly Home Librarians

Please also check out the resources in Chapters IV, XI, and XIV.

American Society of Indexers. PO Box 48267, Department A, Seattle, WA 98148-0267; (206) 241-9196; fax (206) 727-6430; e-mail: asi@well.com.

So you wanna be an indexer? Need some reference materials or classes so that you can create your own indexing systems for your materials? This is the place.

Appraisers Association of America. 386 Park Avenue South, Suite 2000, New York, NY 10016; (212) 889-5404; fax (212) 889-5503.

This organization provides training, certification, and public education for appraisers and the general public. Some members focus on books and libraries.

A new organization for book appraisers is being formed, called the **National Association of Book Appraisers.** Contact Ed Postal, 1445 Glenneyre Street, Laguna Beach, CA 92651, (714) 497-4079, fax (714) 376-3111. The **Antiquarian Booksellers Association of America (ABAA)** (see Chapter VI) lists members that provide appraisal services.

Classification Society of North America. c/o Dawn Iacobucci, Department of Marketing, Kellog School of Management, Northwestern University, 2001 Sheridan Road, Evanston, IL 60208; (708) 491-2722.

They promote the scientific study of classification and clustering, including systematic methods of creating classifications from data.

❖

... those of us who have the extra Messy Gene
need to learn how to repair books
with the help of a patient teacher.
page 173.

Chapter IX — Repair

Being a Recipe Book of the Basic Care Procedures for New and Old Books, Without Resorting to Tactical Nuclear Weapons.

Why Is It So Hard to Take Care of Books?

No matter who I talk with in the book community, from paper conservators with international reputations to the directors of tiny rural libraries, the unanimous opinion is to keep your books clean, dry (humidity around 50 percent), cool (around 60 degrees), well ventilated, and away from direct light and various book-eating and -nesting critters. Prevention is the key to home library care, not restoration.

If you suspect any of your books are valuable, please contact a local expert in fine book repair before you begin your education in book conservation. The centers listed at the end of this chapter are good places to start.

Booklovers are not perfect beings, and they live in imperfect, bookhating climate zones (e.g., Houston, Texas; Portland, Oregon; Kansas City, Missouri; Key West, Florida). Here are the kinds of problems booklovers encounter while trying to repair a book, with some strategies for success.

The "How-Much-Money-Are-You-Going-to-Spend?" Problem

Repairing fine books the right way can be very expensive, but just taking care of books can cost money. Of the dozens of booklovers I surveyed, only one mentioned the cost of caring for her collection in her response, even though boasting about how much or how little money was spent on acquiring books was common.

I taped a paper cover on a book once and the tape later turned yellow and fell off. It was still a book.
—Mike Robinson, booklover, Tacoma, WA

The nemesis of the book repair expert is the family Bible. Those huge showy volumes with the fancy gilt covers and elaborate color plates were usually produced in our grandparents' era by commercial "schlock" printers, who hid poor construction and cheap materials with the book industry version of bells and whistles. Consequently, Bibles are heck to repair, and their size means that those repairs will cost a fortune. A less expensive solution than repairing the book is having a pretty archival box constructed, which will satisfy your desire for an attractive fix and slow the future deterioration of the book.

To lessen the "sticker shock" when you begin to repair your collection, assign a budget based on a percentage of your total book expenditures for a year, as recommended in Chapter IV. This budget should cover the cost of basic cleaning, repair tools, and materials, with some left over to fix your most precious books. You can start inexpensively with tools you find around the house, such as a clean, dry paintbrush, antistatic cloths, and a handheld vacuum, and then, using the catalogs listed in this book, acquire some of the tools and materials of the experts.

When deciding to have professionals repair your books, be aware the expense could be in the hundreds of dollars. Depending on what you need done, the main cost of fixing a book is the amount of time it takes the meticulous expert to fix what is wrong. This is not an assembly-line production job, and the person who does the work is likely to have advanced training and years of experience.

In our family, we pick three or four books each year to be professionally refurbished with new covers, hinges, and endsheets, and with pages cleaned and repaired. Slowly, our best books are being put into their best shape, while I do my best with the rest.

Another strategy, when dealing with cost of repair, is to weigh repairing the book against replacing it. If content is more important than historical or sentimental value, here are some questions to research:

1. *Is the book still in print?* If so, you can find out how much hardback or paperback copies cost from your local new or used bookstore.

2. *Is it available online?* Many classic books are available free from computer services that specialize in capturing and distributing out-of-print books in digital form. See Chapter XII for more information.

3. *Is it available at a number of libraries?* If it is an expensive directory that you don't use very often, you might want to rely on your local public or academic library to order and maintain it for you. A related strategy is to buy the directory and contribute it to your local library, with the understanding that they will not weed it from the collection without telling you. This way, you could get a tax deduction and still have use of the book.

4. *Is the author still around?* I have tracked down authors who had stashes of their own books to sell, after the books officially went out of print. In a related incident, although the author was long dead, I was able to help a friend get one of her favorite books back in print. I introduced her to a bookstore owner who had a connection with a publisher.

5. *Is it in the public domain (no longer protected by copyright) and available for you to make a facsimile copy for personal use?* A facsimile service will make a photocopy of the book and rebind the pages into an attractive and usable copy. Although this technique is most often used to create working copies of fragile

and rare books, it is also a reasonable strategy when a book is falling apart and cannot be rebound because of the poor quality of the paper. A book in danger of total disintegration can be saved this way.

Libraries, museums, and universities with collections of rare books will sometimes have special photocopy machines that can make copies of pages in bound books without hurting the book. The other choice is to take the book apart and photocopy the individual pages. The original is either rebound, or the pages are reverently laid to rest in a custom-designed archival box.

Opening a healthy book, plunking it face down on a photocopier, and squishing it flat by pushing down with the cover of the machine is not acceptable, unless it is an already broken book, with no value other than its content. Otherwise, you will literally crack the spine of the book, which eventually will cause signatures to loosen, hinges to rip, and pages to fall out.

If you must, must, must copy something from a book, copy one page at a time, and let the other side hang outside the copier. And, at the very, very, very least, please never squish an open book face down again. Promise?

6. *Is it available in used bookstores?* Over the last ten years, our family has been able to find all the books we looked for but two out of many searches, and the information about those two is now posted to online book search services. The used books we acquired were uniformly in excellent shape and are now swathed in Mylar. See Chapter VI for some sources for out-of-print and rare books.

Another strategy for handling the cost of repairing books is to put yourself under a book-buying moratorium for a year and use the money to repair and replace. Some booklovers would consider that cruel and unusual punishment; others would welcome the self-imposed discipline.

People who respect books will take care to gently spread open a new book a few pages at a time, so as to let the spine of the book stretch slowly and in small increments. Snapping open a new book is likely to damage the spine, prematurely aging its physical structure, and causing premature page drop. Any new volume will benefit from this ritual, and it should be taught to your children. ❖

The "Even-Experts-Don't-Agree-So-How-Should-I-Know?" Problem

During an all-day regional conference on the preservation of fine books, experts from the audience politely, but firmly, contradicted the statements of various expert speakers. At one point, four people stood and challenged each other on the use of deacidification chemicals.

I have found this kind of discord everywhere in the book community. The most extreme case might be the author of a book on book repair who contradicted himself on the same page. He gives the formula for a cleaning solution as promoted by the British Museum and, in the next paragraph, admits that the recipe destroys books.

The differing views in the book community on book care tend to be generated by two different situations. First, the people involved in the argument have different goals. The most prudent of the preservationists I encountered was a museum conservator, who was in charge of protecting items thousands of years old from decay. Her pronouncements about the necessity of ultra-low light levels in public exhibit halls, which require visitors to navigate in near-blackout conditions, make perfect sense in the context of her work. In this case, preserving the artifacts is more important than the public enjoying them in full sunshine.

A pressure-sensitive tape's threat is not acidity but resins,
which can be pH-neutral and still bleed right through paper.
Anything that involves heat and gooey resins is
outdated, stupid, senseless, destructive, and your own
damn fault these days. You may quote me.
—Douglas Stone, paper conservator, Milwaukee, WI

A book conservator will want to remove dirt from a book so that the dirt does not interact with the chemicals in the paper and cover to further damage the book; appearance is a secondary consideration. A booklover might want the book to "look nice," but scrubbing a fragile book with erasers and cloths can do more damage than the left-in dirt. Cleaning powders, which absorb dirt and oil before being brushed, vacuumed, or shaken off, are superficial cleaners only.

The second reason for the different views on book care is the varied and sometimes contradictory experiences of people in the field. I find the best people in book conservation are the ones who have lots of different kinds of experience, who are active practitioners, who keep learning, and who cheerfully admit to their failings. These honest folks can drive you crazy though, because they have learned the danger of pretending to be certain about much. Also, they can change their minds.

The person who is not an expert needs to cultivate several experts and compare their advice. After a while, it will be clear to you why they are saying what they are saying, and which advice best suits the situation.

Get at least three current references from anyone you plan to use for professional book care. Ask around and find out what their reputation is. The rare book curator might disparage the skills of the book artist, and both might look down their noses at the technical services department of your local library, where books are repaired with cheap adhesive tape and thrown back into active duty. However, you will find a consensus in your local book community about who does a good job for the average home librarian with good books to protect.

Hire only people who have current references from happy and knowledgeable customers for whom they have done the same kind of work they plan to do for your books. Let them do their basic learning on someone else's dime.

The "Oops-This-Cleaning-Solution-Will-Cause-Cows-in-Surrounding-Counties-to-Birth-Three-Headed-Calves" Problem

What about the neato chemicals you can use to clean and fumigate the covers and pages of your valuable books? I wimped out, folks. I kept asking myself if I would want these chemicals in my house, and I didn't, so how could I recommend them to you? If your book needs special treatment, pay a specialist.

The fancy chemicals do several things. They remove grease and other impossible stains from the organic materials that make up a book. They kill the various beasties that can rot your leather, discolor your paper, and shred the threads holding together your signatures. They act as a long-term preservative by changing the chemical nature of the materials in the book. They are used in some of the book arts, such as marbling. They also can buffer the book from the deteriorating effects of acid in the book and its environment.

There have been documented cases in the history of book conservation of chemicals that were unreservedly recommended in one generation and then, a few years later, were found to be hazardous to one's health.

If you want to learn the craft of fine bookmaking and repair, you will find plenty of materials, such as wheat paste, linen thread, fine paper, fine leather, and many kinds of adhesives, glues, and cloth, which are both safe to use and aesthetically pleasing. If you decide you want to use some of the cleaning fluids, deacidification chemicals, etc., please follow the instructions listed along with the package and, ideally, find an expert to help you. Pay special attention to keeping you, your family, plants, and animals from harm. (Remember that birds are very sensitive to volatile fumes.)

If you have a book or document that you are planning to have repaired, please ask the person who is doing the work about the kind of chemicals they plan to use. It might not occur to the conservator that someone might handle the book barehanded (white cotton gloves are de rigueur in rare book rooms) or that someone might lick a finger to turn a page.

One expert says that he does not use the more dangerous of the cleaning chemicals unless the document is encapsulated, which means it is completely protected by plastic sheets. That way he knows no one will be able to touch the document.

The truth is, you will probably have to live with books that keep their stains, no matter how fiercely you attack the problem with the strongest cleaning fluids.

The "I-Have-a-Life" Problem

Question: How long does it take to adequately repair a seventeenth-century leatherbound book?
Answer: How much time do you have?
Question: No, seriously.
Answer: I am *being serious.*

The repair of fine books, as noted elsewhere, is a time-consuming process. If you contact a well-respected professional to repair your precious volume, you may find that you have a six-month wait before he or she can even look at your book. Backlogs are common among the best people.

If you plan to do the work yourself, you may be surprised how long it takes you to do any of the construction work, such as making a new cover. Experienced conservators will warn you that repairing an older book is a little like repairing an older house: You never know what you are going to find when you start taking things apart.

Knowing beforehand the time it takes to fix a book can prevent the heartbreak of missing important deadlines, such as birthdays, anniversaries, and the winter holidays, because you thought fixing up your mom's favorite hymnal would take only a couple of days.

If you have decided to do the work yourself, tackle only those books that would be fun for you to do, so that you don't rush. Otherwise, stick with simple cleaning techniques and focus on preventing further damage.

If you are working with a professional, understand that it will take time. In my experience, fine craftspeople are sometimes not very good at estimating how long a job will take. Always pad their promises with extra weeks (or even months, if you want them to do many books). That way, you can be gracious when they call you to apologize for losing track of time.

If you want to repair a beloved book for a friend, but the conservator cannot meet your deadline, ask if he can make you a pretty book jacket that would fit over the book and a protective Mylar jacket. Present the book jacket in a box, and explain to the recipient that the book itself is at an expensive Swiss spa having a makeover. Don't tell the recipient that book repair can resemble The Betty Ford

Clinic for Books or a Beverly Hills plastic surgery clinic; she doesn't need to know what the book is really going through to maintain its good looks.

I also learned to keep to the simplest projects, to practice first on discarded books, to work on only one book at a time, and to master one product or technique before moving on to another. Because I was already an experienced commercial printer and used to handling machines and paper, I thought that I could pick up bookbinding and book repair in a snap. Wrong. My initial impatience caused many problems. For example, I learned the hard way to smell my hands before I handled a book. The garlic I minced for supper flavored the paper of one poetry book I was rebinding.

Now I know that the kind of repair I can do on a book is going to take a couple of hours at least. I need the time to clean off the dining room table, assemble the tools, practice a little on a discarded book, do the repair, redo the repair, fix the damage I did while doing the repair, clean up, and call my former teacher to see if she has time to take the book in and fix it the right way.

The "I'm-Not-a-Tidy-Person" Problem

For months I studied and practiced bookbinding and repair under the stern but loving tutelage of a talented bookbinder. I created books from scratch, sewed signatures, created cloth covers, scraped leather so as to form shapely corners on my covers, and repaired some well-beloved children's books. I even learned the basics of paper marbling and gold-leaf stamping.

After each session, I would pick glue balls out of my hair and remove mysterious slivers from my fingers. My cuticles hung in ratty curtains, and more than one book was speckled with blood. Whatever room I chose to work in would be a mess. My tutor, unmoved, would merely sigh and tell me that I needed to be neater.

Although I eventually became more comfortable with the tools of the trade, and even became facile with my bone folder, I never became a competent craftsperson. I suspect that some of you reading this book might have had similar experiences with craft projects, and loathe turning your home into a disaster area.

As mentioned elsewhere, those of us who have the extra Messy Gene need to learn how to repair books with the help of a patient teacher. My hands-on lessons allowed her to correct mistakes that are not mentioned in the books, whose authors assume that everyone is a well-coordinated, normally handy adult.

The two book-repair skills that eluded me were cutting the right amount of cloth for covers and using glue without making a mess. It never occurred to me to practice with scraps before I tackled a real project. I wasted a lot of good material before I caught on. ❖

The "Have-You-Ever-Tried-to-Land-a-Plane-Before-Timmy?" Problem

The book repair and book arts manuals suggested in this volume are among the best, and I recommend them all. But given that, almost all craft books have limitations.

1. *The authors are not necessarily technical writers.* Unless they have ferocious and well-trained editors, craft book writers will leave technical terms undefined, skip steps, and write vague prose, such as "Cut a piece of paper so that it fits correctly."

2. *The illustrations are usually either artful or awful, but rarely very useful for conveying information if you do not have life experience in book conservation.* Without very complete instructions, you won't be able to look at a picture and decide which aspect is the most important.

3. *You still need to do it to get it.* A book cannot tell you the heft, the textures, the smells, the physical resistance. Without experience, you cannot create and access muscle memories of the right amount of pressure to place on a glued backing. Now I know how to judge the right tension when pulling a waxed thread through a stack of folded signatures, but that did not come from a description in a book.

I mention these problems because I felt stupid when I first tried to repair the contents of my library based on what I read in books on the subject, and I have to assume that some of you have felt stupid, too. Looking back, I would have started with classes or had a private session with an expert first.

See also the resource section on videos at the end of this chapter.

The "Generational," or "I-Won't-Live-Long-Enough-to-Ever-Know-How-I-Have-Really-Screwed-This-Up," or "What-the-Heck-Do-We-Got-Here?" Problem

Several experienced experts complained to me about the fads that sweep the conservation community promising miraculous results. It is only after a few years that the promoters of the wonder cure hem and haw about the side effects that then surface.

Of course, if it is an insignificant book in your home library, and you don't think you are going to have it around for more than thirty years, you might be tempted to experiment. Go ahead, so long as you realize that you might regret your decision in ten years. A generation is two decades; the warning here is that it is often not apparent what harm a particular treatment or mistreatment is having on a type of book until years have gone by.

Also, you don't know where the book has been and what chemicals linger in the cover and pages. Even the professionals have to make some guesses when trying to repair a book, because it is not always obvious how a leather cover was treated thirty years ago, and what dyes were used in a nineteenth-century color plate.

What about newer books? Contemporary book publishers can choose acid-free and buffered papers, which will please archivists; recycled papers, which will please environmentalists; and inexpensive papers, which will please their cost-conscious customers and their accountants. As of this writing, there are no cheap, recycled, archival-quality papers for the book industry. Many fine publishers are choosing to use less expensive papers in order to keep costs down. In the long run, books printed on these cheaper papers are more difficult to keep in good shape.

One way to tell the paper being used is not archival quality is that information about the type of paper will be conspicuously absent from the copyright page. Also, the book will look and feel "rough." These books will need extra care to make them last.

You will know that the paper is of the highest quality when you see (∞), the infinity sign, which identifies papers that are meant to last several hundred years and that meet the requirements of the *American National Standard for Information Science—Permanence of Paper for Printed Materials, ANSI Z39-48 1984.*

Since you often work blind when you are fixing a book, educate yourself by working on your least valuable books, and practice the simplest of techniques first, such as erasing pencil marks and repairing pages with archival-quality tape.

The rare book conservators proceed with extreme caution and some humility; you should, too.

Tough Issues

Leather

The first few times you apply a commercial leather cleaner to an old cover, you might like the shine as the dried-out leather drinks in the oily brew. But you have no way of knowing until several years have gone by if that cleaner is slowly eating into the leather. Please do not use over-the-counter leather preparations such as silicone spray or saddle soap on your books. The tanning processes used for shoes, luggage, and furniture are different from those used for book leather.

The standard leather dressing in book conservation combines neat's-foot oil and anhydrous lanolin, a formula that is also available through several of the catalogs mentioned in this book. However, balancing the proportion of the ingredients, the amount to apply, and the frequency of application is an art form. Advice about a new book in a home library on the coast of Washington will be different from that of treating an old, previously treated leather volume residing in Nevada. Although dressing the dried-out leather cover of an unimportant book lightly with the neat's-foot oil-lanolin formula will probably not do it any lasting harm, you should check with local experts first; there are too many variables.

Test an inconspicuous corner of the cover first with less dressing than you think it needs, and then let it sit for a few days. Leather dressing can darken leather and dissolve and remove color dyes. I have also seen cases where the leather dressing, instead of saving the cover, pushed it over the edge.

Several book conservators I interviewed had horror stories about leather bindings turning into leather pudding because of the use of "recommended" chemicals. (I could never figure out if it was merely coincidence or covert, malicious behavior that all of the collections destroyed seemed to be law libraries.)

Red Rot Alert: If a leather cover has turned red and become crumbly, there is not much that can anyone can do to save it, except to have a professional impregnate and seal the entire cover with plastic. Yuck. Unless the book is a museum piece and cannot be repaired except under the most stringent guidelines, you could choose to have the cover removed, and replace it with an attractive substitute in leather or cloth.

Odors

Do you live in a humid climate? Do you store your books in a moist basement? Do you smoke cigarettes in your house? Does your male cat like to mark your library as part of his territory? Are you rescuing books scorched from a fire? Odors are the bane of the home librarian. Many book collectors and dealers won't buy a smelly book, because they have given up fixing them.

There are several techniques for deodorizing books, but not one is guaranteed, and all of them have the potential to damage the book. Also, these techniques are at best superficial. They do not affect those repositories of odor-causing chemicals deep within a book. Consequently, a book may smell fine after one of these treatments until it is exposed to humid air, thus reviving the odor.

Burying the tainted volume in absorbent material is a popular method. The most common recommendations are to use clay litter, the same kind used for cats' waste (both scented and unscented have been tried), baking powder, coffee grounds, cedar chips, Fuller's earth (traditionally used to absorb grease; available from janitorial supply houses), and carpet cleaner. This technique can sometimes work for books damaged by smoke in a fire, but you should wrap the book in something that will keep any of these products from actually touching the book (except for the baking soda), such as cheesecloth.

Misting the book with vinegar, Lysol®, isopropyl alcohol, or perfume is another choice, but all these products can stain pages and covers. Worse yet, the damage might not reveal itself for months or even years.

Chemically treated sponges and putties, designed for removing loose dirt from semiporous materials, can remove surface odors. There is controversy in the conservator community about the use of these products, even though some are sold in book-repair product catalogs, because they can deposit their chemicals onto the pages or cover.

If it is not a valuable book, and your only other choice is throwing the book away, sunbathing is a last resort. Exposure to sunshine on a dry, sunny day is ideal for treating a smelly book. The exposure to the ultraviolet rays will accelerate the demise of the book. But sunlight will kill the organisms causing the smells, and the combination of sunshine and fresh air can remove many odors.

1. Remember to support the sides of the book so that it lies open in the shape of a V; this puts less stress on the spine.

2. Protect the book from crawling bugs by placing it on a chair or table.

3. Nonwoven polymer fabric, which is used in everything from museum conservation to organic gardening, is great for protecting the surface of the book from insect poop; it can be purchased from mail-order sources listed in this book, or found in large garden supply stores. However, depending on the variety, the fabric may be too porous and may not shield the book from rain or wet bird droppings, or it may shield the sun too much. You will have to experiment.

4. Some people use a sheet of solid plastic to keep the pages clean, but this can be a disaster if the sun gets hot enough; many plastics give off fumes, become sticky, or even melt in the heat of the sun. Support the plastic shield so it does not touch the surface of the book and so that air can circulate over the pages.

5. Don't use rubber bands to hold the pages open. Clean, white shoelaces; soft, clean, undyed strips of cloth; or a commercial product like Pink Pull Fasteners, mentioned in Chapter VII, are preferred. Some people use soft beanbags; but if the sun is intense, there is always the danger of forgetting about the book and having a negative image burnt into the surface of the page.

6. Depending on the mustiness of the book, the relative humidity, the air temperature, the intensity of the sun, your patience, and probably the position of the planets, the process can take several days. Someone has to go outside and turn the pages of the book, first checking carefully for unmentionables that might have fallen on the page.

What about wet wrinkles? Paper has a memory, and once it has been moistened and allowed to dry without appropriate constant pressure, the fibers will resist treatment. Forever. Unless the wet book is treated immediately, any subsequent work to flatten the pages will have very limited success. ❖

When to Use Duct Tape

[WARNING: Do not show this section to book conservators, preservationists, archivists, rare book dealers, or book artists with weak hearts.]

Are the shades down? Is the door locked? Are you running water in the shower to mask our conversation, in case the book police are operating electronic surveillance equipment outside your home?

I am going to talk about duct tape and books.

Duct tape, and its genteel cousin, filament tape, are evil incarnate to the experts in the book industry. When I polled booklovers about the worst thing that could happen to a book, duct tape was named more often than any other physical disaster. You could murder a beloved librarian, and still a jury of your bookloving peers would forgive you, so long as you did not use duct tape to fix the cover of the book you stole.

It is not just that the chemicals in its heavy-duty adhesive dissolve the fibers of everything it touches. It is not just that purists consider it ugly. The real problem is that duct tape is "common," as in "commoners versus royalty." It is blue-collar versus college-educated professional. It is tuna fish versus caviar. Duct tape is despised based on class distinctions. (But I found it holding together heavily used reference books throughout the National Archive site I visited.)

After all, who uses duct tape on their books? An auto mechanic crisscrosses it along the spine of the last available Nash Rambler repair manual in the county. Summer camp cooks swath the cover of their favorite recipe books to protect them from the spattered grease of thirty years of french fries and donuts. Fishermen and hunters lash their fieldbooks to the outside of tackle boxes by means of a silvery umbilical cord.

Day-care workers, who know that the day *The Blue Bunny Book* falls apart is the day that chaos will rule at naptime, use it to keep Armageddon at bay. Farmers keep the planting records in a duct-taped journal for generations: Granddaughter added her own new layer of duct tape on the same day she made her first written contribution to the family crop diary.

Duct tape is an excellent way to protect the contents of hardworking books in hardworking, dirt-under-the-fingernails environments. It is cheap, accessible, and fast. It comes in colors. It can stand up to the wear and tear of lifestyles that would cause the average ivory-tower archivist to swoon.

Why not use it if it works for you! And, if you are chastised, ask your critic to suggest a product that matches it in price, utility, and ease of application. I am not suggesting that the original copy of the Declaration of Independence be repaired with duct tape, but is it a sin to use it on an old nature guide that will be discarded at the end of the season?

Filament tape, with its indestructible threads, has won favor from the U.S. Postal Service as an approved product for mailing and shipping. Yes, its adhesive will also eat into the cover of that important book. But it can make an incredibly strong hinge material for workbooks that must be opened and closed hundreds of times. (It has kept our business checkbook together for more than a decade.)

Fine book repairs are designed to be reversible; a measure of the success of the repair is the ability to take the book apart for further work at some unspecified future time. Needless to say, fine books are not intended for tough use. In that context, duct tape and filament tape are horrifying, but maybe when it comes to that furniture repair manual out in the shop, they work just fine.

When and How to Write in a Book

1. The purist says never.

2. The rare book collector permits the lightest of pencil marks on the flyleaf, but limits this to bibliographic information that is just and necessary for the identification of the book or, in the case of the rare book dealer, the all-important price. It is possible to erase such marks, but all erasers will cause the fibers in the paper to break. Also, erasers leave behind residues, which can cause staining and fiber damage in the long run. The best eraser to use is probably a name-brand vinyl eraser, such as can be found in an art supply store. But use lightly, please.

I like to write in my books, a fact which makes nearly every bibliophile I know shudder. Reading is not a spectator sport as far as I'm concerned.
—Kathleen Cain, researcher and writer, Arvada, CO

Kathleen Cain © 1996

---

3. The librarian, who must worry about inventory control, marks a book in a thousand places with red, black, green, and blue ink. She stamps the name of the library across the spine and edges of the book, on the title page, and at random intervals throughout the text. Pieces of paper and plastic are taped and glued onto the covers.

She will even emboss selected sheets with a clamping device that raises a permanent scar. Once a book is scarred in this manner, it is forever a library book, even after being sold or discarded, and is identified as such by book collectors in their descriptions.

4. If you are famous, or plan to be, then use the special famous-author indelible ink, which is available at art supply stores and is featured in several of the book supply catalogs in this book. This is an irony of fine book care. The experts complain because you are using a pen, then they complain because the ink fades.

Never dog-ear a book, or write in it other than in pencil. You are merely the custodian of this precious resource, not its owner.
—Peggy J. Noonan, science writer, Denver, CO
Peggy J. Noonan © 1996

---

5. If you do write in your book, here are three critical suggestions:

First, you should do something about your handwriting. (See Chapter XIII for a suitable workbook on penmanship.)

Second, remember to name-drop frequently. Who will know in 500 years that you did not dine with the Queen Mother?

Third, it is fun to confuse future historians by claiming friendships with famous people who are not quite contemporary. They will guess you are lying if you say that you chatted with Theodore Roosevelt about the issues raised in *The Firm*, but you can confuse them deliciously if you mention you discussed *The Bridges of Madison County* with Eva Perón. Therein lies immortality.

What Can You Do to Repair the Average Book?

You have decided which books in your home library need the expert handling. But what can you do yourself?

Cleaning

First, you can clean the book cover and individual pages gently. Dry methods, such as using a name-brand vinyl eraser, a One-Wipe cloth, or the cleaning powders listed in book-care product catalogs, will remove surface grime. Soft natural bristle brushes can remove dirt from between pages and from fore-edges. A small air blower, the kind used to clean electronic equipment, can get rid of loose dirt between the cover and spine of a hardback book.

A chemically treated, dry sponge can remove superficial dirt from the covers of less valuable books, but it can also deposit chemicals on the surface it is cleaning. There are dry cleaning sponges that do not have imbedded chemicals, but I received mixed advice about using them on more valuable books.

The rule of thumb is to remove whatever dirt comes off easily, and leave the rest. When you start bearing down on the eraser to get that last 5 percent, you are likely to damage the book.

If the dirt is greasy, your dry-cleaning efforts will simply move the grime around and drive it deeper into the fibers. This is a typical problem after a fire. Greasy grime is also the kind of dirt deposited on books by stoves and fireplaces. Consult a professional if you suspect oily deposits. You might not want to use the chemicals she uses to remove large amounts of greasy dirt from your collection.

A barely damp, soft cloth or plain, clean sponge (do not dampen a chemically treated, dry sponge) can remove dirt and water-soluble stains from covers, so long as you realize that this process may cause the cover to buckle and remove some dye. Club soda, which is buffered with minerals, is an inexpensive cleaning solution. The trouble with tap water is that either it is filled with iron and chlorine, both of which can stain paper, or it is filtered and is the equivalent of distilled water and does not have the ability to gently counter the acids in paper. Also, even if you have very alkaline tap water, you can't count on a constant chemical balance.

The dyes in old cloth covers are almost always unstable, and almost any cleaning technique will cause the colors to spot, run, fade, or rub off. A simple solution, proposed by an experienced hand bookbinder and book artist, is to use watercolor paint to touch up the cover after it has been cleaned. She claims the watercolors found in tubes at your art supply store do just as good a job as some of the more expensive dyes (which can rub off or run, no matter what the label says). But you need to practice first on "dead" books you pick off the free shelf at your local used bookstore. Also, you may not have the competence of my friend, with her thirty years as an artist and craftsperson.

When you are removing pencil marks, remember not to remove any writing that might have an "association" value. If Samuel Clemens himself made those annoying notes in the margins, leave them.

Ballpoint ink and most organic stains are impossible to remove by amateurs and many experts without physically or chemically damaging fibers in the paper or cover, or causing new discoloration. Last-resort treatments include isopropyl alcohol and hydrogen peroxide. Peroxide, which you can buy in drugstores in a 3 percent solution, needs to be diluted 3:1 to a 1 percent strength. Both products should be applied in minute quantities, watched carefully, and rinsed out completely with lots of plain water or club soda. Some surface stains, such as paint, can be carefully lifted off using the edge of a sharp, slender blade.

Page and Cover Repair

You can repair ripped pages with a recommended product such as filmoplast®. This is one of the few book-repair products that is easy to use and meets the requirements of many experts. It is a paper-adhesive tape for repairing pages, and comes in both white and a tint that mimics the color of paper that has caramelized with age. It is as easy to use as store-bought, clear adhesive tape on a roll.

Filmoplast not only repairs paper, it also protects it from further chemical damage. It is not cheap at $20 a roll about 15 feet long, but a little goes a long way and it will save you money in future repair bills.

All the book-product catalogs listed in Chapter IV carry easy-to-use adhesive tapes and patching material for pages, covers, and spines. Kapco offers the most complete and, to my mind, easiest set of products for average booklovers to use. The kits they offer will repair or reinforce your everyday books in style.

Because many repair products that are the best to use around books are also modest in price, there is no need to use cellophane- or acetate-backed adhesive tape, which is guaranteed to turn yellow and fall off, but not before leaving an ugly stain on the page.

Delicate repair tissue, sold in art stores and through catalogs, and wheat paste, which can be whipped up in your kitchen from a dry mix, are the professional's simple choices for making page repairs. If you are handier than I, there is something soul-satisfying about using the lovely paper and good-smelling paste to patch the page of a favorite book.

Miracle Glues

The ideal book glue is nontoxic, is easy to use, can be removed with water if necessary, and dries clear and flexible. Besides wheat paste, which requires some skill at mixing and applying, the preferred glue is polyvinyl acetate (PVA). This is not the white glue with the cow on the label that most of us knew as children. PVA is a different creature, and so delicate that freezing ruins it, which is why it is never shipped during winter months. It can be used to anchor an errant headband or seal stray threads from a frayed cover. Also, with a little practice, you can use a fine brush to paint a thin line of glue between two pages of a book as an anchor for a loose page.

If you order it from a catalog, make sure you are ordering the finished product and not a professional's version, which is composed of ingredients that must be measured and mixed.

Fixing a Paperback

What is needed to fix a favorite or valuable book with a sick spine, ripped cover, or ripped hinges is beyond the scope of this book. But it is not hard to give a last resort spinal job to a cheap paperback that is losing pages because the glue has dried up. These directions are probably not better than the ones I complain about; fortunately, most book-repair manuals have a version of this system, with pictures.

1. Remove the cover of the book. This might mean slicing it off with a blade or cutting it off with a knife or scissors. You might not be able to save the spine, but you can at least save the front and back cover and reattach them later.

2. Pry off the remaining dried glue on the bare spine, or have your friendly neighborhood printer trim the thinnest possible piece from the edge of the book.

3. Clamp the book between two pieces of wood the same size as the book, with the smooth and flat spine sticking out about 1/4 inch.

4. Using the edge of an industrial razor, slash the edge of the spine several times, from one edge to the other, as if you were drawing several *X*s. The result should be a coarse crosshatch pattern of shallow slices into the spine.

5. Generously paint the bare, slashed spine of the book, which is still held tight in the clamps, with polyvinyl acetate glue. Plain white glue won't work because it will dry stiff.

6. Let the glue dry completely.

7. If the complete cover with spine is intact, you can glue it back onto the spine and clamp until dry. If you only have the front and back covers, you can use a flexible piece of paper and glue the two pieces of cover back together on a piece of paper wider than the width of the spine. That space between the front and back cover is where you apply the glue; it is now the spine of the book. Remember to clamp the entire book and let the whole thing dry thoroughly, ideally overnight. Confused? That is why you need pictures, at the very least, to guide you through the process.

Deacidification

Acid chemicals lurk in the wood-based products that make up most of your books, slowly turning them brown and brittle. It is most noticeable in books manufactured from the middle of the nineteenth century to the early seventies of this century. Books printed on inexpensive paper that has not been buffered are susceptible. An acid condition is also a consequence of the aging process.

You can stop the effects, at least for a while, by neutralizing the acid with a variety of chemicals, including handy sprays and homemade concoctions listed in several book-product catalogs. However, the ready-made stuff is very expensive, the homemade stuff is hard to control, and the spray stuff is difficult to apply uniformly. Professionals can treat your books, but they cannot guarantee that the treatments are not without long-term consequences.

Reserve deacidification for the most important items in your collection that are in desperate need of immediate help, and use the services of skilled and credentialed experts to do the work.

Boxes

You can put a failing book in an archival-quality box to protect it from further damage. Chapter XIV lists several companies that sell ready-made boxes. Do not seal the book in a container that doesn't "breathe," unless it is to be placed in a freezer, and make sure the book is absolutely dry and free of vermin.

The Home Library Disaster Plan

Water and fire are the elemental dangers that could dissolve or toast your home library in a matter of minutes. Here are suggestions for a home library disaster plan, culled from the wisdom of folks who have rescued books from natural and human-generated disasters.

Preparation for the Unexpected

1. *Inventory, inventory, inventory.* Appraise, appraise, appraise. Insure, insure, insure. Then make multiple copies of your records, and store them securely.

2. *If you have truly valuable books and you insist on keeping them in your house, they should be in a fireproof safe and stored above the 100-year flood line.* If you live in the Mississippi River Basin, make that the 500-year flood line. If you think this is excessive, call a librarian in Iowa and ask her opinion.

3. *Rooms that could be flooded should be equipped with warning alarms to alert you that your collection is in danger of being submerged.* Basements and garages are the most obvious locations.

4. *Put your own library disaster kit together from household goods.* The main items include tools and supplies for sopping up water quickly and for keeping it away from the books (white paper towels, mop, buckets, old cloth towels with no transferable dyes), inert plastic crates for moving wet books, inert plastic bags for holding wet books in the freezer, an extra working flashlight with fresh batteries in a separate bag, rubber gloves, a large roll of plastic (the kind you can buy in a hardware store for insulating windows is fine), and a stash of industrial-strength chocolate to console you when you are hip-deep in water, fishing in the dark for drowning paperbacks.

Burnt and smoke-damaged books will need clean, dry boxes, so they can be stored until treated.

5. *Establish relationships with the book experts in your area who could help you, and do it before you need them.* Find out from your local librarians their disaster plans, and ask their advice in locating companies that specialize in cleaning and repairing large quantities of books. The list of conservation and preservation centers at the end of this chapter can help.

6. *Find out from your local library and book people who will take in your books if you need them frozen.* (The books, not the people.) State libraries, historical societies, universities, or museums are likely to have identified companies in your region with large cold-storage and freeze-dry facilities.

7. *If you live in a place prone to tornadoes, wildfires, mudslides, avalanches, storms, floods, or earthquakes (or, simply put, if you live in California), put aside money just in*

case. As I have mentioned elsewhere, most booklovers think nothing of spending a fortune on their books, and yet spend next to nothing on preventative care.

8. *Check with your local fire department about safety advice for your home.*

You may be slouching in ignorance toward a disaster; let an expert audit the number and kind of fire extinguishers you should have and provide you with information about alarms and fireproof material.

When Disaster Strikes

1. *If you are in the middle of a real disaster, save yourself and your loved ones first.* Relief workers tell horror stories of individuals dying because they dashed back to save beloved material objects, including books.

2. *Contact your insurance company immediately.* If you are well insured, it will be in their best interest to help you. Just remember that it might be cheaper from their point of view to replace rather than repair. With the help of your inventory records, they can assess the damage.

3. *When a disaster hits, it is very possible that you will have only a short time to determine which books you can save after the event.* Also, you may have a small budget to apply to repair. It may break your heart to have boxes of wet books in the bathroom, only to watch them decay. Remember, even in a fire, there can be water damage from the efforts of the firefighters to control the blaze. You will have to make hard choices.

4. *Ask for help.* You may be surprised that neighbors and friends are willing to dry books, store wet volumes in their deep freeze, or even help you replace cherished volumes from their own collections. After all, if you love books, probably the people closest to you do, too.

5. *Your main efforts will be to contain the damage by removing books to a place where they can dry out.* Fans and dehumidifiers are the tools of choice. You are racing against time, trying to extract as much moisture as possible before the mold gods are awakened and Götterdämmerung begins.

You will need to have a small city's worth of white paper towels to interleave or place between the wet pages as they dry, and an army of people to gently place the towels in the books, monitor the drying process, and then remove the damp towels at the right moment.

You will be crippled by high humidity, the fragility of wet pages, and the impossible task of gently flipping the pages of the open, sodden books at precisely the correct time. If you get the bright idea of doing it outside in the sun, you will risk cooking the swollen pages into the paper equivalent of tapioca pudding. Also, you will inevitably trap a large, juicy insect between the pages, where it will die a large, juicy death. Refer to my advice about sunbathing or airing your book presented earlier in this chapter.

Rescuing a large number of wet books is almost a no-win situation for a person with no money and no one to help, which is why freezing wet books as quickly as possible is so important. While most of your frozen books slumber, you can retrieve them in manageable numbers.

6. *Not much can be done for a pile of ashes, but books that are smoke-damaged need to be aired out to get rid of the odor.* Refer to the information about odors mentioned earlier in this chapter. The books also need to be checked for structural damage, and you will have to decide how much time and energy you want to spend cleaning off the soot. You may find that the heat from a fire has toasted the fibers in the pages. The result is books with the crackle and stability of breakfast cereal.

Professional companies that specialize in cleaning up after flood and fire damage use chemicals and chemical sponges in their work. Check with a book conservator before you allow them to work on your more valuable books.

One expert author tells booklovers to gently bend a corner of a page and, if the corner cracks and comes off, then the book is too damaged to resew. Another expert tells me that damaging a book to determine if it is damaged is the height of conservator hubris. Nevertheless, it is likely that some of your fire-damaged books will have to spend the rest of their lives in archival-quality book boxes or be replaced with facsimile copies.

The expert solution for protecting precious pages that have been damaged beyond repair is encapsulation, which is the process of carefully sandwiching each page between two sheets of inert, clear plastic. The plastic sheets are held together with double-sided adhesive tape, but no part of the tape touches the page. This is a very expensive process, done by hand. It is usually reserved for documents, drawings, maps, etc., but can be done for color plates and individual pages.

If the burnt book is not valuable, but you want to keep the pages intact for a while, you can try using some of the acid-free plastic lamination sheets sold by several of the companies listed in the appendices. The companies themselves have service people ready to give you advice about what products to use, and their possible drawbacks.

In the aftermath of a disaster, you must juggle cost, time, and quality; you will be choosing among *cheap, fast,* and *good,* knowing you cannot have all three. Also, no rescue process can reverse damage or stop the inevitable decay of organic matter.

Conservation, Repair, and Recovery Resources for BookLovers
Where to Find Serious Help

Some centers for protecting and rescuing books and related materials are housed in museums and libraries, others are nonprofit ventures, and others are parts of state agencies. Some are commercial services. Many people who staff these places might ask for a level of care that is not realistic or affordable for you. However, they can point to local resources and be invaluable in helping you deal with disasters. Many sponsor classes and publish self-help books and pamphlets. Here are a few, chosen to represent the broadest geographical distribution.

AMIGOS Preservation Service. 12200 Park Central Drive, Suite 500, Dallas, TX 75251; (214) 851-8000.

Conservation Center for Art and Historic Artifacts. 264 South 23rd Street, Philadelphia, PA 19103; (215) 545-0613; fax (215) 735-9313; e-mail: ccaha@shrsys.hslc.org.

Northeast Regional Conservation Center. 100 Brickstone Square, Andover, MA 01810-1428; (508) 470-1010.

Pacific Regional Conservation Center. Bishop Museum, 1525 Bernice Street, Honolulu, HI 96817; (808) 847-3511.

Rocky Mountain Conservation Center. University of Denver, 2420 South University Boulevard, Denver, CO 80208; (303) 733-2712.

SOLINET: Southern Library Network. 1438 West Peachtree Street, NW, Atlanta, GA 30309-2955; (800) 999-8558.

Upper Midwest Conservation Association. 2400 Third Avenue South, Minneapolis, MN 55404; (612) 870-3120.

The Association of Records Managers and Administrators (ARMA) distributes the Disaster Recovery Yellow Pages *by Dr. Steven Lewis. $116. ISSN: 1074-0112. It lists emergency services, supplies, publications, consultants, and other resources. A must if you have a valuable collection. Call 800-422-2762 for credit card orders, or see Chapter XIV for ARMA's mailing address.* ❖

Private Centers

These private book conservation centers are willing to work with home librarians and have exceptionally friendly and service-oriented staff.

BookLab, Inc. 1606 Headway Circle, Suite 100, Austin, TX 78754; (512) 837-0479; fax (512) 837-9794; e-mail: booklab@booklab.com.

Unlike some book conservation companies, BookLab produces a catalog that breaks down the prices for its various services. The minimum order is $250, but it is worth it to the person who is watching a precious book or two decay. BookLab, which comes highly recommended by preservationists in the region, provides limited-edition binding, custom box-making, and preservation photocopies.

Thompson Conservation Laboratory (TCL). 7549 North Fenwick, Portland, OR 97217; phone/fax (503) 735-3942; e-mail: tcl@teleport.com.

Besides specializing in the restoration of medieval and renaissance books and art on paper, TCL offers the best selection of educational videotapes I have come across (Istor Productions) and a selection of rare reprints of books on books, mostly going back to the turn of the century and earlier, all at very reasonable prices (Caber Press). There are also a 4,000-volume research library and a very friendly staff.

A Note on Videotapes

In addition to the collection of more than three dozen videotapes from Istor Productions just listed, see Chapter III for information about videos from the Guild of Book Workers and Chapter IV for a basic video from Vernon Library Supplies. Also check with local libraries, schools, museums, and bookstores for their recommended videos on book repair.

Books and Publications on Book Conservation

Many of the books listed in Chapter III on the book arts also apply to conservation and preservation issues.

Basic Bookbinding. A.W. Lewis. *Dover, $4.95 paper, ISBN 0-486-20169-4.*

This is a simple book on bookbinding, which is a great help for understanding the basic construction of the Gutenberg-era book. One school of book repair believes that you can't learn how to repair a book until you have constructed a few, and this book is less overwhelming than many I reviewed.

Bookbinding and Conservation by Hand: *A Working Guide.* Laura S. Young. *Oak Knoll Press, $24.95 paper, ISBN 1-884718-11-6.*

A fat (250+ pages) and easy-to-read text about the care of books. The bookbinding section has useful information on cleaning and repair, and the conservation section has leads to suppliers and technical resources. Uses both photos and drawings to explain materials, tools, and procedures. The large size provides more information than most of the other books mentioned in these pages.

The Care of Fine Books. Jane Greenfield. *Lyons & Burford, $19.95 paper, ISBN 1-55821-003-2.*

If you are looking for one book to help you take better physical care of your library, make it this one. Greenfield covers the basics of care and repair, but she does not expect that you memorize long lists of chemicals or master alchemical book-crafts. I like the simple drawings and her friendly tone. It is noteworthy that almost all the mail-order companies carry her book, but not one of the major bookstores in Denver had the book in stock. I want the best books about book care to be prominently displayed at all bookstores. So there.

The Colorado Preservation Alliance. CPA Education and Public Relations Committee, c/o Jefferson County Public Library, 10200 West 20th Avenue, Lakewood, CO 80215.

These folks produce a comprehensive list of handouts that contain practical advice for home librarians on book care; much of it was written to serve the needs of small public libraries with limited budgets and untrained staff. Because the materials were written by circulating librarians who are also trained in the conservation arts, the information is correct without sounding like brain surgery. Send an SASE and request an order form. Most of the handouts are modestly priced single sheets on topics like *Simple Paper Repair, Drying Books,* and *Shelving Books & Book Trucks.*

Flood Recovery Booklet. Iowa Cooperative Preservation Consortium, State Historical Society of Iowa, 402 Iowa Avenue, Iowa City, IA 52240; $10.

When the floods hit the Midwest several years ago, millions of books were damaged or destroyed. This booklet contains priceless wisdom on how to deal with the aftermath of a flood, from protecting you and your family from disease, to rescuing and repairing damaged art. The success of the booklet is measured by the fact that the state printer is having trouble keeping it in stock. A new commercial edition was in the works as this book went to print. This is a must-buy for any home librarian who might have to rescue his or her collection from water damage.

How to Clothbound a Paperback Book: *A Step-by-Step Guide for Beginners.*
Francis J. Kafka. *Dover, $2.95 paper, ISBN 0-486-23837-7.*
One of the hardest kinds of books to care for are older clothbound books.
Learning how to work with cloth from scratch can give you the confidence and
skill to tackle the more challenging job of creating new cloth covers for beloved
books that are falling apart, but are not valuable enough to hand over to a skilled
(and well-paid) conservator.

The Practical Guide to Book Repair and Conservation. Arthur W. Johnson.
Thames and Hudson, $14.95 paper, ISBN 0-500-27518-1.
Here is where you will find expert English advice, including explanations of
various chemicals, formulas for cleaning and treating books, recipes for most
types of repairs, and those juicy pictures of book bugs everyone loves. Includes
contacts with European suppliers. This book is useful for those who want to
learn and practice advanced book conservation methods and is a good accompa-
niment to the Talas catalog listed in the next section. You might have to search
for this book in a library or used bookstore.

Books on the Health Hazards of Book Conservation

Here are two books that will help you decide if that chemical recommended
by your friendly expert is worth the risk of bringing it into your home and expos-
ing yourself, family, friends, pets, and plants to its effects.

Health Hazards Manual for Artists. Fourth Edition. Michael McCann, Ph.D.,
C.I.H. *Lyons & Burford, $11.95 paper, ISBN 1-55821-306-6.*
This contains the health hazards of chemicals used in the creation and pres-
ervation of all kinds of arts and crafts. It is considered by many to be the Bible of
the field. The author is director of the Center for Safety in the Arts, 5 Beekman
Street, New York, NY 10038, (212) 227-6220.

The Home Health Guide to Poisons and Antidotes. Carol Turkington.
Foreword by Shirley K. Osterhout, M.D. *Facts on File, $12.95 paper,
ISBN 0-8160-3316-1.*
A very complete and easy-to-use guide to the effects of all kinds of products,
including pesticides, cleaning fluids, plants, food supplements, and adhesives.
Includes emergency care information and suggestions on how to poison-proof
your home. Middle-aged booklovers will recognize the names of some dangerous
products, such as benzene and carbon tetrachloride, which once were widely
available for home use.

The Grandperson of Repair Catalogs

Talas. 568 Broadway, New York, NY 10012-9989; (212) 219-0770; fax (212) 219-0735.

Talas is the oldest of the supply companies devoted to book and paper conservation, and it is where the serious book artist and archivist finds serious supplies. The catalog is one of the most complete sources of incomprehensible chemicals and tools. Definitely not for the amateur.

Five BookLovers' Repair Gifts to Buy From Mail-Order Catalogs

Absorene Paper and Book Cleaner. A weird malleable chunk of stuff used to remove surface dirt, soot, and stains from covers. It was originally sold as a wallpaper cleaner and should not be used on your rare and valuable books. About $3 buys an 11-ounce lump in a resealable pail.

Printed Date Due Book Pockets. These are just like the ones in your old school library books, with a little pocket to hold a book card and a grid marked "Date Due." Nice retro touch for those old James Bond paperbacks. The cheapest styles start at about $10 for a box of 500. You can have your name imprinted for about an additional $6 for a box of 500 with a minimum order of 1,000. There is a one-time charge of $15.00.

Blue Wool Cards. These cards can help you measure how light is causing your books to fade and deteriorate. Each card costs $5. Just put the cards on the shelves of your library among your books and watch the color fade.

Paper and Board pH Testing Pen. For less than $3.50, you can test paper for acid levels. Use on a snipped corner from a blank sheet. If the pen turns the paper purple, the paper has a pH of more than 6.8 and will not need immediate treatment. Although not suitable for rare and important books and documents, it can help you decide if that expensive paper is really acid-free, and if your favorite books are really deteriorating.

Tyvek Tape. A fifty-yard roll can take care of your worst book cover repair needs. Tyvek is one of the book community's favorite materials, because of its strength and its inert composition. This is what you should be using instead of duct tape, but your local hardware store probably doesn't carry it. About $6 buys a 1-inch-wide roll that is backed with pressure-sensitive acrylic adhesive.

❖

... approach the issue of collection management
scientifically and objectively ...
page 196.

Chapter X — Weeding

Being an Exposé of Phobias About Weeding; Loans and Theft (Which Are Two Ways to Weed Your Collection); Disposing of Your Collection After Your Death; and the Truths Most BookLovers Don't Want to Hear About Landfills and Composting.

Weeding Your Book Garden

Weeding, the process of removing books from a library, could be the most hotly disputed issue among booklovers. It also generated the most written comments from the people who answered my requests for advice. Here are some of the pros and cons I heard in weeding debates.

Why Weed?

1. To make room for new acquisitions. You can't afford to build bookshelves forever, and there are too many new good books published every year.

2. To ensure your library does not grow larger than your ability to use it well and care for it. Too many books can deteriorate before you notice problems, and even if you do, you will not have the funds or time to save them.

> *We'll just keep that for the good it has been.*
> —Lewis J. Poteet, folklorist
> Reprinted with permission of the publisher.
> Lewis J. Poteet © 1992

3. To improve the value of the collection, by replacing paperbacks with hardbacks, worn copies with fresh copies, and later editions with first editions in fine condition, preferably autographed. Serious collectors promote weeding as a way of improving the financial and aesthetic value of a collection.

4. To replace out-of-date books, such as reference books and technical journals, with more current information.

5. To dispose of the books the way you want while you are still alive, so you can share the recipients' pleasure, and ensure the books are distributed the way you want.

6. To raise money to buy more books.

7. To help build other people's collections.

8. To share some of the enormous wealth of your society with those for whom any book is a rare treasure.

Why Not Weed?

1. All knowledge is precious, and every book contains a valuable and unique perspective on the world, no matter who wrote it. Important books never grow unimportant, no matter how old, and many books contain information that is not found anywhere else.

2. You can't trust the recipient to care for the book the way you do, or love it the way you do.

3. During previous decades, our culture lost thousands of irreplaceable volumes of historical and literary importance, all because they had little value at the time, and so were disposed of by smug critics who labeled them fit only for the dustbin or charity pile. No one is smart enough to know what will be deemed important in 20 years or 200.

4. It is an ecological tragedy to weed books, because eventually they will end up in landfills.

5. Sometime, someone will ask for the book, and you won't have it.

After weighing all the advice, the anecdotes, the few journal articles I tracked down, and the very few books on the subject, I am currently a confirmed weeding advocate for almost all home libraries.

The exception is the true archive, managed by those of you who are meticulously building a comprehensive collection and, because of your expertise and the nature of the collection, have no need to "trade up" old acquisitions for better. You are trained book conservators, with enough time and money to ensure the health and value of your charges. Many of you, as I understand, married into great wealth, and devote yourself to your personal library the way others devote themselves to their sailing or horses. Good for you.

For the rest of us, weeding is a necessity.

I weed and still maintain a home library of significant books, because more and more of the classic books of the culture are being made available in the immortal archives of the World Wide Web, with enough fail-safes and duplications, spread over dozens of locations and thousands of miles, to satisfy the most paranoid of culture archivists. I can use the magic of electronic media to scan and store out-of-print books for future use, without having to keep a Gutenberg-era copy on hand (unless the electricity fails forever).

I weed and still am responsible to future generations, because I build reciprocal relationships with other booklovers, inside and outside of formal institutions, so that the books I discard most often are adopted, not put to sleep.

Now, twice a year, I weed my home library to coincide with the book sales of my favorite charities. The first time I carried fourteen boxes from the house; this last time, I had only two boxes to donate. Some juicy items are reserved for two used and rare bookstores near my home, whose shelves have proven to contain an unending harvest of used books for my home library. To be blunt, the owners share my taste in books.

Some of my books have ended up in prisons, inner-city day-care centers, and the libraries of churches, schools, and nonprofit organizations. I helped to build the resource library for the local YWCA, and now I am shipping books to Siberia on behalf of a psychologist who wants to keep up with the latest information on popular therapy in the United States.

We purge when the books start creeping across the room,
and up and down the stairs, and chase the cats.
—Tom P. Abeles, resident futurist, Minneapolis, MN

Unofficially, I weed continually, usually because a client or friend absolutely must have a book. To this end, I buy multiple copies of my favorites to give away. To save money, I hunt used and remaindered copies of the dozen or so books I think everyone on the planet should own. (It might seem that I am defeating the weeding process by acquiring books to give away, but those books don't last on my shelves very long. That part of my library is more like my permanent gift store.)

As a booklover, I find I am very interested in which books are important to the people I know and love. I know the out-of-print quilting book my best friend from high school is hunting, and I am pretty sure that, at this moment, a stack of history books and naval fiction sits by my father-in-law's side of the bed. Yes, I do check out people's bookcases within minutes of arriving at their house for dinner. A quick scan usually tells me if there is something I have on my shelves that belongs on their shelves.

In this way, weeding is a function of my relationships within my community. Pulling a favorite book off my shelf and giving it a new home with an equally enthusiastic fellow booklover makes up for the temporary hole in my shelf.

Despite acquiring my own copy of almost every book mentioned in this book, plus about fifty more that I needed for general research and the usual twenty to thirty new books that seem to appear like magic on my shelves each month, I have about 10 percent fewer books than when I started this project in 1994. Also, the net number of books on my shelves has remained constant for the last year. And, for the first time in my life, I have an empty shelf, way up high, and no pressing (sick) need to see it filled.

Weeding Theories

If you approach the issue of collection management scientifically and objectively, you can set yourself some simple weeding goals based on percentages, ratios, and numbers.

A percentage goal, used by many circulating libraries, hovers between 1 and 3 percent per year; the larger the library, the smaller the percentage. This might seem arbitrary, but if you acquire new books on a regular basis, you can't expect that you will be able to cram them into your home forever, can you? Even archives and special collections weed occasionally, for reasons of financial need, shifts in academic interest, and space limitations.

A weeding ratio means that for every book you want to bring into your home, you must get rid of one or more first. Then, when you have control of the situation, you stick to a one-to-one ratio, so that you are moving the same number of volumes in and out. Weed before you go to the bookstore, not after.

The numbers game might help those of you for whom weeding is anathema. At the beginning of the audit, set yourself an easy weeding goal, like removing two books, or ten, or even fifteen.

When I first weeded my collection, I started with those books for which I had a specific new home in mind. It was as if I were shopping for gifts at an exclusive used bookstore whose owner had stocked all of my favorites.

There are several formal models used by managers in circulating libraries to cleanse their shelves. One of the most popular is the MUSTY model.

1. *Misleading, inaccurate, out of date.* I use this criterion to discard science, geography, and health books as the authors' theories become discredited.

2. *Ugly.* In a home library, this means worn out physically, but within certain limits. I have some bathroom books that are water-stained atrocities, sacrificed at the altar of my desire to read while submerged in a bubble bath. These books I do not replace, because I do not want other books to share their fate. Nice copies of many of these books reside on shelves where they are kept clean and dry. I have weeded out many old books that were too expensive for me to repair, as compared to replacing them with newer versions.

3. *Superseded.* I was a fan for years of *The True Believer* by Eric Hoffer. But when Doris Lessing's *Prisons We Choose to Live Inside* came along, I lost my heart to what I believe is a better book. I have one lonely copy of Hoffer's book left, while I buy a copy of Lessing's book whenever my budget allows. This criterion works only if you are willing to keep learning.

4. *Trivial.* Most of the books I have found on my shelves under this category were gifts: popular novels from people who do not know my tastes, self-help books from proselytes who wanted me in their camp, and the special category of

"I knew you love books, so I bought you one." This approach works well with chocolate lovers, as in "I knew you love chocolate, and so I bought you some." I have never yet been given the wrong kind of chocolate. I *have* been given books that needed to find a home with someone besides me.

I also have found that my impulsive buying habits have caused me to buy books, particularly during vacations, that did not survive scrutiny in the cold light of my living room.

On the other hand, one reason home libraries are superior to large institutional libraries is that the home librarian is freer to collect and cherish what might be termed "minor works." Home libraries are often repositories for the small treasures of bookdom. When you weed, save a corner of your collection for orphans: obscure topics, small presses, weird theories, strange publishers. These are books that the big libraries won't or can't find room for, unless they are blessed with scholars who care about certain small corners of the world.

5. *Your collection: This book is no longer appropriate for your current passions.* I used to collect nineteenth-century books on veterinary science and cookbooks published by small-town women's organizations. When I hurt my back, I sought out books about back care. Some of those collections have been traded away, and others lie fallow. The world changed, my focus changed.

Here is another weeding model, specifically for home librarians.

1. Have you read it recently? In my library, I have looked at every book at least once in the last five years. What is your cutoff point? Do you have one?

2. Is there someone in your life who would enjoy it more than you, given their current circumstances?

3. Do you have a better book on the same subject with the same information on your shelves?

4. Is the book in such rotten condition that it threatens the health of other books nearby?

5. Has this book (or box of books) floated unopened through the last three moves?

6. Did the book make a positive contribution to your life?

7. Is the book readily available in another form?

8. Is it a book that you think you ought to read someday, as a duty to your third-grade teacher who said that all civilized people should read this book?

9. Do you have it on your shelves to impress people?

10. Do you have too many books and feel forced to make some hard decisions?

11. Is your family threatening you with eviction, divorce, or commitment to a mental institution?

The Weeding

To prepare for the physical act of weeding, follow the advice given in Chapter IV, regarding the library audit, and in Chapter VII, regarding moving and mailing. The main thing to remember is to have a simple method to inspect and clean the books as they go into clean boxes or sturdy bags (depending on how far they need to travel to their next destination).

It is considered a point of civilized behavior not to give away books infested with book bugs, unless the books are very rare and valuable, you have no choice because of time and money, and you warn the recipients. Please clean your discards, and, at the very least, have them thoroughly examined for hitchhikers.

If your books are valuable or you are a serious collector, create an inventory of the books you are pulling. If you have a good cataloging system in place, you can indicate who is receiving the book, and keep the bibliographic information for future reference.

Here are some basic strategies for disposing of books.

Sell Your Books

See Chapter VI for more information about the collectibles market for books. You will probably not get very much your books unless they are in perfect condition, are modern first editions of the kind collectors like, and/or are books of an antiquarian nature. Book dealers either offer a flat rate for hardbacks and paperbacks or figure a percentage of the cover price. You can also try to seek out collectors who might give you a better price than a book dealer.

Garage Sales

1. Sort and price the books based on condition and original price. Resist putting stickers on the books; this will lower the value in the eyes of serious collectors. Instead, post titles and prices, or at least general price information.

2. Take the time to display the better books upright, rather than stuffing everything into old boxes. It might be worth the effort to bring some bookcases outside, even if the bookcases themselves are not for sale. Your best books should be swathed in Mylar and displayed face out on a tabletop, either upright or flat and closed, with the covers slanted toward the customer.

3. Clean the worst of the dust off the top and cover of the book, but don't do a major cleaning job; it is not worth it.

4. Advertise that you are selling books; do mention if they are collectibles.

5. Some professional book dealers might show up early and offer to take your entire collection off your hands for a fistful of dollars. Their offers will be based

on how much profit they think they can make, selling the books to the same people you hope to reach. There is nothing wrong with this; they are in business to make a profit, and they can save you time and energy.

The rudest dealers show up at dawn. They will flash rolls of bills and, with rueful and disparaging smiles, suggest that you won't do any better. It can be tempting, but it can mean losing at least 50 percent of what you could make if you sold the books to individuals. My technique is to agree to sell them the whole shebang with no discount. (Be prepared for scathing insults. Keep smiling.)

Have love affairs frequently. Weeding usually comes at the end of these affairs. If you reside in a house or apartment owned or rented by your partner, you'll probably have to get out relatively quickly when the end comes. Grabbing the books most important to you becomes intuitive, and intuition in such situations proves more sure than selection under serene conditions.
—Karl Young, poet and publisher, Kenosha, WI

Or, tell them that if they come back after a particular time, you are willing to chat. Even if you have books left over, you will come out ahead. Part of the fun of a garage sale is meeting your neighbors and seeing items find new homes. Selling the books before the sale starts defeats that purpose.

6. Put a sign on your door the night before explaining that you will not make any sales until the official, advertised opening, and that you will not appreciate early morning visitors. This will dissuade all but the most aggressive buyers.

7. Pricing? If you have very valuable books, based on what you know the local rare book dealers are getting for the same items in the same condition, stick to your best price. The individual collector will be more interested in acquiring the book than in finding a bargain.

8. If there are used bookstores in your immediate neighborhood, set your prices slightly under their schedule, particularly if you are trying to unload lots of genre fiction, such as westerns, romance, science fiction, and horror.

9. Try to have a bargain bin for booklovers with small budgets.

10. Unless it is a true collectible, I would encourage you to sell your children's books as inexpensively as possible. In fact, why not be generous and enjoy the pleasure of giving them away? In our neighborhood, there are always families struggling to make ends meet, and books can feel like a luxury. While Mom and Dad shop for used clothes and dishes, let the kids go through the free book bin and keep a book that catches their eye.

11. Garage sales are usually busiest on the first morning of the first day. To generate more sales, post signs offering discounts on books after 3 p.m. Some people offer their discounts on the second day; they prefer having the books sold rather than carting things back into the house.

Open a Used Bookstore

Many used booksellers started their businesses out of their homes by creating a catalog of their better "weeds" and sending it around to prospective buyers. Of course, this doesn't move those books out of your house immediately, but it could lead to a second career and, most important, provide you with a terrific excuse to acquire even more books than you have now! Cool, huh?

Charitable Donations

There are several nonprofits that support the donation of books to needy charities. These charitable clearinghouses prefer to deal directly with publishers; two exceptions can be found at the end of this chapter.

Because of the latest Internal Revenue Service regulations, you will need to keep a record of the books you donate to tax-exempt organizations, with a list containing the value of each item, if you expect to withstand scrutiny during an audit. Many organizations that receive items will provide you with a suggested range of values and a complete receipt. If you have valuable books you plan to donate, please check with a tax advisor.

The main categories of charitable giving are:

1. *Charities, libraries, and institutions that will take your books and sell them at their book fairs to make money.* The growing hordes of insatiable booklovers, looking for bargains and treasures, can keep some cities busy with book sales every weekend.

2. *Charities, etc., that will keep the books and add them to their collections.* In these cases, you should get to know the charities, etc., and see what they need. Some collect books for the personal development and entertainment of employees and clients. Others build special collections around subjects related to their mission.

Many of the books you might discard from your collection will not be suitable for a public, school, or academic library. An example is fiction bestsellers. A public library might have a waiting list of 100 or more people wanting to read the book, but two years later, nobody cares. So, unless you give that steamy bestseller to your library within a few weeks after you purchased it, the book will not end up in their collection.

3. *International charities.* The good news about the overseas market for used books, particularly in English, is that there is a urgent need for donations, and whatever you have to offer, even ancient medical and physics texts, are very welcome. Since English is the international language of commerce, teachers in small villages are desperate to help their students learn it. Consequently, they will take any book, no matter how outdated, so that they can build libraries to teach English.

The bad news is that it costs a fortune to ship books overseas. The best way is to take advantage of the "M-Bag." It is available from post offices in every nation, and is designed to help lower the cost of sending books overseas. You pack your books tightly in one or two medium-sized boxes and mark them "Gift Books." Place them in the M-Bag with the special address card supplied by the post office. You can send 11 to 66 pounds of books that way for about 79 cents per pound. Some people remove jackets from hardcover books to lighten the load.

Churches and international relief organizations are good sources of leads for people who need books, though it is doubtful they will have the budget to send them themselves. Perhaps you could save something out of your own book-buying budget for people whose home library shelves are empty, and who can love books and knowledge only from a great distance. See the entry at the end of this chapter for the international nonprofit, Tranet, that can help put you in touch directly with people who would love your books.

Books for the blind can be sent to any country free by surface mail in up to 15-pound packages. Contact your post office for more information.

Book Exchanges

You can trade the books at used bookstores, and use the credit to buy more books. Most bookstores will offer better terms for exchange credit than for cash.

You can also run your own exchange. Invite other booklovers over for an afternoon of books and good food. (I served cake and sherry at my last event.) Participants bring their weeded books, which are donated to the exchange, and then have the privilege to take as many books as they like. This works best among friends who are devotees of genre fiction. A variation on this model is to have families come together for children's book swaps. Part of the fun is mulling over books with a bunch of fellow addicts. Any leftover books can be donated to a worthy cause.

College Textbooks

If you are weeding your library with the notion that you can sell your old textbooks for big bucks to the local bookseller, realize that nothing loses value in the book world faster than a textbook, except for a textbook in which you have highlighted every other word in Day-Glo™ yellow.

Textbooks become out-of-date very quickly. Also, some people think that the price of many new textbooks is highly inflated, because the professors can demand that students purchase a particular book for a class and there is no competition between editions to keep costs down. Consequently, it is very difficult to find someone who will want to pay what you paid for the book and who does not *have* to buy that particular volume within a particular length of time.

College bookstores have very stringent rules about returns so they will not be flooded with books they then have to dump. Screaming at some work-study student because your $55 textbook on the psychology of zinnias is no longer being used in the business department will not change the situation. Used bookstores that set up shop near campuses are blessed by a flow of educated buyers, but cursed by students and faculty trying to unload textbooks.

Your best bet is to try to get a tax deduction by donating the books to a nonprofit program, such as those supporting literacy programs that serve populations with few resources. New tax rules will require a detailed inventory. If the books are very recent purchases, you can try to sell them directly to students before the semester starts. If you want to keep the resale value as high as possible, lay off the underlining and note-taking in the margins.

I have seen several attempts on the World Wide Web to promote the exchange and sale of books between students of different colleges, but volume is very low at this time.

The End of the Line

Booklovers don't want to hear what eventually happens to most books, in the same way that pet lovers don't want to know what happens to many cats and dogs dropped off at the typical animal shelter.

Most recycling plants will not take books because books are poison. The witches' brew of chemicals used in the printing and binding of the product makes reclaiming the fibers very expensive. Adhesives are most often mentioned as the main culprits. "We don't know how to deal with the glue" is the litany of recyclers. The one recycling company I found in our community that would take books would not pay for them. You must deliver to them, at your own expense, a pile of books. The covers will be pulled off and the insides will be shredded and shipped off to a pulp mill. See nationally known recycling expert Jim McNelly's report on the art of composting books later in this chapter.

So how do books travel to their final resting place? Librarians have been known to wrap and seal books in small packing cases, and then spirit the innocent-looking packages away to dumpsters in the dead of night. Some rip and shred the books in-house and transport the shredded product. Larger institutions have unmarked trucks back up to the loading dock.

Book publishers also visit the dump. The saddest recycling story we heard was from a well-known author and illustrator, who found himself one day strolling by a city landfill in northern California. Innately curious, as all good researchers are, he decided to explore the less deadly-looking of the piles. While he was standing in the midst of the rubble, a dump truck backed up and proceeded to unload hundreds of books at the feet of the author. His own books, to be exact, dumped by his latest publisher, whose marketing efforts on his behalf had fallen far short of the mark.

The sacredness of the book in some people's minds demands that the printed word deserves an eternal resting place, much the way devout Jews treat any document that contains the sacred names of the Almighty. But where the religious community prepares special resting places for their holy documents, the typical community expects perpetual care for book collections without raising the money to pay for it.

Here is the truth: Not every book will find new life. If you took seriously the theory that most books eventually end up in landfills, would it change your acquisition habits? Would you bring home books that you plan to keep forever?

More than one booklover proposed a radical solution for the problem of too many books: Only buy and read books with a shelf life of 500 years.

Carol Moran owns the Living Tree Paper Company, which has produced the first commercial hemp-content, tree-free paper in the United States. Her paper consists of hemp, esparto grass, argo residues, and post-consumer recycled fiber. For information and a brochure, call (800) 309-2974. For a copy of *Talking Leaves*, her magazine on ecology and activism that is printed on this new paper, send $5 to the Deep Ecology Education Project, 1430 Willamette Street, Suite 367, Eugene, Oregon 97401.

Dunn and Company in Clinton, Massachusetts, works with publishers to rescue commercial quantities of books that would otherwise be destroyed. These are books with misprinted covers and pages, and books that need to go from being hardcover books to paperbacks. David Dunn runs what he calls a Book Trauma Center, which can take off covers, insert new pages, and rebind the books, thus rescuing them from the dump.

And what does the company do with the leftover covers? Dunn's three daughters have started a company called Legacy Publishing Group, which takes the discarded bookboards and uses them to create gift items with folk and antique art themes. Legacy's products, which include coasters, magnets, ornaments, and address books, are sold in gift stores throughout the country.

Composting Books
By Jim McNelly, President,
NaturTech Composting Systems, Inc., St. Cloud, MN

Books are not easily recycled in programs to recover fiber. Recovering books as fuel is practiced at some solid waste facilities. Another less practiced recovery option is to return the books back to soil and humus products. All organic materials eventually "decompose," and books, which are made largely from paper and cloth fiber, are no exception.

Rapid and controlled decomposition, or composting, is widely practiced as a means to convert organic materials, such as yard trimmings, wastewater biosolids, manures, and other organics, into compost. Composting has also successfully decomposed a variety of paper products, including newsprint, corrugated containers, mixed paper, and phone books. But a review of available literature and the library at the Composting Council in Alexandria, Virginia, reveals no studies on composting significant quantities of discarded books.

There are several "mixed waste" composting facilities operating in the United States and Europe that include books in the process stream. At mixed waste sites, unsorted refuse is shredded or tumbled to reduce particle size sufficient for composting. Books are factored in the overall paper stream fraction and decompose without any known adverse effects to either the composting process or the compost product. The cost of mixed waste composting ranges from $45 per ton up to $90 per ton, with limited value for the finished compost.

New generations of "source separated" waste composting facilities require the waste generator to separate their organics from inert materials, such as metals, glass, plastics, and grit. The organic fraction of the total solid waste stream is more than 70 percent, and a full 40 percent, including

Prior to 1970, some North American printers used lead printing plates. Foreign books and older printings can have lead concentrations as high as 2,000 parts per million (PPM), leading to toxicity problems when paper is composted. Background lead levels in the soil are around 50 PPM, and 250 PPM is considered to be the maximum level tolerated in compost that is intended to be used in vegetable crops.

Diluting books with other paper products, using book-based compost in non-food chain applications, or avoiding adding suspect printings to the composting process can reduce the problems associated with lead in the soil.

paper, food scraps, and yard trimmings, is considered to be separable at the source. The resulting compost from source-separated sites is of higher quality, and the cost of "clean" composting is lower, ranging from $15 to $60 per ton.

Books pose unique problems compared to other paper products and are similar to telephone books, which are also difficult to recycle. Books are too large to compost and must be shredded or pulped before composting. They are also low in moisture, less than 20 percent, and must be amended up to 50 percent for proper decomposition. All paper products are high in carbon and need to be blended with a nitrogen source to stimulate microbial activity. While cloth and linen in books should decompose fine, glues and plastic fibers may cause a concern. Generally speaking, if the material is not a biohazard and is not a perceptual problem, glues and plastic fibers should not be a problem in either liability or marketing.   ❖

Who Gets Your Library When You Pass On?

If you are the kind of person who "never" gives away, sells, or throws out a book, you are passing the task on to the next generation. And unless they have inherited your inclination for impassioned and indiscriminate book storage, and have the space and income to indulge in same, your family will give away, sell, or throw away your books en masse.

If you are putting together your will and you have books, talk to friends and family today. You may be surprised at who wants what. Those fancy leather-bound editions may mean nothing to your children, who covet instead the worn-out children's books of their youth. Consider breaking up the collection before you die, so that you can share their enjoyment now.

If you don't have books to bequeath to specific people, and you have valuable books, publish your own catalog and sell the books before you go. Another strategy is to hold an auction, which is considered by many the best way to get the highest prices for collectibles. The emotional tension helps loosen purse strings and can send prices skyrocketing.

Appoint someone to formally oversee the disposal of your library. Build a relationship with a respected book dealer, which means you have done business with that person over several years. Make her a partner in helping you decide what to do with your collection, and reward her well for her help.

This person should be someone knowledgeable about books in general and your collection in particular; a librarian is another possibility. Ideally, you should meet with the person you have designated as the executor of your estate and the book person, to go over details such as alternative plans—in case your fantasy auction fails, for example—and how the book person will be compensated for his or her time.

Do some research. You may find that an academic library in another state is more than happy to take your books on mushroom diseases and will give them a stable home for many years. But realize that there is no way that any institution, no matter how well intentioned and/or how well endowed, can predict accurately what might happen to your collection in the future. Libraries can lose their funding; endowments can be siphoned, legally or not, for other purposes; and the entire focus of a special collection can change.

Another problem, from the library's point of view, is that the donation rarely comes with enough funding to guarantee that the books will be examined, repaired, cataloged, displayed, and maintained. The catch-22 is that people who donate their collections often do so to realize tax benefits; neither they nor their estates have the cash to support their gift.

One academic librarian told me that the generous gift of 10,000 volumes she received from a wealthy benefactor would cost her library anywhere from $30,000 to $100,000 to deal with adequately.

"A gift this size would keep two people busy for a year," she explained. I met with her just before she sent off a proposal to the giver, hoping he would help the library by supporting his gift with money for extra staff, let alone shelving. She was not hopeful, even though the benefactor is very wealthy.

Still another problem, which is a sensitive issue for both givers and recipients, is the gap that can exist between the giver's view and the recipient's view of the gift. You might think your collection is important, but that is not always the case.

I once tried to help an elderly man find a home for a collection of popular nonfiction he had collected over three decades. His collection turned out to be little better than mulch. Not only were the books musty and dirty, but the contents of most had long since been superseded by better volumes. Also, the contents were redundant, with information duplicated dozens of times.

You may decide that you will let the worst happen. Book dealers will scour the collection at open sales for the best volumes, which they will buy from your unsuspecting children for pennies and sell for a fortune. Some priceless books will be lost or stored away forever. But you will be in Library Heaven, reading through eternity.

Here are comments from some booklovers about the challenges of providing new homes for a collection of books.

Karl Young, poet and publisher, Kenosha, WI

I have made tentative plans twice, at times when death seemed imminent. My main consideration in this is where would the different parts of my collection be of most *use*. I have not drawn up a will because I am carefully watching a number of institutions to see what they would be most likely to do with the books. I have a large collection of facsimiles of pre-Columbian and colonial Mexican and Central American manuscripts and inscriptions. Should they go to a library where they will be available to scholars and advanced students—or would they be of more use in a school or library with a large number of Chicano or Guatemaltec students who might get a better sense of their heritage and hence build their sense of self-esteem?

The thing I watch for is collections in active use, not collections that exist for the sake of a catalog. I'd like to see more bibliophiles take similar attitudes and make them known to potential recipients. This could do a great deal to change the attitudes of librarians and curators. I have made it clear to the alumni association and the library of one of the universities I attended that their anal-retentive lending policies have lost them books they would like to have. I would like to see other bibliophiles do the same.

Donation of books only to those who will make good use of them would be the best way to honor the writers, artists, and publishers whose efforts went into these books, a way of thanking them for what they have given to others.

Of course, those remarks apply only to rare books, the kind that survive love affairs, midnight moving parties, more orderly changes of residence, and many of the other adventures and traumas that make a life. The plainer books make up the major part of my library or the libraries of many people who read this.

Al Lehmann, booklover, Terrace, British Columbia, Canada

My father is growing very old now, both in body and in attitude. As he is probably the primary influence in creating my book addiction, it's interesting to see what he is doing with his library. He is literally mailing it away. Every other day or so he goes to his shelves or into another of his trunks, takes out a book or two, and scans through them (doubtless remembering all kinds of things from the first excitement of exposure to new ideas to the taste of the roast beef he had for dinner before first reading it). Then, decisively, with paper and string, he wraps them up and sends them to some unsuspecting recipient. (I am no longer unsuspecting, as he has sent me a good many volumes this way.) Occasionally the receipt of such parcels is just a nuisance, but I have often tried to fathom the meaning these books must have had for him.

Susan Spragg, writer, Denver, CO

I donated all my women's history books to the then-women's college, Loretto Heights College in Denver. One of the faculty had been collecting women's history books for years, and so I decided that my collection would be a good addition. Several years later they decided to integrate all the women's history books into the general collection. Then, the college was bought by a Japanese, male-oriented group. God knows what happened to all my carefully selected and expensive books.

Elizabeth Gardener, water conservation officer, Denver, CO

My sister, Rebekah, was told she would not live past July 1994. Well, today is 1996, and while she is very sick, she is still alive. She, too, is a book collector and has told me that I may inherit all her books that I want to keep. So, even though it feels very strange, I have been clearing out spaces and old collections to make room for three bookcases of treasures. Some are duplicates of my own collection. It's a sour/sweet situation: losing my soulmate sister and gaining all those books.

Protecting Books From Unintentional Permanent Loan and Other Forms of Theft

The home librarian is more likely to destroy books through neglect than lose them to armed robbers.

Some experts believe that a system of marking and recording books can deter thieves and, if a book is stolen, can help with its recovery. A methodical system can also be seen as a flag to the casual visitor that you take your library and its contents seriously. For example, academics who keep their libraries in their offices on campus might have to deal with "undocumented borrowing." If a student or colleague knows that theft prevention systems are in place, it may make a midnight raid less attractive.

Everything comes back to haunt you—except loaned books.
—Tony Delcavo, pre-rare book dealer,
Bella Luna Books, Highlands Ranch, CO

If you do not have the budget to protect every book in your collection, the following methods can be applied to those few you decide are most valuable. Start with methods that encourage the prompt return of loaned books.

1. Custom dust jackets, made of paper, cloth, or plastic, can be marked with your name, address, and phone number. This system protects hardback and larger paperback books you give out on loan, and provides a strong visual

reminder to the honest but absentminded borrower. Put a Mylar slipcover over your homemade dust jacket for extra protection.

If the book has a dust jacket, you can remove it and keep it in view to remind you the book is on loan. Meanwhile, your book is swathed in a Mylar jacket, with a label proclaiming its true home and appropriate contact information in case it strays.

2. Paperback books can travel in their own box or marked bag. If you dump them in an old plastic or paper bag, it is psychologically easier for the other party to think they are a permanent loan or just some old books you are throwing out.

3. Bookmarks are an inexpensive way of reminding people of your ownership. One clever system involves a booklet with perforated pages. Each page can be removed and used as a bookmark, leaving a tab in the booklet with a place to note the title of the book, the date it was loaned out, and the person who borrowed it. See Chapter VIII for a list of some pretty gift bookmarks.

4. Bookplates are a minor controversy in the book world. Strict archivists frown on them, except those that already exist in a book as part of the historical record. Not-so-strict archivists request that you use acid-free paper and a minimal amount of wheat paste to attach them to an expendable page. An artist will demand that you use your creativity to create something aesthetically meaningful.

I could not find any evidence that an attractive bookplate will shame someone into returning a book faster. And the chemicals in most pressure-sensitive labels will eventually destroy the page. There are archival-quality pressure sensitive labels available through many of the catalogs listed in Chapter XIV, and a mail-order source of lovely bookplates at the end of this chapter.

5. Registering books you loan out is a necessity. How you do it depends on the importance of the book and the importance of the relationship you have with the person to whom you are loaning the book. Write down the name of the book, the name and phone number of the borrower, the date of the loan, and— many booklovers told me this is very important—an agreed-upon date for its return. As mentioned above, this information can also be recorded on a bookmark that has your phone number and name prominently displayed.

It can also help to make a little production out of the process. If you are casual about lending your books out, the people who borrow them may be casual as well. You can't count on them taking the matter seriously if you hand the book over without writing down any information about the transaction.

Circulating libraries indelibly mark the books they lend out a dozen ways, much to the despair of archivists and collectors. The main methods are inks and embossing tools. Every outer surface is covered with rubber-stamped and written information, and inside the book, information is stamped at various intervals.

And still, books get stolen.

The invisible mark is a way of identifying a book as yours, if it surfaces in a book dealer's or collector's collection. Special inks, which can be revealed only under ultraviolet light, are one way to mark valuables. The reason you want the mark secret is that the thief is less likely to notice it and remove it. Another way is to place some secret mark in an obscure place, such as the inside of the spine of the book, which would be impossible to detect unless the book were examined with a flashlight or, in extreme cases, taken apart.

Book Contracts
By Peggy J. Noonan, science writer, Denver, CO
Peggy J. Noonan © 1996

What should a contract between a book lender and book borrower contain? First and most important, a promise that the borrower will care for the book as ardently as its owner would. If the borrower doesn't understand how the owner feels about the book, or how the owner would care for it, then he should not borrow it. Subsequent "I'm sorry" pleas will not make up for the breach of contract if a borrower fails to render the expected care.

Second, the borrower should place that book on his top priority reading list and actually read and return the book as quickly as possible. He should do that regardless of how many times the owner says, "Oh, there's no hurry, whenever you get to it." If you want to keep the book forever, go buy it yourself; when you're borrowing, you have an implied agreement to return it promptly.

Third, the borrower should be willing to talk about the book with the lender—good or bad reviews don't matter; it's the sharing that counts, or else what's the point of lending?

Does it sound as though the cards are all stacked on the side of the lender? You're right, they are, and I think that's exactly where they should be. Anyone kind enough to part with the wondrous treasure of a book (speak that word in hushed and reverent tones) should be afforded the same respect given to the lender of the world's most precious diamond or giver of the last piece of heavenly (eat your heart out, Godiva) See's chocolate candy.   ❖

The Book Loan Contract

Today's date: Date by which book will be returned:

Name of book owner:

Name of book:

Book will not be lent without completing all the information below.

Borrower's information:

Name:

Address: Net worth:

Social Security Number: Location of car title:

Description of tattoos and scars:

Any mental illness in the family?   Where will book be kept?

References: Name, Address, Phone, Relationship with Prospective Borrower, How Long Each Reference Has Known You

1.

2.

3

4.

5.

I agree to return this book in two weeks, which is a reasonable length of time for reading a book on loan. If I fail to return the book on time, I will be hunted down by mad dogs and ripped to shreds, a just consequence of my thoughtlessness. Also, here is a bunch of money, in case you can't find the book after I am dead, and must replace same. Also, I will be really sorry I did not return it on time.

Signature of Borrower / Date

Signatures of Four Witnesses / Date

From *The Bloomsbury Review BookLover's Guide.*
Copyright ©1996. Published by Owaissa Communications Company, Inc.

Resources for Weeding and Related Issues

Homes for Old Books

International Book Bank. 815 Central Avenue, Suite F, Linthicum, MD 21090; (410) 636-6895; fax (410) 636-6898.

A nonprofit organization founded in 1987 that ships about a million books per year to various organizations in eastern Europe, Africa, Asia, and the Caribbean. Books are donated to IBB and made available to recipients who commit to distributing them to other nonprofit institutions. The receiving organization agrees to conduct an evaluation of the project and share this evaluation with IBB. They provide a detailed and very useful set of guidelines of what they can accept.

Tranet. PO Box 567, Rangeley, ME 04970-2252; e-mail: tranet@igc.apc.org.

A twenty-year-old international network of people interested in alternative and transformational movements. Send these hardworking people $10 and they will send the names and addresses of people all over the world who need books for their village libraries and schools. I have known these folks for almost as long as they have been in existence and can vouch for the good work they do, spreading useful and provocative information.

The Real Weeding Story and Additional Books That Can Ease the Pain

Garage Sale Manual and Price Guide. Dana G. Morykan and Harry L. Rinker. Photographs by Harry L. Rinker, Jr. *Antique Trader Publications, $12.95 paper, ISBN 0-930625-37-4.*

The authors tell you how to hold a garage sale and how to shop them, so that you get the best value for your dollar no matter which side of the transaction you find yourself on. The best advice is an unsentimental approach to garage sale leftovers: Get rid of them!

Nolo Press Self-Help Law Books and Software. 950 Parker Street, Berkeley, CA 94710; (800) 992-6656, (510) 549-1976; fax (800) 645-0895, (510) 548-5902; e-mail: nolonews@aol.com.

The best source of reasonably priced and accurate advice concerning wills, trusts, estates, legal forms, copyrights, household inventories, and other legal matters of concern to booklovers are well-established and well-respected self-help legal presses. You can find print and computerized versions of all the information you need to put together a simple will, at a fraction of the cost of going to a lawyer. Also, the books will tell you when you need a lawyer, and some of the pitfalls you need to pay attention to under the laws of your locality on a variety of practical subjects.

Weeding Library Collections: *Library Weeding Methods.* Third Edition. Stanley J. Slote. *Libraries Unlimited, $42.00 cloth, ISBN 0-872676-33-0.*

If I shamed you into getting your weeding act together, this book will give useful advice, although much of it is aimed at circulating libraries. The introduction in this edition has a number of checklists of weeding criteria, which you can then match against your own ideas. As of this writing, the publisher is producing a new edition, but you should not have any trouble locating this and previous editions in large libraries or through the interlibrary loan services of your local library.

Tools for Weeding

Book Jackets™. PO Box 3077, Culver City, CA 90231; (310) 202-0293; e-mail: bookjac@primenet.com.

A line of attractive, cloth book holders in two sizes and several styles. My favorite is the "Jacketeer," which has both handles and pockets. The covers feature dozens of fabrics, from romantic florals to formal designs that look like they were lifted from a shirt factory. Are you surprised that the Kitty Kat design is one their bestsellers?

Book Lovers' Borrow Book. *Starhill Press, $6.95 paper, ISBN 0-913515-24-8; PO Box 21038, Washington, DC, 20009-0538; (202) 387-9805.*

A bound booklet of bookmarks, with a place to record the book, date, and who received it. The bookmark has a place to write the name of the person who owns the book (I would add the phone number as well).

Bookplate Ink. PO Box 558, Yellow Springs, OH 45387; (513) 767-2042.

A lovely and extensive collection of bookplates printed in dozens of styles. I particularly like the ship motifs. If you are not concerned about the effects of self-adhesive labels on your books, you will be very pleased with the assortment of traditional, religious, and contemporary book themes. You can also create your own custom bookplates and/or have the standard bookplates personalized.

❖

Become familiar with the many different
kinds of libraries in your state.
page 218.

Chapter XI — Other Libraries

Being a Guide to the Diverse Flora and Fauna
That Inhabit the Greater Library Ecology Outside the Walls of Your
Own Book Zoo and Some Advice About Creating a Real Library.

You Are Not Alone:
Part One — Plugging Into the Library Community

If you have obeyed the advice of the book and home library experts, every one of your books has been repaired, cataloged, and appropriately displayed. Your library has been weeded down to a lean, mean, reading machine.

You now have the time to lie back in the your new, crushed-velvet lounge, with a glass of your favorite beverage by your side, and read for the rest of your life. Or, as I often do, you can soothe your fevered brain by staring at the patterns the spines of the books make across your shelves, the same way you would watch telephone poles flash by the window of a moving train.

Another choice is to start weaving yourself and your home library into the formal web of professional library people and their organizations. Peek behind the scenes, and learn how you can extend your library into the greater world.

I think the best tools for a home library are a
public library card and a credit card.
—Scott VanGerpen, inveterate reader, Auburn, WA

You love books. You love libraries. You might have even dated a librarian or two. But unless you are someone trained and experienced in the library workplace, or have married a librarian, or were born into a library family, you probably know very little about what happens in "real" libraries or about the people who work at the various levels of the library food chain.

Trust me. I am a librarian groupie. Under various pretenses, since 1979, I have attended their professional conferences, sat through training programs and staff meetings and public hearings, and listened to their stories. Without really meaning to, I often gave the impression that I was one of them. Thus, in the best anthropological tradition, I have been let in on secrets usually reserved for those who have subjected themselves to ancient rites, chemical brainwashing, and years of strenuous education, which normally take place in a spaceship in orbit behind our moon.

At least, that is how I have sometimes felt. Like any other discipline, the practice of librarianship is fraught with peculiar belief systems that don't really make sense to people who are peering through the smoky glass of ignorance and innocence. What is Truth in the library community might seem like Myth to the outsider.

On the one hand, some of the best people I know work for libraries. I have watched people do outstanding work, year after year, making personal and financial sacrifices that other professionals would scorn. You should know that some studies demonstrate that degreed librarians will make less on average than any of their counterparts in other professions requiring advanced degrees, including schoolteacher, pharmacist, physical therapist, and engineer. When I think of the stereotypical librarian, I think of an intelligent and hardworking individual motivated by the desire to be of service and by the love of books and information.

On the other hand, I have heard the silliest statements emanating from the mouths of some professional, college-educated librarians. There was the oil company librarian who didn't want the scientists in her company to use the reference books in her library, because when they took the books off the shelves, the empty spaces broke up the attractive pattern created by the leather bindings. Really. Or the rural, public librarian who did not want to visit the people in her community. Keeping her library open every day, even when no one visited for hours at a time, was more important than getting books into the hands and hearts of the people who wanted to read but had no way of getting into town.

The Real Librarian

Do you believe, as I once did, that a librarian is someone who works in a library? That people who work in the children's library are one and the same as the people who run libraries in schools? That all librarians are alike in education and training, and that they all get together frequently, no matter what kind of library they inhabit? That librarians spend most of their time reading? That they are gray-bunned spinsters, corseted in whalebone, and wear only sensible shoes? That they "shush" people and stamp books, but not much else? That they know everything in the world? The world sees librarians as a nineteenth-century cartoon of the "schoolmarm."

Only those with an American Library Association accredited Master's of Library Science degree can be called *librarians*, according to the True Believers. Someone with doctorates in information science, quantum mechanics, and children's literature will still be referred to by the euphemisms *paraprofessional, paralibrarian,* or *support staff.* There are libraries where the director forbids anyone without a master's degree to give the even simplest information to patrons, such as the location of the bathrooms.

Deciding who is a librarian these days is an important issue for the library community. Employers such as school districts, law firms, hospitals, and research firms, are firing the more expensive degreed librarians and replacing them with less expensive file clerks and aides in order to save money. Librarians are being challenged to justify what they do and to explain their value to the customer. This is a painful experience for people who have spent their lives serving others.

In addition, the purpose of a physical location called a library is coming into question. Why do we need to spend money on public libraries, when there are such things as used bookstores and CD-ROMs? Why do lawyers need law libraries, when they can do their own database research from their desks?

I'm a libertarian readaholic who opposes book worship.
—John Ohliger, co-founder, Basic Choices, Inc., Madison, WI

Part of the responsibility for the demotion of librarians and the downsizing of some libraries falls on the librarians themselves. As a professional group, they became a little smug and insular and did not respond as quickly as they could have to new technology. Until recently, leading library schools did not teach classes in computer science, and many librarians were more concerned with creating the mathematically correct library catalog than responding to the needs of the customers. In fact, more than one serious home librarian has confessed that the main impetus for creating a private collection was frustration with the lack of service and resources at local libraries.

Although individual librarians and libraries have done a terrific job at becoming leaders in the Information Age (these, of course, are all my personal friends in the library community), the formal library community as a whole is playing catch-up, in terms of both technology and customer relations.

Some tension exists in the library community between the people who have the MLSs and the people who don't. Wise library managers know that it does not take an advanced education to point to a shelf and say, "Big red book, third from the left," and that many of the skills learned in library school can be picked up on the job. But, at the same time that people with advanced degrees are being laid off, the library profession is insisting that those advanced degrees be required in more and more libraries. So, while private-sector librarians with an MLS are being fired and replaced with less expensive personnel, library workers without credentials in public and academic libraries are being told to earn their degrees or lose their jobs.

The library profession has not learned how to separate the traditional acquisition of the formal degree and the documentation of the competencies of people who, without that degree, have done an excellent job of running their libraries. More than once, I have been introduced to library directors who have won the respect of their colleagues and patrons with high standards of service, only to have someone whisper later that the person did it without formal library training. Couldn't some of the library schools award credit for workplace accomplishments? In discussing this issue with people in high positions, I discovered that this idea, which has been embraced in many universities and college programs, is not yet conventional wisdom in the library world.

Besides the issues of who has a degree and whether libraries will survive in their current form, there is the curious divisiveness among the different flavors of librarian and library worker. I did not realize that public librarians and *special librarians* (the term that describes the kind of librarian who works in specialized libraries for private industry, government agencies, law firms, etc.) rarely speak to each other. No, they don't snub each other on the street. But there is an alphabet soup of professional associations for each designated type of librarian, and the lack of communication and collaboration is astonishing to the outsider.

Given this slightly soiled private laundry, I am still an unabashed supporter of all kinds of librarians and libraries. I am not too worried about what form the profession will take in the next few years, as it struggles with the transition from the Gutenberg era to the Silicon era. Most of the librarians I know are successfully meeting the challenges of selling the need for their expertise to their constituencies.

So, how can the average booklover and home librarian build bridges to benefit themselves and the greater library community?

Here are some suggestions that will help you get along better with your librarians and library workers. They will also help you understand some of the controversies that are affecting your ability to access information.

Know How Your State Public Library Community Operates

Become familiar with the many different kinds of libraries in your state. You most probably have a *state library* office. The state librarian and staff help set standards for the publicly funded libraries, provide training, run special projects, deal with the other segments of state government, including lawmakers and the governor's office, and assist with everything from cataloging to computer networking to job searches.

Your state could be carved up into smaller *library regions* or *systems;* these offices address some of the same issues that a state library does, but on a smaller scale. Some work only with public and school libraries, and others are *multitype systems;* these work with everybody from academic libraries to corporate information centers to small rural libraries.

The next level is usually a public library district, which can be defined by the boundaries of counties and cities. These districts raise money and might operate many different public libraries in different towns. School districts run the school libraries, which are usually now called *media centers,* just as a school librarian is now called a *school media specialist.*

Individual libraries take many forms. A public library can be run by a city, a foundation, a nonprofit organization, a county, or a district. Funding comes from several sources, including property taxes, municipal and state budgets, endowments, and donations.

Knowing your public library service providers means that you know who makes decisions about your libraries. More than once, I have solved a problem for a client regarding library service, simply because I knew who to call. Finally, this knowledge will provide a road map for finding libraries you can support with your time and money.

Know Your Local Resources

Do you know where the best business library collection resides in your area? Do you know who has the best books on gardening, job hunting, taxes, home repair, or health? Do you know what academic collections are open to the public? Which ones charge? Who has classes in book conservation? Who can find you an appraiser? Who has the best book sales? Who will help track down a difficult interlibrary loan?

One of the simplest techniques for learning about your local library resources is to make friends with librarians. (Or library workers; you don't have to ask if they have the correct degree!) What a concept! Talk to the people behind the desk. Tell them about your own library. Ask for help. Bring them gifts. (Chocolate is preferred.)

Remember that valuable libraries are often hidden. Most museums have wonderful research libraries, as do professional associations, religious institutions, nonprofit organizations, and government agencies.

Growing a Home Library Up and Out

A home library is a mirror of the hearts and minds of individuals, a family, or a tribe. Even if it grows in size, it can stay a home library because its purpose has remained the same, hearth-bound by the love within four walls. For example, your home library may be a personal refuge from the world, a single-minded mass of favorite murder mysteries and science fiction. Even when it grows beyond the bookshelf next to the bed and takes over the family room walls, it is still a personal collection of terrible and fantastic vistas.

However, sometimes a home library grows into something else. As you were warned in Chapter VI, the home library can evolve into a book business. It may start innocently. You sell a few fine books at a local rare book establishment and use the money to purchase a few more, which are just a little bit better. Soon you are worried about tax numbers and your listing in the Yellow Pages. By the time you have your own storefront, with your name carefully lettered in Gothic type on the glass door (outlined in gold), you are a professional, credentialed, licensed, bonded, and insured antiquarian bookseller, with a bank account and cash flow, and if you are hardworking and lucky, People Are Giving You Money to Spend Time With Books!

Another type of metamorphosis is when your home library, with a lowercase *l*, becomes a Real Library, with a capital *L*. A Real Library is more than the beautifully cataloged and annotated private collection of a great scholar. A Real Library is one where its caretakers nurture relationships with other people who, in turn, create their own dialogues with the books. A Real Library is visited and cherished by individuals who relish the judgment of the caretakers about what is worth collecting.

As explained in Chapter X, many booklovers hunt for a suitable home for their collections in existing libraries or archives, with the idea of letting go only after infirmity or death. In other words, they are willing to part with their collection when someone has to pry the books from the grasp of a cold, albeit literate, corpse. But you don't have to wait for the medical examiner's approval, and you also don't have to give up your library, in order to share its treasures.

Almost every great library, until the recent past, started as someone's private collection or, in the case of the state or institutional libraries of the past, someone's private passion made public. In making your library more formal and accessible, you will join the ranks of royalty, popes, and geniuses of every scholarly stripe.

Sometimes, the home library grows into something more because of love. Steven and LaVerne Ross met on a blind date. They discovered a shared interest in alternative healing practices, each borne out of a personal, successful experience with unconventional healing. Each brought to their subsequent marriage a sizable home library of books and other documents relating to healing and health. Within a few months after they married, they invested their life savings to create a visionary organization to share their information with others.

Today, the World Research Foundation, located in Sherman Oaks, California, is an internationally respected nonprofit network that provides information about both alternative/complementary and conventional health treatment options available worldwide. Supported by grants and the modest fees paid by patients and practitioners, the organization provides hundreds of pages of information to clients needing help with health problems.

When I availed myself of their services during a bout with sciatica, I received hundreds of pages of data, with references to many international sources long out of print. It was as if my own personal professional librarian had searched the world's libraries for information, just for me. By the way, much of the information is not contained in existing computer databases, and in many cases, the books themselves—arcane texts from other countries—do not appear in a conventional medical bibliography.

Neither Steven nor LaVerne Ross was an academically trained librarian; they were just home librarians with a passion for helping others. (Send $5 and a written request for introductory information to the World Research Foundation, 15300 Ventura Boulevard, Suite 403, Sherman Oaks, California 91403. Their phone number is (818) 907-5483, and the fax number is (818) 907-6044. Hours are 9:30 a.m. to 1:00 p.m. Pacific time, Monday through Friday.)

After the taking of Carthage, the Roman senate rewarded the family of Regulus with the books found in that city. A library was a national gift, and the most honourable they could bestow.
—Isaac Disraeli, eighteenth-century booklover
from *Curiosities of Literature*. Bradbury, Agnew & Co., 1839

Sometimes, your home library grows into something more because if you don't do it, no one else will. When Maida Tilchen, a teacher in Somerville, Massachusetts, started collecting lesbian pulp fiction, "Everyone else seemed to think they were worthless. At that time, I was able to find one published article about the genre, and that was in a very obscure periodical. I knew gay literature professors in the mid-1970s that thought the pulps were beneath contempt."

Maida's library grew from a book she "literally stepped on ... at a party." She gathered more than a thousand volumes, and was successful partly because it was before the market for such books attracted swarms of interested collectors and partly because she was living in the rural Midwest, where bookstores stocked inexpensive pulp fiction.

The books, which were mostly published in the fifties, have historical and cultural importance. However, the books themselves were deteriorating rapidly, and Maida did not want to let people handle them, let alone lend them out.

"I felt bad hoarding the books, and I wanted to open the minds of those who had a negative, pro-censorship response, so I put together a slide show [that] features the covers, both front and back, and has a tape of women reading the passages from the books, as well as a narration explaining the history of lesbian fiction." By creating the slide show, Maida presented the essence of her library to hundreds of people.

As the collection grew, Maida ran into the classic home librarian problem of having more books than she could care for. She gave about 700 books to the Lesbian Herstory Archives, sold off some duplicates, and keeps the rest in cartons in her closet, where they are brought out only on "the rare occasions when someone comes to visit them." The library launched Maida's career as a writer, and became the starting point for what ended up as hundreds of articles on "lesbian/gay, Jewish, and antinuclear topics." The library lives on and inspires her words.

There are numerous examples of how home libraries have grown into something more. Many legal and medical professionals have started their organizations' research libraries by setting up their own collection in a public space. University libraries grew from the private stocks of students and faculty. One source of books and documents in earlier centuries was debating societies, whose members took winning very seriously. The members pooled their research so as to give their members the winning edge in fiercely fought public debates. These evolved into private libraries, which, because of their popularity with students, were invited to merge with the "official" college library.

How to Grow a Real Library

The library philanthropist Andrew Carnegie was said to have been inspired by a generous man who opened his home library to boys who wanted access to knowledge, at a time when libraries accessible to the general public were few. Could your love of books, your skillful acquisition of same, your ability to classify and catalog, and your knack for publicity create an accessible library that inspires someone to greatness?

If you want to grow your home library into something more, you need to ask two important sets of questions.

First, you need to find out how your collection stacks up against other libraries. Your collection does not have to be unique, but it should be unusual enough within your geographic area to create a draw for potential visitors. A one-of-a-kind library could draw people from all over the world. For example, if you are planning to make public the only existing copies of How to Punch Cows books written and published by nineteenth-century American cowboys, expect German and Japanese Western Americana scholars to be knocking at your door.

To ensure that it will be worth the time and effort to make your home library into a Real Library, talk to knowledgeable individuals of many perspectives in the book and library communities. These would be in addition to those individuals who are experts in the subjects on which your library focuses. Remember that the owners of new and used bookstores don't necessarily chat with people who work in libraries or universities. A restaurant owner might not know that the local public library houses the region's best collection of menus and cookbooks. Likewise, it may shock the local college library staff to discover that the much maligned, national chain bookstore has a terrific collection of books on philosophy.

You also need to measure your collection in terms of its physical condition. Could your books stand up to constant use? Are they physically in shape? If they are really valuable, are they housed in archival-quality boxes under ideal environmental conditions and, at the very least, shielded in Mylar dust jackets?

> *I keep people from borrowing stuff by just saying,*
> *"No, I need it for my work." As I am a*
> *sociologist, I need everything for my work.*
> —Professor Barry Wellman, University of Toronto,
> Toronto, Ontario, Canada

A collection of books does not become a Real Library until someone puts some thought into how the books are organized, which leads me to the second set of questions: What do you want your library to become, and what do you want to spend your time doing?

Let's do some visualizations about having your own library. You see yourself in your own Real Library, directing the proper placement of the walnut bookcases, the antique brass lamps, and the crushed velvet lounges. You revel in images of yourself ordering every book you want from thousands of catalogs. You look forward to those times when patrons bring you tasteful but extremely expensive gifts in gratitude for creating the monument to culture and world civilization that is Your Library.

Don't be shocked, but there is more to library management than spending the family fortune. Few people outside of the professional library community realize how much boring work is involved in establishing and maintaining a formal library. For every fun activity regarding furniture and customer service, there are a thousand bookkeeping details, most of which involve dusty manual labor.

Refer to Chapter IV, and pretend that your whole life becomes a series of Library Audits. You are surrounded by books, but you have no time to read them yourself. You examine them for damage and enter bibliographical information about them into ledgers and databases. You stand on a ladder and hunt for an elusive volume, while an extremely impatient Ph.D. candidate, who repeatedly reminds you that she drove 50 miles in the rain because you assured her you had the book, drips on your best upholstered chair. You are no longer a Booklover but a Library Worker; you know the contents of books only by their reputations in book review magazines.

Also, you are going to have to decide the legal structure of your library, its location, and what kind of access you will allow. How about those pesky details such as budget, zoning laws, building codes, permits, licenses, and signs? Oh, and have you asked your family and neighbors what they think about your plan?

If your library is in good shape, if you are convinced it has value for others, and if you have a realistic understanding about the amount of time and money it will take to run a small library, STOP RIGHT THERE. Before you do anything else, go volunteer at someone else's Real Library for a while. Learn about the tasks firsthand. Attend library conferences. Take classes. Read the books professional librarians read.

Are you still eager? Are you really ready? My parting advice is, take your time. Start with limited hours, and run the public part as an experiment. If it doesn't succeed, tell your supporters that you learned a lot, and renew your official status as an amateur booklover.

Building the Community Library

What if your goal is to create a public library? Perhaps your small town has suffered without a library for years, or previous budget crises have forced the library to close. Maybe you live in a commuter subdivision, one of the housing tracts that starts with rows of houses, instead of a main street and a downtown. Now there is a pressing need for a local public library in Heather Rose Dale Wood Creek Park, which a few years before was just cow pastures. Or, perhaps library service to your neighborhood was cut off because of budget issues.

Larry Wilkinson, who with his late wife Betty, was the seminal force behind the public library in Telluride, Colorado, has seen his community's public library grow from a shelf of old books to a brand new building that has quickly become a center of community life. Almost ten years later, the new building is bursting at the seams, reflecting the health of this lovely mountain town.

Larry, a successful businessman, learned very quickly that the key to building a public library (as opposed to a private research library) is collaboration; the secret is remembering the word *public*. Without strong, active, and influential support on the part of many key citizens, the library will fail. Even if you decide to take the radical approach of creating your library under the umbrella of a nonprofit, with the intent of not taking any government funds, you will still have to spend your time building coalitions among a diverse public.

Now, maybe you are not a Larry, a skilled negotiator whose cheerful presence fills a room with goodwill. What will you need to do to help your community library grow and prosper? The successful directors of many small, start-up, and growing libraries have revealed their secrets to me.

First, assume that you are going to have to work with everyone in the community. *Everyone* means the neighbor you hate, the politician you detest, and the businessowner you can't stand.

Second, build a team. You will want to have the key decision-makers on your side from the beginning. These include elected officials, members of wealthy and influential families, and, of course, the media. But don't forget that the library is for everybody. Avoid the taint of elitism, and make sure that the average citizen has a role. Involve people from the school, religious, ethnic, senior, and arts communities. Make sure if someone shows up to volunteer that there is a way he or she can make a meaningful contribution. You want everyone in town to walk into the new building (or the old building with the new paint) and be able to feel that it is their library.

There have been ages when, for the possession of a manuscript, some would transfer an estate, or leave in pawn for its loan hundreds of golden crowns; and when even the sale or loan of a manuscript was considered a sale of such importance as to have been solemnly registered by public acts.
—Isaac Disraeli, eighteenth-century booklover
from *Curiosities of Literature*. Bradbury, Agnew & Co., 1839

Third, if you don't have the talent for asking for money from almost everyone you meet, you need to either acquire the skill or find a partner who has it. This is not about only writing grant proposals, where you can hide behind a piece of paper. You will have to ask people one-on-one, face-to-face, for money.

You will encounter the mythology that cripples the health of many of this country's best public libraries: People tend to think that information is free. They tend to ignore the fact that the outcome is to create a publicly accessible location so that people can find the information they need to create a better life for themselves and the organizations and community they serve. That relatively free outcome (unless you have huge overdue bills or try to reproduce a phone book at the copier) happens because of an input of money. And tax dollars, as many communities are discovering, are not enough.

Also, tax money tends to be attached to political strings. I have seen governing bodies threaten to cut a library's funding because someone on the city council or legislative committee has taken exception to something a librarian said or did. Healthy fundraising lowers your reliance on the goodwill of elected officials.

Fourth, if you don't already have a well-respected advisory board of library experts, start cultivating it now. In rare cases, you might find that officials from neighboring libraries will take exception to your efforts. Indeed, it may make more sense to create a branch library within an existing district, rather than start from scratch. In any event, the success of your public project depends on the support of the greater library community.

Fifth, marry for money, give up your social life, pack the kids off to camp until they are married, and forget about making a fashion statement until you are tucked away in the nursing home. Library development is a full-time job, and it takes years. By the way, almost every full-time librarian and library worker I know laments their lack of time for reading.

Sixth, remember that it is not *your* library, even if they do put your name over the door. You might find that the professionals who run it have very different ideas about how to organize the stacks. You will have to retreat to the womb of your own home library to be able to regain that sense of control. You will glow when you walk into your public library and realize that you helped create this bulwark of democracy and the American Way. But when they kick you out for weeding the shelves without authorization, you might feel put out. Get over it.

Finally, beware of success. I have been reading a recent report issued by the Wilkinson Public Library in Telluride. (Yes, you might get the public library named after you if you are very, very good). One of the themes is that the gracious community feel of the library—the open spaces, the plant collection—has been replaced by shelves packed with books. Ironically, in the beginning, patrons did not understand why there were so many empty shelves! Now, if a new book is purchased, a book needs to be taken off the shelves to make room.

Resources From the Real Library World

Books About Libraries

Almost all the books I could find about libraries were written by librarians about the operation of publicly accessible libraries, were written in jargon thick enough to slice, or were too expensive for the budget of the average booklover. Lots of books, for example, are written about helping patrons use a library, but they are written *by* librarians, *for* librarians, in much the same way that twenty years ago books on health were written *by* and *for* doctors, not patients. Some of the books on the history of books and libraries listed in Chapter II provide interesting cultural highlights. The following books are reasonably priced and interesting reads.

The Community of the Book: *A Directory of Organizations and Programs.*
Third Edition. Compiled by Maurvene D. Williams. Edited and with an
Introduction by John Y. Cole. *Library of Congress, $8.95 paper,*
ISBN 0-8444-0807-7.

A compact directory of more than 100 nonprofit, government, and professional trade organizations related to the book. A nice snapshot of the library, book, education, and literacy communities. Published by the Center for the Book.

Cultural Gems: *An Eclectic Look at Unique United States Libraries.* Mary
Buckingham Maturi and Richard J. Maturi. *21st Century Publishers, $29.95*
cloth, ISBN 0-9607298-1-X; 1320 Curt Gowdy Drive, Cheyenne, WY 82009;
(307) 635-5511.

A pictorial architectural survey of dozens of interesting libraries. The accompanying text provides a patchwork-quilt history of the growth of libraries in the United States, with insights into how different communities decided to provide public library service. From the red brick, hexagonal library in Madison, Maine, to the pueblo-style adobe in Lordsburg, New Mexico, from the library chateau in Scranton, Pennsylvania, to the former stone church that houses the library in Kiowa, Colorado, every kind of library building is represented.

Future Libraries. Edited by R. Howard Bloch and Carla Hesse.
University of California Press, $16.00 paper, ISBN 0-520-08811-5.

The essays are already more than three years old, several lifetimes by the measure of the speed by which libraries are changing. However, the concerns of the authors, which range from issues of the use of library space to the problem of copyrights in a paperless society, are still being argued at library conferences and boardrooms. This will give you a good idea of some of the main concerns of the professional library community and how these concerns might be affecting your local library world.

Rare Books and Special Collections in the Smithsonian Institution
Libraries. Ellen B. Wells and Leslie K. Overstreet. Foreword by
Barbara J. Smith. Introduction by Nancy E. Gwinn. *Smithsonian Institution Press,*
$19.95 paper, ISBN 1-56098-625-5.

An elegantly designed coffee-table paperback that highlights the treasures housed in several libraries associated with the Smithsonian. The editors have wisely chosen exquisite examples and presented them in full color, when appropriate, so that the reader can appreciate their beauty. My favorite selection is the first issue of *The Cherokee Messenger,* an 1844 publication printed in the Cherokee alphabet.

Library-Related Organizations

These organizations include several professional membership organizations for the library community that might not invite you in as a voting member, but can provide support for your best home library efforts by means of publications and online services. Also, if you make friends with local representatives, you might find that you can attend their workshops or at least visit the exhibit halls at their conferences. I have attended many such programs over the years, and no one seemed unduly upset that a mere mortal was allowed on the premises. However, I am especially well behaved in public.

American Library Association (ALA). 50 East Huron Street, Chicago, IL 60611; (800) 545-2433 (choose option #6); fax (312) 440-9374; e-mail: pio@ala.org; Press Officer: Pamela Gooders (312) 944-8520. web site: http://www.ala.org

The mother of all library organizations, billed as the oldest and largest library association in the world. The public information office is willing to help the home librarian with publications and information regarding libraries and books. Many of the most interesting publications that apply to home library care are published by the ALA; although expensive, they are obtainable through inter-library loan programs through your local public library.

Association of Independent Information Professionals (AIIP). 245 5th Avenue, Suite 2103, New York, NY 10016; (212) 889-6750; fax (212) 481-3071; membership: $85/year (Associate member); e-mail: aiipinfo@aiip.org.

These folks act as private librarians and researchers for mostly business, technology, legal, and financial clients. Because their accomplishments are measured and rewarded directly by their customers and not by professional associations, the independent information professional is less likely to have an MLS degree. Also, they are more likely to have degrees and experience in other professions. A doctor becomes a forensic researcher and writer for legal firms. An economist does research for technology firms. A city planner specializes in searching online systems for inventors. And, yes, there are a few MLS librarians going into business for themselves. This group is the closest thing I could find to an organization that serves the needs of the home librarian who wants to turn professional researcher.

Association of Research Libraries (ARL). 21 Dupont Circle NW, Washington, DC 20036; (202) 296-2296; fax (202) 872-0884.

This organization focuses on the needs of libraries found in research organizations, the overwhelming number being universities. The most valuable resource for the booklover or home librarian is the publication catalog, which publishes the collective wisdom of its member libraries, on subjects ranging from copyright issues to photocopying policies to preservation and disaster preparedness. The prices reflect their main audience (people who are used to being overcharged for 50-page pamphlets), but the information is top-notch.

Friends of Libraries U.S.A. (FOLUSA). 1700 Walnut Street, Suite 715, Philadelphia, PA 19103; (215) 790-1674; $25+ a year, depending on size of library and level of support.

Libraries need help. They need people to weed their gardens and wash their windows. They need people who can check out books so that the staff can go to workshops and conferences. They need trustees and fundraisers, lobbyists and people to make crafts with the kids on Saturday mornings.

Friends of Libraries groups help libraries, and Friends of Libraries U.S.A. shows you how to create one. If you are planning to grow a community library, this organization should be your first stop.

Independent Research Libraries Association(IRLA). Hagley Museum and Library, PO Box 3630, Wilmington, DE 19807; (302) 658-2400.

IRLA includes the American Antiquarian Society, American Philosophical Society, the Folger Shakespeare Library, the Hagley Museum and Library, the Historical Society of Pennsylvania, the Huntington Library, the Library Company of Philadelphia, Linda Hall Library, Massachusetts Historical Society, the Newberry Library, the New York Academy of Medicine, the New York Historical Society, the New York Public Library (Astor, Lenox, and Tilden Foundations), the Pierpont Morgan Library, and the Virginia Historical Society.

The IRLA was established in 1972 in order to address the future of independent, privately supported research libraries. Three common threads unite IRLA's members: (1) their libraries house collections of national or international significance that are capable of supporting sustained research in a variety of interrelated subjects and of attracting scholars from all over the world; (2) they are organized as privately endowed, independent institutions, each with its own act of incorporation or charter, its own board of trustees, and a full-time chief executive officer; (3) their primary purposes are to collect and to make available the records of the past, to promote research in them, and to share those materials with scholars and the public.

Librarians at Liberty. CRISES Press, 1716 SW Williston Road, Gainesville, FL 32608; (904) 335-2200; 2x/year; $10/year.

There is ongoing controversy in the professional library community about how books and materials are selected for public access. One issue is how much material a library should carry that is not part of the mainstream of political thought. Publications like *Librarians at Liberty* lament the lack of a significant presence of progressive and left-leaning alternative and small press literature on most public and academic libraries' shelves. This magazine publishes reviews of other magazines, books, directories, and indexes. It also keeps subscribers up-to-date on alternative publishing with interviews and coverage of events, and invites input from librarians who are dealing with these issues.

Libraries for the Future. 521 Fifth Avenue, New York, NY 10175-1699; (800) 542-1918.

A national nonprofit organization that initiates and supports grassroots organizing, demonstration projects, research, and public awareness activities to focus attention on the public library. I have found the staff to be intelligent and appropriately assertive in their defense of public libraries.

Library of Congress (LC). Washington, DC 20540-0001; (202) 707-5000.

The more I researched the Library of Congress, the more astonished I became. It is the world's largest library, for one thing. Although its first priority is to the United States Congress, it is best known for its research library, its management of programs such as the Copyright Office, and special services regarding the needs of the "thinking and creative public." The **Center for the Book** was established "to heighten public awareness of books, reading, and libraries and to encourage the study of books and print culture." It can be reached care of the Library of Congress, Washington, DC 20540-8200; (202) 707-5221; fax (202) 707-0269. The Library and the Center are the heart of the American library community. Many states and regions now have their own centers.

The Libri Foundation. Ms. Barbara J. McKillip, PO Box 10246, Eugene, OR 97440; (541) 485-8532; fax (541) 485-9688.

In states like Colorado, the majority of public libraries serve communities of less than 5,000. And, either because of politics, distance, a lack of experience, or a lack of clout, these small libraries can be neglected by funding organizations. Libri donates new, quality hardcover children's books to small, rural public libraries by matching locally raised contributions with books at a value of two-to-one. Started by a librarian who cares about rural libraries.

Special Libraries Association (SLA). Information Resources Center, 1700 Eighteenth Street, NW, Washington, DC 20009; (202) 234-4700; fax (202) 265-9317; e-mail: sla@sla.org.

The special librarian works either solo for a variety of customers, or within an organization, serving that organization's needs, and is likely to have degrees in both library science and the subject in which the library they work with specializes. I know special librarians knowledgeable in math, biology, history, and geology. They can be experts in tax law and Russian politics. Like the ALA, SLA can supply information of use to the home librarian, particularly if your collection is focused in technical or business subject areas.

University Microfilms International (UMI). 300 North Zeeb Road, PO Box 1346, Ann Arbor, MI 48106-1346; (800) 521-0600.

One of the best sources for establishing a "just-in-time" library. Instead of acquiring books against future need, you only order books as the need arises. This service takes several weeks, but it can cut the number of "what-if-I-should-want-this-someday" books from your shelves.

Books on Demand™ provides more than 134,000 out-of-print books, copied for you on acid-free paper from the microfilm negative of the original book. First, the helpful staff will send you a list of the current subject catalogs, which range from *African-American Studies* to *World History.* Then you order the free catalogs; rarely have I encountered type this tiny that is still legible. The current *Engineering* catalog has 129 pages, organized by general categories such as motor vehicles and nuclear engineering, and the books within each category are alphabetized by author's name. Each extremely small entry lists the basic bibliographic information and provides a price. The only catch is the price, which is a minimum of $25 per book, at 28.5 cents per page. But you will find books here that are impossible to find anywhere else. Call the number above and ask for Books on Demand or dial extension 2239 to request a subject catalog.

UMI Dissertation Services provides a similar service for accessing copies of 1.2 million dissertations and master's theses. Its extension number is 3736.

❖

These webs of wire and oceans
of invisible waves make up
the heart of a community hearth.
page 234.

Chapter XII — Electronic and Online Books

Being a Snapshot of the Internet and Computer Resources,
for Those Who Regret the End of the Gutenberg Era.

You Are Not Alone:
Part Two — The Electronic Community

Sit by the fire, and listen to the stories around the flickering light. This is the best way, of course, the tribal ritual—warm voices, gestures emphasizing a point, smiling faces, shared laughter, an arm around the shoulder—the words break into song, and even the oldest get up and dance.

When the first books were introduced, there was wonder and anxiety. It was wonderful that the words of the storyteller, the trader, the king, the shaman could be translated into animal tracks on clay, or knife bites on a carved stick, or dyes rubbed into the hide of an animal, and carried from one fire to another. At the other fire, those tracks and bites could be translated back into words, song, and dance, so long as those people knew the key.

A person requests information about where to access a century-and-a-half old publication from Transylvania (Romania or Kentucky??). And then you people jump on it like a dog on a bone. First someone points out that there's a university by that name in Lexington, Kentucky. Then another mentions that it has the oldest medical school west of the Appalachians. Then the publication is cited. Almost immediately thereafter a medical librarian offers to send the issue. Hard on the heels of that offer is direction to a London-based medical history museum that would probably have the work on microfilm. Whew! You folks are really amazing. My compliments on your wisdom and collegiality. (In my world—marketing—such cooperation is unheard of. Too bad for us, I'm afraid.)
—Jerry Silverman, president, The Silverman Agency and
collector of oriental rug books, Chicago, IL
Jerry Silverman © 1996; from the *exlibris* listserv, 14 May 1996

But, said some, it is not right that the complex nuances of the spoken word, the performed song, and the physical dance be captured so inadequately in a medium that simplifies and distorts the original experience. I am sure that some of those anxious people considered banning the book altogether.

Consider electronic communication. Beginning with the click of a Morse Code message in the last century, it has evolved into a crazy quilt of telephone lines carrying voices and faxes, computer services, television cables, satellite transmissions, and the infamous Internet, by which the computers of thousands of organizations communicate. The World Wide Web allows users to hop from site to site on the Internet, so that each site can become an active catalog of other related sites. A few clicks of a computer key or mouse bring you information from physical locations thousands of miles apart.

These webs of wire and oceans of invisible waves make up the heart of a community hearth. The difference is that now the fire is grown to the size of a young sun. You can send words, songs, and moving pictures across cities and oceans. A phone call from Mom or an exchange of e-mail with my best friend from college is not as satisfying as a physical visit, where we hug and break bread. But, it is better than no visit. And it is amazing how the shifting of electrons and the vibrating of molecules can be translated into love.

This chapter on the electronic book was the hardest to write, because there is too much going on. Any one person's window onto this world is very, very small, and I felt that I could only echo the work of my betters.

Also, I still think the main point of having a home library is to have the books near you that you love to read, even if your library is primarily an investment or a gallery of the book arts. Consequently, any activity that causes me to spend money or time on something besides reading and caring for my books has got to be pretty compelling. I had to convince myself that I could find useful tools online that would serve the needs of the person who wants to spend most of their time reading, not getting software to work.

If you are already looking at book-related information on the Internet or one of the commercial online services, you can find resources by typing the word *book* or *library* into a program designed to search millions of records and files. You can get connected to several hundred thousand choices (but not necessarily the one you want). You don't need a new list of hot book discussion groups if you are already going blind from peering at your screen for an entire evening.

On the other hand, if you don't already know enough to know what I am talking about, this book is not the place to learn the technology; refer to the resources listed at the end of this chapter to get you started or head for the classroom where you can learn about computers firsthand.

What I *can* do is share my answer to two questions of the day: Is the Internet useful to booklovers and home librarians, and at what cost?

The Light Touch: Herding BookLovers on the Internet

How does someone deeply committed to freedom of expression govern an online discussion among hundreds of articulate, opinionated booklovers? On the one hand, she does not want to lose the elusive, rich ecology of a free market of ideas and goods, but on the other hand, she does not want that ecology overrun and destroyed by the terminally clueless. Here is how Shoshana Edwards, owner/moderator of the Internet's *bibliophile* list, balances freedom and structure.

Bibliophile *is a subscription mailing list specifically for dealers and/or collectors of books of all kinds. Anyone with an interest in preserving the printed word in all its glorious and interesting forms is welcome to participate. Participants are encouraged to offer books and ephemera for sale, to search for titles, and to engage in discussion of topics specifically related to the buying, selling, and collecting of books of all kinds.*

Please confine yourself to two postings every day. With nearly 1,000 subscribers, if everyone decided not only to post every day, but to post multiple times, we would be in deep trouble.

We all love a good joke; however, the sheer volume of the mail on this list precludes the advisability of posting such material. Please send jokes, vignettes, etc., to your friends; not to the bibliophile *list.*

Personal attacks of any kind will not be tolerated on the open list. Posting of private e-mail to the list without the explicit permission of the author of the e-mail is forbidden. Either of these acts will result in immediate expulsion from the list.

The moderator of the bibliophile *list will handle all problems regarding inappropriate postings or problems with the mailer. If you feel something should be dealt with, please address your request to me. This, of course, does not apply to personal exchanges which might occur between yourself and another member of the list. Please keep private correspondence private.*

—Shoshana Edwards, **Books from Bree,** Scientific and Technical Books, Beaverton, OR 97008; (503) 644-7218; e-mail: bree@auldbooks.com; web site: http://www.auldbooks.com.

Reprinted with permission of the author; from the *bibliophile* listserv, 20 Feb 1996

The Online BookLover

My view of the electronic campfire has been shaped by almost twenty years of experience as a computer user, which is skewed, I admit, because I have been sheltered from most of the mundane disasters that plague the average home computer user. I married a man who has found me the best computer systems at moderate prices, and he fixes them for me when they don't work. On deadline. At midnight. For free. (Sorry, our marriage is doing fine, and he does not make house calls.) Unlike many booklovers I know, I spend my time running my computer, not getting it to run, which leaves me lots of time for reading books.

I love my computer. It appeals to my lingering girl-nerd persona, the one who got straight As in math and science. But, this affection is balanced by a stubborn conviction that computers, like books, are tools to serve my purposes, not the other way around.

For example, I love the fact that I have the full text of all of Shakespeare's works on my desk in digital form. It is great fun to browse all the works at once for certain words or phrases, or to sit in a darkened room and play with the typography of the sonnets on a lit screen. But having the ability to print out the full text in any typestyle I choose is not going to get me to give away the volumes of Shakespeare that sit on my shelves. As one publisher told me, sometimes what you want is a book to hold.

Books are important, but not substitutes for people.
—Mike Robinson, booklover, Tacoma, WA

It surprises me how much time I spent traveling the wires on electronic lists, the Internet, and the World Wide Web for this guide. Every day I was communicating one-on-one with contributors via e-mail, searching various sites and lists for specific information, and participating in group discussions with booklovers from all over the world.

But now, a disclaimer: I have neglected the specifics of some important online services, such as CompuServe and America Online, for three reasons.

First, although the various bulletin boards and online services are sites of great activity in the book world, I never participated enough to have an opinion. In fact, I cheated several times by asking friends who were already skilled and knowledgeable on different services to hunt for information for me. (For the same reason, I do not review any of the programs that browse the World Wide Web, because the only system I know is the one I use, which I think is the best, but runs only on NeXT computers.) Also, you can find book and library resources through the print magazines associated with each commercial service.

Second, even as I write these words, so many mergers are being announced (and cancelled) that I don't know how to predict the identity of the survivors.

Third, the one trend I can predict is that most of the remaining companies either will be moving their resources to the Internet, or will create such seamless paths between their services and the Internet that the average user will not be able to tell the difference.

In addition, I did not have a convenient and reliable way to personally test the book-oriented software I came across in my research.

Here are some home movies from my journeys.

Reel One: Online Services for BookLovers Are Not Cheap Fun

Being online still costs too much for most booklovers, whether you are searching for or providing information. I am not talking about e-mail, which is worth the bother because it is cheap to use and enables you to communicate with an increasing number of booklovers all over the world. I am talking about the hardware, software, online services, training, and midnight grief connected with getting online to browse different sites or participate in group discussions.

Most of the booklovers I met who spend a lot of time using the resources of the Electronic Book and Library either make their living from the information or are subsidized in some manner. About every publisher, researcher, editor, and author I know spends time every day online, mining information they can sell in books and magazine articles, or using e-mail to communicate with clients and colleagues. True, some of them spend more time than can be justified by the pursuit of profits, but business users are able to write off the cost.

The rare book dealers, bookstore owners, and publishers have swarmed to the Internet, and their collective presence grows every day. My own impression is that the used and rare book people are seeing profits faster than their new book counterparts or the publishers. This is because each dealer has a unique and constantly changing inventory, and the collectors and other dealers know that they have to search for the books they want. Searching the "buy" and "sell" listings in print catalogs has been part of the book dealer's life for decades, so it has not been a big deal to move those activities into the electronic marketplace.

The dealers and collectors also appreciate the speed and convenience. A request or offer will be seen by thousands of potential buyers and sellers in a matter of hours. Also, because online services have dramatically lowered the cost of conducting business with overseas booklovers, even one-person operations can go international in a big way.

To sell new books, which already can be ordered through most existing bookstores, and to promote new books that no one knows about yet, are bigger challenges. The stores and publishers that seem to be doing the best are those that already had a strong following before they went online; for these book businesses, online sales are gravy. The niche stores and publishers, whose customers are a small but active market AND are likely to use online services because they are already computer-literate, also do well. Despite the problems, most business owners feel they have to be present online, with the assumption of future profits, as the markets grow and tools become more sophisticated.

Other booklovers you will find online are the members of the scholarly, professional, and trade associations relating to books and librarians. The Internet is *thick* with librarians. Just about every organization listed in this book uses e-mail and has web sites to inform their membership and promote their causes to the general public. The most exciting use is the trend toward making the technical and scholarly libraries of their organizations available on the Internet. Much of this information is available nowhere else. The costs of these sites are paid by the membership and have become a necessity for even small groups with only local memberships.

Subsidized BookLovers Online

The subsidized booklovers range from college professors, whose tools and time are paid for by their institution, to students of all ages, who have access to their school's equipment and computer accounts. These booklovers aren't seeking a profit from their online time, but they also do not write a check every month to the company providing the services. Mom, the graduate department, or an employer is picking up the tab. In the case of students and children, it is easy for them to forget that all of this cool electronic gear did not come down the chimney with Santa Claus. (And when did you finally realize who paid for that shiny, new bike?)

My impressions might seem to contradict the conventional wisdom that everyone in the world is going on the Internet. Until recently, "everyone" was graduate students, professors, Unix hackers, and government officials. Now, "everyone" is businesspeople, researchers, students, and all flavors of computer enthusiasts. But I have watched most of my college-educated, middle-class friends spend *months* getting online. ("But the salesperson *swore* I did not need an upgrade to use this software.") And, as most of the reports I have read underscored, just because 30,000 people visit a computer site every day doesn't mean they spend enough money online to net the site owner any profit.

A lot of people are still subsidizing the diggings in this gold rush. As in the collectable book business, it is the people selling the tools who are making most of the reliable money, not the people panning for sparkling ore.

Online in Small Bites

The biggest mistake I have seen average booklovers and home librarians make is to buy equipment and services before they know what they are doing. If you are intrigued by what is online and want to know more, you have several sources of cheap, if not free, help.

Are you blessed with friends and relatives who will let you learn on their equipment? (It is considered good form to offer to pay for the time, which is usually only a dollar or two an hour at the most.) Make sure you are not just getting a quickie lesson; you want to spend several hours with your hands on the keyboard, seeing if this makes sense to you. Do the exploration in several sessions, but spend enough time every time to get confused and have to ask lots of questions. Also, if you know nothing about computers, it is very useful to make lots of mistakes and see what grief your friend goes through to fix whatever you did. *If the software blows up, it is never the user's fault.*

Other good resources are the academic and library institutions in your community, although you don't want to just take classes. You want the time to figure things out on your own. My belief is that unless you have a hefty budget to blow and lots and lots of time to spend, you should not buy any computer equipment to get online until you have become comfortable with this world on other people's machines. You should mess around in both Macintosh® and Windows® environments, (which are your main choices these days), preview several different online services, and not just rely on the Internet; all this before you spend a dime.

Reel Two: Online Services Are Mostly Junk but So Are Most Books

Online media is being shaped by people who want their information in flash-card format with lots of colored lights. But, to be fair, most of the books that are published each year are not of the highest quality either. And you know what? THEY NEVER WERE! Physical memory has been flawed for thousands of years. Older people in each generation start noticing the mistakes because that is what older people do: Notice mistakes. Now that I am spending less time dealing with raging hormones and more time savoring the life of the mind, I find myself mentally blue-penciling the classics.

"Why *did* Kipling use *that* word," I fume.

The Internet and other online services are full of wrong information. There are thousands of sites, filled with pictures of pets and personal autobiographies of no interest outside of a family reunion. A spiritual kinship exists between self-indulgent online sites and the vanity presses, which overcharge authors for publishing their books.

Also, as the professional librarians have warned us for years, online services are not cataloged. Librarians find it amusing that someone will spend an expensive five hours hunting on the World Wide Web for data that a research librarian could retrieve from a reference book in minutes. They are also extremely concerned that students are being taught how to harvest the Internet, not how to critically judge the reliability of the data and opinions they discover.

Another sin is that indexing is not complete. Interesting sites can be "lost" when they are mysteriously deleted from the indexes used by major search programs, and new sites can take months to include. Also, very few people bother to delete information about dead resources, so a good percentage of the resources you find will have vanished before you have a chance to check them out.

What about all the book-related *listservs, chat rooms,* and *newsgroups?* These are all online means for booklovers to share information and conversation with a group of people; what you type in response to someone else's entry might be read by one person, or one thousand. Participants discuss everything from removing cat urine from leather book covers to the history of the pun to the application of copyright law to an unpublished diary. The upside is that every group swarms with kind, brilliant, good-humored, and articulate people who act as if they were put on earth to help you solve your book problems. The downside is that the online services are also infected with mean-spirited, pompous, and just plain nasty people who love to take offense at the most innocent remarks. Even the scholarly online groups harbor unmedicated demons.

Outside of the scholarly and professional association sites, which are worth the cost of admission for the booklover who wants to do serious research, most of the award-winning commercial sites I visited do not live up to their implicit promise of "everything about the book world."

I have found more than one commercial site guilty of not linking to significant other sites that are the competition. This contradicts decades of friendly cooperation among most booksellers, who take pride in directing a customer to another store. I found one glaring case of an online bookstore that did not list a competing service's published book. Also, the commercial sites tend to be limited to the needs of the booklover who buys only bestsellers and genre fiction.

Also—and this is perhaps my biggest complaint about the organization of information on most sites—the content focuses on the medium. This means, for example, that a major university library in Wisconsin does not list the physical location of the library in its web site, because, you know, it doesn't matter; because, you know, we are, like, online. Cosmic. After forty-five minutes of reading every piece of posted information (I timed it for your edification), I called directory assistance (none of the listed phone numbers I tried connected me with a human being). I finally reached a student working at a circulation desk; she had to go outside and read the address off the front of the building. My nefarious purpose, by the way, was to send the library a donation of a book I had written.

Too many web sites list information only about other web sites. The designers forget there is a physical world where an online booklover, browsing on a public terminal in a library, might want to print out a list of names and addresses.

Online Services That Make It All Worthwhile

Following is my short list of the web sites I visited over and over, the ones I squealed about in pleasure. What is nice is that these web sites will lead to great books and to other quality sites, both on and off the Internet. This is not to say that people I did not list aren't wonderful, you understand. This is just my opinion on a warm summer morning in 1996.

I did not find a single scholarly or academic web site that I did not like. These web sites, which tend to be run by graduate students with no social lives or tenured professors who can do what they want anyway, are light on fancy graphics and dense with all kinds of useful information, including learned papers, announcements of meetings, and totally engrossing discussions. My personal faves.

But how to find the best of the book- and home library-related web sites? My favorite source for information on scholarly and book arts information online is the *Oak Knoll* web site. Behind every great web site is a great person, and Oak Knoll's treasure is Esther Fan. She has gathered hundreds of pieces of information about magazines, organizations, societies, associations, and other web sites, with a special emphasis on book arts, book history, fine book scholarship, and book collecting. Also, she has the information organized so that you can print out a useful list of names and addresses; the information is not limited to resources only online. And the pages are legible. The web site address is *http://www.oakknoll.com.*

What if you are looking for new books? *Amazon.com Books* has organized almost everything in print so that you can search by different methods, such as ISBN number, title, author, and subject. Other commercial sites have similar search programs, but I like Amazon's the best.

Like any other system, it is not absolutely perfect; I checked on a book last night that is technically out of print, but is available through other online bookstores, and Amazon did not list it. But I have found books that I thought were long gone, the same editions of books with different titles, and books that have skipped around among several publishers. I also found a number of books that are probably going out of print but are still warehoused by publishers. They will also tell you via e-mail if a book in your selected category has been made available. And most of what they sell is discounted. The current web site address is *http://www.amazon.com.*

What if you are looking for a discussion about books, particularly collecting, selling, repairing, and locating used fine books? I had the most fun on *bibliophile*, the listserv moderated by Shoshana Edwards (see her words of wisdom earlier in this chapter). Most of the thousands of messages you will read are about buying and selling used, and some new, books. But booklovers should scan it for the wonderful discussions regarding the book world. I have learned about book thieves, conferences in England, removing soot from rare volumes, pricing books, book fairs, and the identity of authors and publishers. Amateurs and newcomers are treated kindly, for the most part, but the conversations can get spirited. There is a modest yearly subscription rate.

The related web site features the wares of book dealers from around the globe; it is the best place to hook up with the *bibliophile* discussion group. The web site address is *http://www.auldbooks.com/biblio/index.html.*

Resources for the Post-Gutenberg-Era BookLover

Other Online Sites

When web sites are shifted from computer to computer, the dogs of havoc are unleashed. Links collapse, and booklovers surfing the Internet curse. These addresses are current as I enter these characters: Good luck. For the associations listed in these pages, contact them firsthand to learn their current web site addresses and the correct nomenclatures. Some sites have changed addresses several times since I started researching this book.

BookWeb™ is the web site for the American Booksellers Association (see Chapter V). It features information for publishers, booksellers, and booklovers. The web site address is *http://www.ambook.org.*

The American Library Association web site (see Chapter XI) can lead you to information about library community, including a bookstore of ALA publications. The web site address is *http://www.ala.org.*

Bookport and the Internet Book Fair provide links to many resources in the book and publishing communities, including book fairs, online editions of books, and antiquarian booksellers. The web site address is *http://www/bookport.com.*

BookWire™ is one of the seminal sites for the new book and publishing communities online. The web site address is *http://www.bookwire.com.*

BookZone provides online catalogs the book catalogs of more than 600 publishers, plus publishing resources, book news, and classifieds. The web site address is *http://bookzone.com.*

LISZT claims to have a list of 54,787 e-mail discussion groups, located on 1812 sites, as of August 1996. The web site address is *http://www.liszt.com.*

The Publishers Marketing Association (see Chapter V) provides a place to learn about hundreds of independent publishers and their books. The web site address is *http://www/pma-online.org.*

ReadersNdex provides direct links to books and publishers. The web site address is *http://www/readersndex.com.*

The Virtual Book Shop® is a starting point for linking with booksellers who specialize in rare, antiquarian, first edition, and collectible books. The web site address is *http://www.virtual.bookshop.com.*

At the Scholarly Societies web site are the location of hundreds of scholarly societies. The web site address is *http://www.lib.uwaterloo.ca/society/webpages.html.*

Books for the Electronic Community

The proliferation of Gutenberg-era books about the end of the Gutenberg-era book, computers, online services, etc., presents a delicious irony for booklovers. Hundreds of books are available about the Internet, CD-ROMs, and online services, most of which are either too technical or not very good. These kinds of books have a brief half-life, which starts ticking away as soon as the ink hits the page, so I have only chosen a scant few; magazines are a better source of up-to-date information about what is happening in the new electronic memory market.

As with the books about conservation and the book arts, there is a limit to how much you can learn without the help of several knowledgeable technology-savvy human beings. I have found that the percentage of computer consultants who are reliable and effective is about the same as the percentage of auto mechanics you want to bring your car to a second time.

The Book Lover's Guide to the Internet. Evan Morris. *Fawcett Columbine, $12.95 paper, ISBN 0-449-91070-9.*

An easy-to-understand introduction to Internet resources, focusing mostly on resources for readers and the acquisition of new books. The big commercial web sites are here, as are listings of the different online discussion groups. Lacking are the resources for collectors, book arts, and conservators.

The Little Online Book. Alfred Glossbrenner. Illustrated by John Grimes. *Peachpit Press, $17.95 paper, ISBN 1-56609-130-6; 2414 Sixth Street, Berkeley, CA 94710; (510) 548-4393; fax (510) 548-5991.*

Alfred Glossbrenner has been educating average folks about information services for almost fifteen years. His many books provide a gateway into the Information Age, and, unlike many of his contemporaries, he is not fixated on the Internet as the only game in town. This is a good book for technology beginners.

The Online 100. Mick O'Leary. *Pemberton Press Books, $22.95 paper, ISBN 0-910965-14-5; Online, Inc., 462 Danbury Road, Wilton, CT 06897-2126; (800) 248-8466; fax (203) 761-1444.*

A directory of the most important online information services, with lengthy descriptive reviews, facts about cost, and availability through different media. Although some of the services listed in the year-old edition I saw have already changed, this is still a valuable book for the researcher or technical booklover who needs their data hot. The prices may dismay amateurs who still think information is free.

Magazines for the Electronic Community

There are, at last count, 14 million different publications relating to the use of the Internet to find books about baking chocolate chip cookies; I did not have time to research any further. To make your life a little easier, I have picked two magazines. Most of the large companies and computer services have their own newsletters and publications, so I looked for general-interest subscription magazines that were written for the average bright person and that had useful information. Just to make sure, I subscribed to each for at least a year to see if I continued to find them interesting and useful. Both survived the test.

internet world. PO Box 713, Mt. Morris, IL 61054; e-mail: info@mecklemedia.com; monthly; $29/year.

It was difficult to find a magazine about online services (*internet world* does cover services besides the Internet and World Wide Web, and many of the top vendors advertise in their pages) that addresses the needs of home computer users, not just hackers. I like the friendly redundancy, meaning they assume that any issue you pick up is the first issue you have seen on the subject; the many educational articles; and the interesting lists of web sites. Every issue will whet your appetite for more online adventures.

WIRED. PO Box 191826, San Francisco, CA 94119-9866; (415) 222-6200; fax (415) 222-6399; e-mail: subscriptions@wired.com; monthly; $39.95/year.

This magazine will pin back your ears. The graphics and language bleed off the page, with disregard for most of the conventions of the Gutenberg era. But it is not just adolescent ramblings. The top thinkers of the age are invited to participate in weighty interviews, while readers mouth off about the concerns of the digital age: Woman, Man, Birth, Death, Infinity, The Future of the Book. Cool web sites to visit. A tolerance for the vulgar language and images of the late twentieth-century is required.

Computerized BookLover Services

Interloc™

Interloc™ is part of a minor computer empire, serving the serious, collectible book community. The software is designed for the professional collector or dealer who needs an electronic marketplace; all of its related services focus on buying and selling. The organization runs training programs at sites around the country and demonstrates wares at book fairs as well. I sat through two demos of the main product, which combines software that resides in your machine and paid access to an active online market. I liked the service-minded and honest attitude of company president Richard Weatherford. Fees are tied to usage, and are affordable for people who treat their collections as business ventures. For free information, write **Interloc, Inc.**, PO Box 5, Southworth, WA 98386, or call Richard Weatherford at (360) 871-3617, or e-mail him at weatherf@interloc.com.

CD-ROMs and the Virtual Book

I am suspicious of the lifespan of the CD-ROM as a technology product. Although it can pack huge amounts of data into a small space, and it is neat to have your encyclopedia talk to you and play movies, why have a dead piece of data taking up room on your desk, when you can have the same information live on the Internet, a commercial service, or a database? My sense from spies in the industry is that the CD-ROM bubble has burst and, with new online technologies, including the monster collaborations among cable companies, phone companies, television production companies, book publishers, libraries, and whoever else is selling information, entertainment, and access, the CD-ROM may not be a significant part of your home library in ten years.

On the other hand, the virtual book, second to e-mail, is the most important reason to be online. There are more than a score of organizations devoted to putting the full text of books online, from new, self-published poetry to the Greek classics. Some charge; others give the work away, just for the sheer pleasure of sharing information.

My favorite is the Gibson Digital Library. It can connect you with the Gutenberg Project, which plans to have 10,000 texts online by the end of 2001. (The Gutenberg Project can use your financial help, by the way. Write to Project Gutenberg/BU, PO Box 2782, Champaign, Illinois 61825-2782.) The web site address for the Gibson Digital Library is *http://kcmo.com.gdl.*

❖

... most of you learned to read
by being read to out loud
by fond older family members.
page 249.

Chapter XIII — Children and Books

Being a Guide for Parents and Other People Who Love Children and Who Want to Infect Them With a Passionate Love for Books.

The Gift

It is a birthday, a holiday, an anniversary, or a celebration, and you want to give a book to a child you love. Just as there is not only one kind of love, there is not one way to decide which book to give.

Models based on childhood development theories (and it is very difficult at times to remember that these are only theoretical models, not edicts from a Supernatural Being) provide year-by-year guidelines. The more obtuse of these have phrases like "enhances the immature ontogony vocabulary functionality modules." At least, that is what I think it said.

> *I made a deal with my youngest daughter when she was age six. In exchange for no television in the house EVER, she could have any book she wanted as long as she read it. We now have around 3,000 hardcover books in my little house, and they are pushing me out. When the second child came along, there was no choice as to TV. Both girls were raised without it, and as a result, are voracious readers and have a depth of knowledge far beyond their contemporaries. Sure, they have missed some good stuff and are not up-to-date on the latest fads, but the fads pass and the books remain.*
> —Philip LaBerge, writer, Concord, GA

At the other extreme is the reassuring pap of recommendations that say nothing, but say it nicely. One nameless expert suggested "buying books appropriate to the age of the child," and then moved on to more interesting topics, like the color of the gift wrap.

The secret of giving a book to a child is simple: Know the Child, and Know Children's Books.

Buying a book is part of the relationship you have with that particular short human being. It is where your awareness of the child as a full-fledged personality with likes and dislikes is tested. The child, on opening your gift, will know if you have taste, wit, and sensitivity. Your gift will be met by the child's discovery of who you are and your likes and dislikes; the child will be able to tell if he or she is visible to you. Have you been paying attention to what the child says and does?

The best book present I received before the age of eighteen was a book of poetry. We had just moved to a new state only three weeks before my fourteenth birthday, so I knew my gifts would be limited to those from the immediate family. This meant new clothes for school, since I would not yet have made friends my own age, who would know what a teenager really wants.

My father's new business partner, a charismatic and gallant Welshman named Hugh Wilson, took me out for ice cream. Unlike family, who tend to take one for granted, Hugh asked me questions about myself as if I were important.

So, when his book arrived, my family assumed that the nerdy youngest was getting another science text. Instead, the thick volume was a deluxe version of *John Brown's Body*, Stephen Vincent Benét's Pulitzer opus. Hugh had taken the time to find out about my new interest in poetry. The fact that he also chose a book that was an important adult book with some hot love scenes made a big impression on an adolescent girl. It was a book that mattered because I mattered to Hugh as a real person, even though he had only just met me.

Does this mean you should never give a book to a child just because you love the book? Like any other gift, the question is, whom do you intend to benefit? If you want to give a piece of yourself, be prepared for it to be rejected. If you really can't resist, make sure the child understands that it is a keepsake book, one that tells the child something about you, whether or not the child takes to it. It helps if you can share an anecdote about why you loved the book, or if the book becomes a starting point for storytelling.

Will the child be likely to read a hidden moral lecture into your intention? A book on fashion might be welcomed by the girl who fancies a career in modeling, but it might crush her sister who fights with her mother about wearing dresses.

Is the book a perfect gift for the child, only you are five years too late? What does it say to your favorite nephew that you forgot he passed through his obsession with cowboys months ago, and now is into football?

Sending a book to a child you have never met is fraught with danger. It is too likely that your impressions are based on what the parents say, and you can be placed in the unwitting role of "Uncle Tim, who wants you to be a teacher just like him," as the distant voice of the parents' own unspoken wishes.

Knowing children's literature is tricky. Spend time in the children's section of local bookstores and libraries. Without getting arrested for being strange in a bookstore or library around children, you can listen in on the conversations children are having with their parents about books.

Which books are causing children to squirm off of laps versus the ones that have the kids totally mesmerized? When are the adults dominating the conversation, telling the children how much they ought to like a certain book, and when are the children telling the parent about the joys of the book? Which books are being toted to parents over and over again, with small demanding people asking for them to be read out loud? Which books can't the librarian and bookstore manager keep on the shelves? Old favorites can make great gifts, but it behooves you to keep current, especially with older children.

Storytelling

Storytelling prepares children for loving books. It helps build their vocabularies for reading, and it whets their appetites for more stories.

First, there is tribal storytelling, as when you get to tell your family once again about how Rex the cocker spaniel ate the entire Thanksgiving dinner. These are the stories that bind us to our family trees. There is creative storytelling, like my mother's made-up stories about an Irish setter whose big feet could walk on top of deep snow. Even now, I can remember curling up in the back of the family car, listening to the adventures of Lopchik, the Wonder Dog.

My mother often read to my sister and me before bed, and I very early got the idea that books held the key to worlds of light far beyond the tiresome life of frustrated dreams. If you have a small child, make sure you have a chair that's big enough for both of you, a comfortable lap, and a pleasant reading voice.
—Philip Normand, graphic designer and illustrator, Denver, CO
Philip Normand ©1996

Then, there is storytelling that is the reading aloud of stories in books, and the child begins to figure out that the magic words are coming from the pages. Most children will want to hear their favorite stories over and over again, until they begin to tell the stories themselves, moving fingers along sentences in imitation of the storyteller.

And just when the parent or big brother or grandmother cannot stand to read the story one more time, the child has learned to read. Mixed with the sense of relief is the sense of loneliness, underlined by the empty lap.

I will bet that most of you learned to read by being read to out loud by fond older family members. Storytelling should be part of every family home library, and it shouldn't stop when children can read on their own. Storytelling can be straight oratory, or a collaborative effort, with many interruptions and sidebars. Let the little guys read stories to the big guys. Let family members take turns reading to each other. Read the classics out loud and discuss them. Read books that surprise everybody.

The sound of a family home library can be the moth-wing whisper of turning pages, or the soft hesitant voice of the eldest son reading out loud from Ray

Bradbury. Language saturates the air of a well-used library, condensing into storms of words, whether from Shakespeare or an old Joni Mitchell song.

How to Make Sure Your Kids Will Hate Books

1. Lecture them frequently and at great length about how they ought to read for the Good of the Future of the Republic. Discourage them from thinking that reading has anything to do with personal pleasure. Reading books should be seen as a civic duty such as voting, attending school board meetings, picking up trash on Neighborhood Clean-Up Day, or obeying the speed limit.

2. Ridicule their taste in books. Put children down for reading books that are "too childish." Carefully check the "age-specific" information on the cover of the book or in the copyright information, and make sure the child knows how he or she stacks up against the norms. You might have to throw out books they love while they are away at school, to wean them from those that are too simple.

3. Likewise, ridicule them if they fall in love with one author and only read books by that author. You read all the books by certain mystery authors or popular self-help gurus because of the superior writing style of the author. Convince yourself that young people cannot possibly have the aesthetic sophistication to prefer one author to another.

4. Likewise, ridicule them if they read the same book over and over again. You read the same books repeatedly so that you can relive the magic moments in a favorite book. Children do so because they are lazy and don't want to challenge themselves with new experiences.

5. Likewise, ridicule their reading habits in front of other people, such as their friends and adults in authority. Make the issue of reading another battle-front in the family.

6. Make sure that they understand that all books, including the cheapest of paperbacks, are to be treated as if books were more important than people. To this end, children should never be exposed to the bad habits of booklovers, such as reading in the bathtub, reading while eating, reading in bed, reading on picnics where books may get grass stains, etc. Instead, have your child focus on the importance of white cotton gloves and deacidification. Send them off to book conservator camp as soon as possible.

7. Never read to your child. You are a busy person with lots of important responsibilities, and the child will never remember your reading to them anyway. For that matter, never read out loud to anyone. Never read romantic love poetry out loud to your significant other; never read thrilling mysteries out loud to your family. They should never hear your voice caressing language or listen to you break up with emotion over a touching or funny passage.

8. Never take your children to bookstores or libraries. They should learn that reading is something they ought to do, but not something adults choose to do.

9. Never tell your child about books you love. Books should not be a discussion topic at meals or bedtime.

10. Never buy your child books, but if you do, make sure they are books you think the child ought to read, because some expert told you so.

11. And never, ever let your child catch you reading. Never let her see you leave dishes unwashed, bills unpaid, lawns unmowed, phone calls unanswered, television shows unwatched. Never let him see you compelled to finish a chapter, even when dinner is on the table. Never let her hear you say that you prefer reading to renting a video.

The Librarian's Puppy
By Susan Hartman, technical services librarian
Grand Junction, CO

About three weeks after moving into a new house, I went out and adopted a puppy. If you're one of those people who saves everything imaginable, you know what kind of a field day that six-week-old puppy had!

We got the bookcase up in the living room and decided which books to fill it up with several evenings earlier. This particular evening we decided to eat dinner first and work later, so I was busily working away in the kitchen. I looked up just in time to see Munchkin (the puppy) coming around the corner into the kitchen carrying her new discovery: a book.

Now this wasn't just any book from the bookcase—it was a kid's book, and it was bigger than she was. She was struggling to hold it in her mouth and still see where she was going, but she was just as proud as punch with this giant treasure.

After gently taking the book from her and reprimanding her with something about Mommy's books, we headed into the other room where we had been working through boxes. I cut the spine and covers off an old Reader's Digest Condensed Book that was on the weeded book stack, cut the stories apart, and gave them to her. She now had five books all her very own to carry around or to do with whatever she wanted.

I thought she would chew them to shreds before the week was out, but for the next two years she very often greeted me with one of those books. She never chewed them up and only on rare occasions would a page come loose, but they were one of her favorite toys. She's the only dog I know who was given her own books—and took care of them! ❖

Intershelving
**By James LaRue, director, Douglas Public Library District
Castle Rock, CO**

In the roughly 150 years that public libraries have been around, there have been at least two real revolutions in service. For a long time after public libraries began, all the books were kept in areas that were open only to staff. When you asked for a book, the librarian got it for you. If you wanted another one, you asked again. This was called "closed stacks."

Somewhere around the early 1900s, that changed. We adopted "open stacks." The books were set free, the people invited in to browse. Not surprisingly, the use of public libraries soared.

The second revolution was a wildly radical idea called "the children's library." At the time it was advanced (around 1930), the presence of children was barely tolerated in public libraries. Whereas the "open stacks" notion was adopted fairly rapidly across the country, children's materials were admitted only grudgingly to public library shelves. But once they arrived, there was again a big jump in library use.

These days, a public library that didn't have kids' books wouldn't seem like much of a library at all. Librarians and the people they serve have come to understand the importance of early and frequent exposure to books.

Nonetheless, there are some problems with maintaining a discrete children's collection. Sometimes, separating materials makes sense. Jumbling the picture books in with fiction for older children, for instance, would just confuse and inconvenience people. But lately I wonder if it isn't time for a third revolution in service: combining or intershelving the adults' and children's nonfiction.

Let's look at the adult perspective first. About ten years ago, I got curious about the Black Plague. When I went looking for books about it, I was dismayed to find mostly scholarly tomes. But then I saw a reference in the computer catalog: There was also a book in the children's area. Feeling a little foolish (this was before I had a child of my own), I wandered into the section. To my surprise, there were several books on the subject. So I checked out all of them, and read a couple over lunch.

While I cannot recommend reading about the bubonic plague as an appetizer, this is when I made a great discovery. Children's nonfiction is some of the best, most wide-ranging, writing you'll find anywhere. Children's books concentrate on the most essential and interesting facts. Then they stop. I like that.

Since then, I've realized that a lot of adults come in looking for something, then leave without it, just because they didn't look at the kids' books. Or to be more precise: They don't find what they really want, because we've hidden it from them in another section.

Now let's take the case of a child. Suppose he or she is looking for books on hamsters. There are plenty of hamster books in the kid's section, but there are a lot of them in the adult section, too. Again, just as some adults feel foolish in the children's area, some kids are intimidated by the adult shelves. So they go home without the books they need, too.

Here's another advantage to a combined collection of nonfiction: If you're an adult with a reading problem, you're more likely to find something you can use. Or on the other side, if you're a child who's ready for a more challenging book on a subject that interests you, it's right there. In brief, combined shelving provides a broad range of materials and reading levels, all assembled in just one location. Add to this the staff perspective: Why catalog, mark, and shelve books on the exact same subject in two different places?

We gave this a try at our Highlands Ranch Library (located in a suburb of Denver) since it opened in 1991. It was an experiment. How well has it worked? On the whole, very well.

There are some problems, of course. The shelves probably get a little messier. And the thinner children's books sometimes are hard to find if they're wedged between two adult books.

On the other hand, when libraries went to open stacks, a lot of books got stolen. And when we let the kids in, it got noisier. But it just might be that a third revolution would have the same kind of positive payoff: greater convenience for the whole family, and a consequent jump in use.

I think it's worth it. Look for this to happen in all of our libraries over the next several years. And then look for it to happen around the country.❖

Books not suitable for children, as well as poisons, should be filed at the very top of the wall shelves. Books especially for children should be filed near the floor, unless your family includes a puppy, rabbit, or ten-month-old baby who might chew the books.
—Clara Lou Humphrey, writer and speaker, Lakewood, CO
Clara Lou Humphrey © 1996

The Worst Thing That Can Happen to a Book
By Sharon W. Saxton, English teacher, Santa Ana, CA

When I first began teaching, I indulged my passion for books. At a time when I paid $180 a month for an apartment fashionably close to the beach, I spent $200 a month on children's books. I bought beautifully illustrated editions of *Sleeping Beauty* and *Snow White*, fairy stories illustrated by Arthur Rackham, everything of Leo and Diane Dillon, stories about teddy bears, and the collected works of Beatrix Potter in both English and French. I rationalized that someday I would have children of my own, and this expenditure was an intellectual bank account I was starting for them.

A few years later, it became clinically clear that I would never be able to engender the readers for my library. Shortly thereafter, Kelly and then Patrick joined my brother's family. If I was not to be a mother, I would be a literary fairy godmother. Each birthday, Christmas, and special holiday activated its own gift of a beautiful book or two or ten. But they all seemed to disappear. Each time I returned, I noticed no evidence of the gifts of the previous visit.

Finally, one trip revealed the hiding place. As I wrapped my coat around a hanger and prepared to thrust it into a closet, the stacks of books I had brought winked to me from the back of the closet in dusty oblivion. I was visibly shaken. My sister-in-law, observing my reaction, came to see the cause.

"Oh," she shrugged, "messy things, books. Leave them down where the kids can get a hold of them, and they will be strewn underfoot. Can't have that now, can we?"

She walked away purposefully. The children and I stood peering mutely into the black maw at the silent treasures, in the dark, beyond our reach—our books.   ❖

Storytelling abilities complement an interest in reading. Ask the children in your life to tell you the stories they find in the books they read, and share your favorite stories with them. Tell them what you liked about their stories, but also tell them what you liked about the way they told the stories. Another extension of reading is theater. Some children find it easier to act out a story with puppets.   ❖

Resources for BookLovers Who Love Children

The Children's Book Council. 568 Broadway, Suite 404, New York,
NY 10012; (212) 966-1990; fax (212) 966-2073; e-mail: cbkkidlit@aol.com or
cbkkidlit@msn.com

The Children's Book Council is a nonprofit trade association of children's book
publishers. The purpose of the Council is to promote the use and enjoyment of
children's trade books and to disseminate information about books for young people about trade book publishing. It offers a number of printed materials, including
"Children's Choices," a bibliographic list of the year's most popular books selected
by 10,000 children nationwide, issued by the International Reading Association–
CBC Joint Committee. Send a 9" x 12" stamped self-addressed envelope to: International Reading Association, PO Box 8139, Newark, Delaware 19714-8139.

Magazines About Children and Books

Book Links: *Connecting Books, Libraries, and Classrooms.*
434 West Downer, Aurora, IL 60506; (708) 892-7465; bimonthly; $22/year.

The American Library Association's resource for classroom teachers about
books. For laypeople, this means access to information about the latest children's
books and book-related resources, including magazines, contests, and software.

Children's Book Review. PO Box 5082, Brentwood, TN 37024-5082;
(800) 543-7220, (615) 776-3172; fax (615) 776-3256; 4x/year; $12.90/year.

An oversized, full-color magazine of ads and reviews for all kinds of children's
books. The graphics are enticing, with color shots of the covers and, when appropriate, samples of illustrations and photographs.

The Horn Book Magazine: *Recommending Books for Children and
Young Adults.* 11 Beacon Street, Boston, MA 02108; (617) 227-1555;
fax (617) 523-0299; 6x/year; $35/year.

An extremely intelligent source of information about children's literature,
with an emphasis on the finest books available in both fiction and nonfiction.
The reviews are longer and more detailed than you find in many book review
magazines, and, although the tone is sometimes scholarly, if not "librariany," the
average person interested in children's books will find much of value, even if he
does not work in a "real" library or school. See Chapter II for information about
how to order a real horn book.

Books About Children and Books

Some of these books focus on homeschooling, a growing force in improving nonfiction for children. Whether or not you school your children at home, the emphasis that the homeschooling movement puts on reading and books provides all parents and children with useful book lists and suggestions.

A Book of Your Own: *Keeping a Diary or Journal.* Carla Stevens. *Clarion Books, $7.95 paper, ISBN 0-395-67887-0.*
A simple and moving book to encourage readers to become writers. The author has collected some interesting examples from the youthful diaries of writers, famous people, and fictional characters, and has good advice aimed at the young person.

Books and Libraries. Jack Knowlton. Pictures by Harriett Barton. *HarperTrophy, $5.95 paper, ISBN 0-06-446153-X.*
For a small, illustrated children's book on libraries and books, this has a surprisingly complete history of the book, with references to everything from clay tablets to computers. Look for it in school and children's libraries.

Classroom Publishing: *A Practical Guide to Enhancing Student Literacy.* Laurie King and Dennis Stovall. *Blue Heron Publishing. $22.95 paper, ISBN 0-936085-52-5.*
The best experience of my public school career was working on the school newspaper. Learning about newsletters, newspapers, and books by producing real products that were read and judged by my peers gave me a sense of accomplishment that has lasted my whole life. If your schools are not providing these opportunities for your children, this book gives resources and guidance, whether or not the work is done in a formal classroom.

Continuing Education Press. Portland State University, PO Box 1394, Portland, OR 97207; (800) 547-8887, extension 4891, (503) 725-4891.
Inga Dubay and Barbara Getty have created almost a dozen books about handwriting and calligraphy, including **Write Now:** *A Complete Self Teaching Program for Better Handwriting ($12.95 plus $4.00 shipping and handling, ISBN 0-876780-89-3)* and **Italic Letters:** *Calligraphy and Handwriting ($15.95 plus $4.00 shipping and handling, ISBN 0-876780-91-5)*, that could transform the written communication skills of your entire family. Their basic model is an easy-to-learn and extremely attractive and distinctive italic style, which is superior in several ways to the systems most of us learned.

Both books address an important aspect of the book arts—hand lettering—and are the kind of books the whole family can use. As someone who was told by her third grade teacher that she would never make it to fourth grade because her handwriting was so bad, these books were a revelation.

Family Book Sharing Groups: *Start One in Your Neighborhood!*
Marjorie R. Simic and Eleanor C. Macfarlane. *EDINFO Press, $6.95 paper,*
ISBN 1-883790-11-5; Indiana University, PO Box 5953, Bloomington, IN 47407;
(800) 925-7853.

Unlike other guides to reading groups, this one focuses on families and children. A variety of activities are proposed, and the authors cleverly provide a structured agenda for several meetings. This is a useful book for families and organizations that support family activities, such as churches and neighborhood associations. It is also useful for homeschooling families who are looking for collaborative projects.

How to Stock a Home Library Inexpensively. Third Edition. Jane A. Williams.
Bluestocking Press, $14.95 paper, ISBN 0-942617-18-5.

I became acquainted with Jane Williams several years ago, when we exchanged letters and phone calls about economics, book publishing, homeschooling, and book reviewing. (See a listing for her catalog at the end of this chapter.) This book focuses on catalogs and resources for homeschoolers, but you don't have to be a homeschooler to find useful ideas on buying books inexpensively, or finding resources for helping your children achieve.

My First Year in Book Publishing: *Real-World Stories From America's Book*
Publishing Professionals. Edited by Lisa Healy. Foreword by Samuel S. Vaughn.
Walker and Company, $11.95 paper, ISBN 0-8027-7425-3.

Honest and often humorous accounts of that first year in a new career, when everything is fresh and scary. The contributors share the mistakes they made, their triumphs, and why they went into book publishing in the first place. This book will broaden a young adult's idea of the book publishing industry, because it covers everything from writing to sales.

Raising a Reader: *Make Your Child a Reader for Life.* Paul Kropp.
Doubleday, $12.00 paper, ISBN 0-385-47913-1.

Now that you know what not to do, here are statistics, resources, recommended book and author lists, and reasonable expert advice to help you instill a love of reading in the children you influence in your life.

Write Your Own Curriculum: *A Complete Guide to Planning, Organizing and Documenting Homeschool Curriculums.* Jenifer O'Leary. *Whole Life Publishing Co., $12.95 paper, ISBN 1-883947-24-3; PO Box 936, Stevens Point, WI 54481-0936.*
Even if you don't homeschool your children, you may have to supplement your children's education at home. This book provides information about activities and resources, including texts, that can support any child's education.

Beginning Books for Children on the Books Arts

All of these book are well written, profusely illustrated, and reasonably priced. Many can be found in the teacher education section of your local bookstore or library. If you are lucky enough to have a teacher's resource store in your community, you will find these books and many more.

Get Set . . . GO: *Printing.* Ruth Thomson. *Children's Press, $4.95 paper, ISBN 0-516-47992-X.*

How to Make Cloth Books for Children: *A Guide to Making Personalized Books.* Anne Pellowski. Foreword by Robbie Fanning. *Chilton Book Company, $14.95 paper, ISBN 0-8019-8398-3.*

The Letter Book: *Fun Things to Make and Do With Letters.* Ivan Bulloch and Diane James. Photography by Toby Maudsley. *Simon and Schuster, $4.95 paper, ISBN 0-671-73887-9.*

Making Books: *A Step-by-Step Guide to Your Own Publishing.* Gillian Chapman and Pam Robson. *The Millbrook Press, $6.95 paper, ISBN 1-56294-840-7.*

Read! Write! Publish!: *Making Books in the Classroom.* Barbara Fairfax and Adela Garcia. Illustrated by Terri Rae. Edited by Janet Bruno. *Creative Teaching Press, $7.98 paper, ISBN 0-9917485-4-9.*

Step-by-Step Making Books. Charlotte Stowell. Illustrated by Jim Robins. *Kingfisher, $6.95 paper, ISBN 1-85697-518-5.*

If you want children to enjoy the book arts, set them up for success from the beginning. Keep projects simple, and don't confuse them with too many choices of materials at first. This will make clean-up easier, too. ❖

Papermaking Kits

(See Chapter III for a brief description of the papermaking process.) Each kit comes with instructions and a two-piece papermaking screen. The variations in price reflect the differences in packaging and in the construction of the screen.

Denise Fleming's Painting With Paper. Denise Fleming. *Henry Holt, $16.95, ISBN 0-8050-3528-1.*

This award-winning author shows how to create vivid art by placing wet, colored paper pulp directly onto the wood-framed papermaking screen. A brightly illustrated poster provides dozens of clever craft ideas.

Paper Anew. Woodrose Design. *$24.95. Distributed by Chasley, Inc., PO Box 19202, Seattle, WA 98109.*

The most elegant of the three kits. The emphasis is on pretty, natural-looking papers laced with botanical materials, such as seeds, leaves, and flower petals. (My kit included lavender petals and dried parsley!) In addition to the two-part papermaking screen, there is a mold to create cast papers. This kit will appeal to older children and adults with a strong interest in gardening and the decorative arts.

The Paper Book and Paper Maker. Shar Levine. Illustrated by Joe Weissmann. *Hyperion, $12.95, ISBN 1-56282-235-7.*

The plastic papermaking screen is sturdy and easy to clean, inviting lots of experimentation with natural dyes. The enclosed booklet includes a friendly history of paper, and several different paper-related crafts to try. Designed for younger children, ages five to ten.

Pop-Up Books

Many popular books for young children are, from the purist's point of view, not "real" books. Some adults grumble that children should be exposed to real books at an early age, and that children are shortchanged by adults who insist on buying them gimmicky books. Here are two pop-up books that defy the critics.

The Christmas Alphabet. Robert Sabuda. *Orchard Books, $21.95 cloth, ISBN 0-531-06857-9.*

Orchard is one of my very favorite children's publishers, and this book is their bestseller. The intricate and charming examples of papercraft that illustrate each letter are an extraordinary example of the book arts in a mass-produced book. A knowledgeable adult friend who examined the precision of the cuts told me seriously that the book would be impossible to manufacture!

Gutenberg's Gift: *A Book Lover's Pop-Up Book.* Nancy Willard. Illustrated by Bryan Leister. *Harcourt Brace, $20.00 paper, ISBN 0-15-200783-0.*

The author admits that the details of this little story were made up and presents the few facts that we really know about Gutenberg's life in a coda at the end of the book. The value here is twofold—in the richly colored illustrations and in the idea of books being something precious.

Book Catalogs for Children's Books

Are you liberal or conservative? Do you homeschool your children or send them to public school? Are you and your kids interested in religion, art, or science? The diversity of choices is dazzling if you decide you want to buy children's books through catalogs. One type of catalog listed is from publishers who are willing to sell books directly to the public. The other type is from bookstores and mail-order houses, which have selected books based on quality, price, or how they fit into a particular value system. Here is a sampling of both.

When buying books from catalogs, I suggest that you start by using the them to identify books that look and sound interesting to you and your children. Then use your local libraries to find the books and test them at home. Let the children help you decide if the book is worth more than two weeks' worth of reads.

August House Publishers. PO Box 3223, Little Rock, AR 72203; (800) 284-8784, (501) 372-5450; fax (501) 372-5579.

August House is devoted to books on storytelling, with collections organized around ethnicity and story type, and information about storytelling training techniques. The paperback editions are very affordable.

Bluestocking Press. PO Box 2030, Department 7, Shingle Springs, CA 95682-2030; (800) 959-8586, (916) 621-1123; fax (916) 642-9222.

Bluestocking focuses on books about history, government, and politics, with some emphasis on traditional, libertarian, and conservative viewpoints. The hundreds of books listed are often award-winning, with excellent writing and scholarship.

Charington House. PO Box 9661, Bradenton, FL 34206; (941) 746-3326; e-mail: 73307.2636@compuserve.com.

A mail-order catalog of fine books in several categories, covering picture books, multicultural, and special needs issues, such as illness, fear, and "being different."

Children's Book Press. 6400 Hollis Street, Suite 4, Emeryville, CA 94608; (510) 655-3395; fax (510) 655-1978.

For twenty years, the Children's Book Press has focused on multicultural literature for children. The picture books feature exciting imagery, influenced by the cultures they portray. Families from Asian, African, Jewish, Caribbean, and Hispanic cultures can find books that reflect the folklore, language, and lifestyles of their peoples. Many of the books are bilingual, with titles available in Spanish, Korean, Khmer (Cambodian), Vietnamese, and Chinese.

Chinaberry Book Service. 2180 Via Orange Way, Suite B, Spring Valley, CA 91978; (800) 776-2242, (619) 670-5200; fax (619) 670-5203.

This catalog organizes its hundreds of handpicked books into broad categories related to age and development, so that the neophyte has gentle guidance without guilt-provoking edicts.

Enjoy-A-Book Club. 555 Chestnut Street, Cedarhurst, NY 11516; (516) 569-0324; fax (516) 569-0830.

Jewish families who don't have access to big-city libraries or a well-stocked religious bookstore will appreciate this service-oriented company. Many of the books are award-winners, and all emphasize a strong, positive Jewish content.

The Family Travel Guides Catalogue. PO Box 6061, Albany, CA 94706-0061; (510) 527-5849.

The claim of this mail-order book catalog is that the books selected will help you "go anywhere with your kids." Some selections are organized by geographic regions, others by topic, such as general how-to information. Parents will appreciate the books and games designed to occupy hours in cars and motel rooms.

Free Spirit Publishing: *Self-Help for Kids®.* 400 First Avenue North, Suite 616–54, Minneapolis, MN 55401-1730; (800) 735-7323, (612) 338-2068; fax (612) 337-5050.

Books that focus on learning materials for improving the lives of families and children. Good materials for children who are experiencing personal crises.

Home Education Press. PO Box 1083, Tonasket, WA 98855; (800) 236-3278, (509) 486-1351; e-mail: homeedmag@aol.com.

In addition to books and pamphlets, Home Education Press publishes *Home Education* magazine (6x/year, $24/year). Their catalog is generous with its information on resources for homeschoolers, including support groups and resources.

John Muir Publications. PO Box 613, Santa Fe, NM 87504; (800) 888-7504; fax (505) 988-1680.

This press publishes several series that add a compelling twist to nonfiction topics with great graphics and photography. The Extremely Weird series focuses on animals that look and act weird, from bats to spiders. The Bizarre and Beautiful series does close-ups of parts of an animal's body, like tongues and eyes. The Rough and Ready series is devoted to cowboys, lawmen, and loggers.

Klutz®. 2121 Staunton Court, Palo Alto, CA 94306; (800) 558-8944; (415) 424-0739; fax (800) 524-4075.

Books, toys, and fun are integrated into a set of extremely silly and successful products. Face-painting, juggling, shadow puppets, and really cool science stuff. This is what happens when goofy people start a business out of their home and it accidently becomes successful.

Zephyr Press. 3316 North Chapel Avenue, PO Box 66006-B, Tucson, AZ 85728-6006; (520) 322-5090; fax (520) 323-9402.

Many books for children and families are available only through academic and school presses, which usually charge much higher prices than the so-called trade publishers. This press will sell to individuals, and the prices are moderate.

For the Compulsive Young Readers in Your Life

If you ever tried to read with a flashlight under the covers, you know how hard it is to manipulate book, blanket, and light. Here are three solutions.

Mini Beam and Read®. *EK Success Ltd., $11.95 suggested retail.*

This nifty little light goes around your neck and gives you a bright light, enough to read comfortably. Runs on two AA batteries, and comes with two extra lights.

Snakelight™. *Black & Decker®, $25.00 to $50.00 suggested retail.*

One of the best new household products in recent years. A bright beam sits in a sturdy, snaky device that can wrap around a tent pole or arm. Comes in several sizes.

Swivel-lite™. *Rayovac®, $12.00 suggested retail.*

A pivoting head rotates in a 180-degree arc. Perfect for holding up the top of the blanket while illuminating the entire area with an extra bright light.

A new trend in the book community is the appearance of young home librarians who decide to organize their collections for the benefit of friends and neighbors. The budding Carnegies seem to be fanatic readers who love to share. Of course, a concerned adult can find dozens of reasons to discourage this kind of philanthropy. What if a favorite book is damaged or lost forever? How much time will it take to organize the books? And will a frustrated soccer parent want to send the eager book-lover to junior library school to make sure the cataloging is done the right way? You can, if you like, suggest a trip to an art supply store for some book repair materials. Also, you can search for a children's librarian who wants to share in the fun and provide not more than fifteen minutes of really good advice. Otherwise, count your blessings. Then, ask your child if you might be issued a library card. Nothing will compliment your young librarian more than a sincere request from a favorite adult for the loan of a book from his or her personal collection.   ❖

❖

*Having good records
is the first rule of disaster management.
page 267.*

Chapter XIV — The Home Archives

Being a Revelation About the Differences Between Home Libraries and Home Archives, and Why You Should Care, With Special Resources for Preserving Your Personal History.

Stuff: Why You Can't Park the Car in Your Two-Car Garage Anymore

How much Stuff do you have? You know, Stuff. You bought, borrowed, inherited, and were given the books for your home library, but in addition you have created, inherited, and accumulated a lot of other Stuff (excuse the technical jargon). Stuff includes family photos, medical records, financial information, maps from trips, diaries, and letters. How about the notes from your children's teachers, term papers, and government records, such as passports and Social Security cards? Stuff is also magazines, file folders filled with newspaper clippings, sheet music, and business papers left over from your last three jobs.

Actually, that is just the Paper Stuff. You probably own at least a modest collection of audiotapes, records, CDs, videos, software, and CD-ROMs, which are Electronic Stuff. You have Fabric Stuff, such as antique quilts, baby clothes, and a wedding gown tucked away. (I still have my winter prom dress, circa 1966.) You might have Real Art Stuff: paintings, sculpture, etchings. You have a rock collection, a toy train collection, and a doll collection, which are Collector Stuff.

Parents have to keep everything.
—Elaine Ricklin, artist and
art educator, Denver, CO

The secret spaces of many homes resemble Sourdough Trixie Rose's Roadside Reptile Museum and Postcard Boutique, where it is very evident that the owner could profit from recent psychopharmacological research. Trixie, who never met a garage sale she didn't like, never throws anything away. And unlike her book-loving cousin Pat, who contemplates starting a used bookstore to finance her addiction, Trixie is making money off a giant junk drawer masquerading as a gift shop. Her collection is housed in an ancient gas station that died when the interstate was built. She sits, cheerful and totally mad, amidst dusty moose heads and musty old blankets. This is not creative disorder; this is insane.

If you want to take care of that home museum of yours, listen to what the experts say. Archivists and records managers are the experts at taking care of Stuff. (Although I emphasize archivists in this chapter, records managers, their professional first cousins, are also sources of information for the home librarian.)

265

Archivists tend to hang out in archives (this isn't brain surgery), which are not necessarily well publicized or visited by you or me on a regular basis. Compared with a typical library, an archive is about the physical records that pertain to particular people and institutions, as opposed to a collection of books about a subject. An archive is a storage facility, while a library is a place where the items circulate. An archive tends to be files, drawers, and boxes of papers in nonbook form, rather than shelves of books. Archives also contain physical objects not on paper, such as paintings, sculpture, archeological remains, etc.

An archive tends to organize information by date, while a library is more likely to organize information by topic. An archive is less likely to be organized by Dewey decimal or Library of Congress, and tends to have its classification systems based on time, people, and place.

Formal archives tend to be run by people with degrees in history rather than by people with degrees in library science. An archivist is likely to collect everything, such as every item in a sequence of tax records, while a librarian must pick and choose according to what are the best books for a particular audience.

An archivist thinks about the historian who will need a particular letter in a hundred years, while a librarian thinks about the next two years in the life of a nonfiction book on home health care.

Archivists have to deal more with Stuff produced for another purpose, such as a piece of business correspondence or a collection of photos. It is very unlikely that the person who created these items was very concerned at the time about how legible the signature was, or if all the photos were identified and dated.

A librarian has the advantage of dealing mostly with books, which the publishers will have had cataloged by the Library of Congress even before they are printed. The book will be printed in a form that is similar to other books, making shelving and organization much easier.

Archives are more likely to be found in government offices, museums, historical societies, and professional and trade organizations. Although some librarians are archivists, and some archivists are librarians, the organizations that support these professions have different conferences, associations, missions, education, etc.

So What?

A home librarian is more like an archivist or a records manager than a librarian. A home library, for example, is less likely to have the same circulation problems as a public library. And in the management of an individual's life, the location of the most recent version of Aunt Edna's will and the verification of her signature by her lawyer might be more important than the location of the misplaced copy of *An Exaltation of Larks*.

What is the value of becoming a good home archivist?

1. *Having your Stuff in order will save you time.* You will not have to spend hours tracking down lost birth certificates, Social Security cards, passports, and medical records. Being well organized is a blessing in an emergency.

2. *Having your Stuff in order can save you money.* If you sell your home, good records mean that every dime of money you put into the house is accounted for, as well as the date and extent of each repair. Also, it means you can prove how much you paid for a previous repair on an appliance or figure out where you bought that cat door, the one that is finally breaking down after twelve years of heavy use.

3. *Having good records is the first rule of disaster management.* The second rule is that all the records need to be duplicated off-site, so that the only copy of the fire insurance policy is not lost in a fire. On the simplest level, several of our neighbors and family members have a copy of our emergency list, which includes the names, addresses, and phone numbers of insurance agents, family members, doctors, a friendly electrician, the pharmacy with records of my medication, and most important of all, our veterinarians (we have three).

4. *Good record management can save a life.* What is the name and phone number of the nice neighbor who lives near Dad and can check in on him if he doesn't answer the phone? What was the name of that cancer Mom had twenty years ago; does current medical wisdom suggest you need to have a screening?

5. *Keeping photos in good shape means that you and your family can enjoy the positive emotional links with generations of relatives and friends.* My favorite family photo shows a turn-of-the-century baseball team, with the familiar steely eyes and lanky limbs marking certain players as blood relatives. My mother's high-school graduation picture is of a young beauty, which helps me understand the lively, seventy-something square dancer I know today.

6. *Your personal archives may become part of an important historical archive regarding your family, town, religion, or profession.* You don't have to be famous to have documents and artifacts that some historian may find useful in understanding the success of a fundraising drive, the origins of a trade association, the failure of a business, or the look and feel of a city decades ago. All this information could be buried in your family archives.

This chapter focuses on several kinds of record management and archival concerns. First are pointers about dealing with specific nonbook materials, such as photographs, manuscripts, paintings, sheet music, and electronic media. Second are suggestions about dealing with different kinds of vital paper records, such as tax and medical records. Third are pointers to national archives, and some of the best places to begin your genealogical research, an important archival function. Last are some of the premiere mail-order catalog resources for archival supplies, plus books and professional associations you can turn to for help.

The general advice for managing Stuff is the same as managing your home library, with a few key differences. Even though you probably can reduce the number of books you invite into your home, you don't have those choices when it comes to medical records or correspondence with loved ones. For that reason, the use of archival-quality storage materials is more important. You can buy special boxes and wrapping materials to store anything. As with your books, archivists ask you to keep your collections of Stuff clean, cool, dry, and dark.

The Care of NonBooks

Photographs

The physical care of photos, as with books, is about conservation. The problem is that your photographs are the most likely artifacts in your home to have suffered physical abuse over the last forty years. Remember the day you let the kids tape a bunch of vacation pictures into a black paper album? Remember all the times you stuffed photos into old envelopes, promising yourself that someday you would do something about them? Remember the grimy fingers, smearing hamburger grease and grit onto the images during countless picnics?

Three factors make photo conservation very difficult.

1. *Photographs and negatives are cesspools of self-destructive chemicals, and it is even more difficult to repair a photo than it is most books.* The heartbreaker is that even if you did what you thought was best for them twenty years ago, including gluing them into albums, your past efforts are probably the worst thing possible you could have done. I worked in a fine photo store thirty years ago, and I shudder to think about the advice I gave people at the time and what photo storage tools I sold them.

2. *The average home has lots of photographs. Thousands of them. Tens of thousands of them.*

3. *You will never be guaranteed a picture-perfect memory in this lifetime.* Consequently, unless you carefully annotate your negatives and prints as soon as they return from the photo shop, you will never remember who those people are in the photos or where the photos were taken.

When rescuing a photo collection, you will have to do several things at once. See Chapter IV for advice on doing an audit of your library; much of that information applies to photographs as well.

The piecemeal approach suggests that you start with one box, envelope, or album of photographs at a time. This gives you a project that has a beginning and an end.

Set a time, such as Sunday afternoon, when you can focus for a couple of hours. Discard duplicates (send them to friends and relatives). Take the photos out of their albums, unless the albums were created using archival-quality products and processes, which means the photos are not glued in and the products used in the manufacture of the album are either inert or buffered against acid. If you don't know, check with an expert at a museum, historical society, government archive, or university.

Remove as much of the old adhesive tape and glue from both the front and back of the photos as you can, without ripping the photographs. Discard the old plastic and paper albums. Remove rotting photographic material. Unless you have money to invest in the services of a professional conservator, you will not be able to save the more damaged photographs and negatives, and the chemicals released by dying photochemistry can damage the rest of the collection.

Write descriptive information on protective envelopes *before* you put the clean photographs and negatives into them, and then put the envelopes into protective boxes. As you label the photographs, create catalogs of negatives and their images so you can find them again.

Although archival-quality products are not cheap, they will make a difference if you want to preserve your photos for future generations; you can spread the cost over several months or years. Photos and negatives need to be in a clean, dry, dark, and chemically neutral environment, where none of the photos and negatives are touching each other or any other surface that is not inert.

The prevailing mood in museums is: Don't do anything, wait for the miracle cure which someone will magically come up with any second now. We are still waiting.
—Douglas Stone, paper conservator, Milwaukee, WI

The heritage approach is for people who have some cherished photos that are in danger of total destruction. Rummage through the entire collection and pull out the most valuable photographs, particularly the older photos most in danger of complete disintegration. Rescue them first, and then work on the rest of the collection. Rescuing might include sending elderly damaged photographs to a photo conservator, or having fresh copies made. Restoration services can make old images look much better in a new copy and format.

The total immersion approach is for people who like tackling big tasks in one big clump. Take two weeks off from work, unplug the phone, and do the whole collection at once.

What about photo albums? Reserve them for duplicate photographs, and if you do create albums, use the best archival-quality materials. What about glue sticks, which many people are told are appropriate for attaching paper to paper? In fact, they are sold for that purpose in some of the catalogs in this book. Glue sticks have resins and other complex molecules that can break down. The expert advice I received ranged from the "best-kept secret for repairing comic books" to "Don't use them on anything you care about."

The problem is there is evidence that the mix of chemicals used in the typical glue stick can cause problems, such as the genesis and migration of stains, but these problems might not appear for ten years. Until there is better agreement among the experts, keep glue sticks away from photographs and fine printed material.

Manuscripts

Papers fall into two categories: paper and manuscripts. Paper is just paper, but manuscripts usually have historical or aesthetic value. (Technically, the term refers to handwritten papers.) Your son's third-grade essay on flowers becomes a manuscript once he wins the Nobel Prize forty years in the future.

To take care of fine paper artifacts, follow the same rules as for taking care of books and photos: clean, dry, free of critters, cool, dark, low humidity, constant environmental climate, etc.

Mounting manuscripts and paper, such as autographs, watercolors, fine prints, etc., for display, has been made easier, because the materials can be ordered precut. However, if the document is in any way damaged or looking sickly, it is better to take it to someone who has the experience to fix what ails it and make it look good. Just as you did when you were hunting for a competent book doctor, look for someone with experience, lots of references, and testimonials from customers for whom they have done the same kind of work.

Paintings and Other Artwork

Our family loves art, and the walls of our modest home are covered with original paintings and prints. No old masters, although we are counting on our favorite artist to become an important contributor to late twentieth-century aesthetics, thereby ensuring we can all make a lot of money someday.

Our artwork suffers for the same reason our books suffer. Direct sunlight falls on them. They are dusty and dirty. Cracks appear in the surface of the paintings, which are being sucked dry by Denver's high desert plateau climate.

And, once in a while, something happens to one of them. A careless game of flag football in the dining room cracks a glass. A wire loosens and a painting falls with a crash. Some small insect lives out a short, lonely life under the glass of a fine print, and its entombed corpse slowly spreads a delicate stain across a critical area of the print before it is discovered.

Many fine art and history museums will provide appraisals for the public for a small fee or for free. What is more important for the home art collector is having a piece appraised for possible damage or decay. Art museums can also tell you the names of the conservators they use. But please don't damage the piece in transporting it to the museum or workshop. It might be worth it to pay someone to come to your home to evaluate it for cleaning or repair.

A home is not a museum. Anything very valuable should be in some kind of archival storage, but I hope that you have the pleasure of ownership *and* use. When we bought a nice painting a few years ago, I had it hung in the living room over our nonfunctional fireplace. It is there for me, my friends, and family to enjoy every day. Yes, the ceiling might fall in on it, some exotic desert insect might take up residence behind the backing paper, or a clumsy encounter with a mop or broom might put a hole in it. Or I could put it in a storage case and take it out only on my birthday, in leap years.

Sorry, the painting and I will chance it, thank you anyway.

Sheet Music

Both human members of my household studied music theory and piano, and for decades both of our mothers faithfully kept every single sheet of music. The sentimental value of these music collections was and is enormously high, so we were grateful when boxes of piano sonatas, exercise books, and show tunes arrived at our home.

The collection resides in stacks in our respective offices and on the old upright that dominates our front room. And every single sheet, most of which are thirty to forty years old, is in rotten condition. Many are approaching the brittle state where any touch causes pages to shiver and turn to dust.

---

*Our really enormous library of music scores is housed in
what used to be our son Fred's toy shelves, with folding doors.*
—Harry Davidson, piano instructor,
Sherwood Conservatory of Music, Chicago, IL

When I started writing and editing this book, I became inspired. I had great plans to repair every book and document I own. Now, I am not so sure. My current plan on this fine autumn day?

1. I will work my way through the entire collection of music and discard everything that falls apart when I touch it. There is no reasonable way to rescue a sheet of paper when it becomes that fragile, no matter what its sentimental appeal. (It is one less thing for my heirs to do after the funeral.) Since I am not a

famous musician, there is no historical value in saving the piano exercise books of Patty Jean Wagner, age nine.

2. I will give away any piece of music I have not opened or played in twenty years. (There goes half the collection.)

3. I will make a list of the pieces I want to keep, and check their availability in current editions. If necessary, I will replace iffy documents with new copies.

4. I will use the resources of the wonderful archival catalogs at the end of this chapter to bind and preserve the best of what is left. I particularly like the many cleverly designed binders for sheet music, pamphlets, and small books that require no skill or special tools.

Sheet music is a textbook example of what happens when poor-quality paper is subjected to active use over the years. I can sympathize with those who feel compelled to photocopy their own music for their own use, just so that they don't have to deal with rotting piles of yellow and brown paper.

Electronic Media

All forms of electronic media can and do deteriorate, sometimes at a faster rate than paper records. It is easy to imagine that videotapes, computer software, etc., are immortal, but that is not the case. Heat is the worst culprit, with physical damage a close second. But electronic storage media can die just sitting there.

Many forms of electronic media pick up dirt and grit from the machines in which they are used, causing scratches and chemical damage. Some experts suggest that electronic media be stored in wooden or special plastic cases to eliminate the danger of electrostatic charges that could zap the contents of an audiotape or computer diskette.

While I've had and enjoyed a home library for years, my most recent fascination has been with books on audiotape. My inquisitiveness began during my sixty-minute round-trip commute, motivated by a growing dislike for the news and music programs on the radio. Like water dripping from a leaky ceiling, I felt the intrusion of these dour newscasts, trivial sportscasts, and banal music too much to bear. I've immersed myself in novels, lectures, and poetry. What was once an onerous task has been transformed into a literary retreat from my daily concerns and the subtle burden of network news and vapid social affairs programs.
—David Soister, university administrator, Denver, CO

The best advice came from an expert who thinks that collections of electronic media need to be cleaned and used frequently (on equipment that is also frequently cleaned) so that any deterioration can be recognized and dealt with immediately. This means checking the media by using it once a year, and, if necessary, buying a new copy or transferring the data to another medium ASAP. "Use it or lose it" was his original advice.

Unfortunately, no one I talked to was optimistic about a cost-effective way of retrieving and repairing the contents of damaged electronic media, unless you have access to the kind of expensive equipment used by law enforcement agencies and the movie industry.

The Fine Art of Recordkeeping

If you can't afford archival-quality boxes and file folders to store your fragile Stuff, then, at the very least, clean and change the storage materials at regular intervals. In one of the worst horror stories I collected for this book, silverfish destroyed a banker box wall of business records, stored in a garage. The industrious insects turned months of paperwork into papier-mâché. Each time they finished dining on one year's worth of invoices, they chewed their way down through the bottom of the box, through the cover of the next box, and so on.

Why didn't the owner check on her precious records? The owner looked only for water damage on the outside of the boxes. Since the front walls of the sturdy bank boxes survived untouched, it never occurred to her to open them and look inside. The silverfish, meanwhile, dined in silence, uninterrupted.

Besides looking for insect and water damage, archivists will urge you to remove any Things that can damage your Stuff. Things include rubber bands, metal paper clips, adhesive tape, and the kind of cheap thermal fax paper that curls up and turns grunge-colored with age. Make a plain-paper photocopy of any fax printed on thermal paper. Thermal paper not only self-destructs quickly, but it has been known to damage other documents in the process, so that any paper document touching the thermal fax can be stained.

As simple an act as throwing out paper files needs to be planned. Some landfills have very strict laws about flying debris. If you dump old files, and papers with your name on them are found scattered, you may be held accountable for littering, even if you can show you packed up the materials and disposed of them responsibly. The answer, besides compulsive recycling, is to shred the paper before you dispose of it.

More and more families are transferring their files to their computers through digital imaging with photos of the pages of data kept on the computer, or by typing in the data. Home computer records, in my opinion, are neither more nor less vulnerable than paper records. One expert in computer archival storage suggests that all home systems should have triple backups containing all of the software and data that would cause you pain if lost. At least one of those copies should be off-site.

Consider keeping historical backups, so that, for example, you have a copy of your financial records as they existed several years ago. Frequency is up to you, but if you are making important changes to the your computer data every day, you should make copies of those changes every day. If you think this is excessive, talk to people who have spent weeks restoring lost data.

Irreplaceable Stuff should be kept in secure storage, such as a safe deposit box. If you really like to caress your negotiable bonds, make copies to fondle at home, and store the originals at the bank. Make copies of photos, art, and frequently used documents to use while the originals slumber away under lock and key. Don't count on the fact that something has no financial value to a thief to protect it. Young thieves will steal used lipstick, cheap costume jewelry, and plastic knicknacks.

If you can't afford an on-site fireproof safe and you must store valuables in your home, consider buying a broken refrigerator that still has a functioning seal. Clean the refrigerator carefully, and make sure you can have a lock bolted to the outside to prevent children and pets from turning it into a deadly playground. A clean and intact refrigerator can store several cubic feet of paper records and offers protection in case of fire or flood.

Use color to help organize your files. How about green for health records, red for insurance, black for taxes, blue for savings, brown for house records, white for wills and trusts, banker gray for important letters?

Insurance

Insurance records need to be kept at hand, but in a protected place, on-site, yet out of danger, and accessible in an emergency but protected from fire, flood, etc., etc., etc. My favorite insurance agent says you should keep every piece of paper you receive pertaining to every policy. (He says, under the cloak of anonymity, that he does not trust the insurance companies to keep perfect records.)

Insurance records can be stored in a safe deposit box, but that requires a certain discipline. You need to make copies of all the records so you have them in an *accessible* place, which is in addition to having them in a *safe* place.

Medical Records

Most families need to keep several kinds of medical records. Vaccination histories, medical test results, and information about allergies and drug reactions are useful if you change doctors or have to reconstruct medical information for an insurance company. The medication each person uses, your doctor's phone number, and health insurance information are what you need for the midnight trip to the hospital emergency room.

If your family has been challenged with bad genes or a series of medical crises, I recommend keeping an active diary of medical questions and answers. During a series of illnesses, which I affectionately dubbed my "disease of the week" era, I would type up a list of questions for the doctor to answer during each visit. That way I would not leave his office having forgotten to ask him something. Although he feigned irritation at first, my doctor liked the idea. He even began putting a copy of my question list into my file.

Another kind of record is medical genealogical records. Do you have brothers and sisters who are also struggling with high blood pressure? When did your elderly blood relatives die, and what did they die of? You can't always rely on the consensual mythology of your family to pinpoint cause of death. Grandpa's heart attack may have actually been a stroke, and did you ever learn the truth about Cousin Rose's "secret" ailment?

Another type of medical record is insurance and financial records related to health care. I have had billing companies contact me a year after the fact to contest a payment, but because I had all the right pieces of paper, I was able to prove that I owed nothing in a matter of minutes.

Medical records should be living documents, referred to and used.

Legal and Tax Records

Keep everything. Make copies. Keep the copies. File them. Keep the files. Make copies of the catalog for the files. Catalog those. File the copies of the catalogs of the files. Or ...

Many law and accounting firms are offering the service of copying paper records into digital form and keeping those records for you. If you are overwhelmed by your legal recordkeeping demands, you can opt to move the records off-site (i.e., out of your house) to a place designed for managing records.

Car Records

Don't keep them in the car, where they are subject to Death of Paper in Car Syndrome. People think that federal law requires them to drive around with ten-year-old repair invoices in their glove compartment. Car records can be kept in the house (not the garage or toolshed) with the rest of your home records.

Home Records

Home records include, of course, leases, deeds, mortgages, and all correspondence with landlords, mortgage companies, and government entities. You keep all the records of repair and improvement. But you also keep the name of the paint you used on the front porch and the special kind of fuses for the fuse box. All of the warranties on your appliances and electronic equipment can be part of your home records.

Credit Cards and Bank Records

All the experts warn against keeping a written record of your PINs (Personal Identification Numbers) with your financial records, which can allow a thief to drain your bank accounts and wreak havoc with your credit cards. Also, you should carefully destroy old credit cards and any records and information by shredding them before you throw them out. Crooks may go through your garbage, hunting for financial information they could use to get rich off your good name.

Genealogy Archives

If you live anywhere other than in certain neighborhoods in Africa and Australia, chances are your folks came from someplace else. Most English-speaking countries are home to fanatic genealogists, either fueled by religious convictions or by the delight in locating family connections hundreds of years old.

Genealogy materials include diaries, correspondence, business records, deeds, wills, marriage certificates, school papers, newspapers, photos, and military and immigration records. Some of the public records you can use to track down or verify data include fire insurance atlases, records of building permits and tax assessments, social registries, old phone books, clipping files, and church registries.

I remember the thrill I felt when I was able to track down the newspaper report of the celebration of my great-uncle Harry's birth in Hartford, Wisconsin; it took me only about an hour to locate the actual newspaper in the town library's files. Before I found the newspaper files, however, I was told by officials, in no uncertain terms, that "Jews had never lived in Hartford."

Fortunately, Harry's father (my great-grandfather) had resided there long enough to have been written up in the paper several times, which left a clear paper trail. Even the self-appointed historians could not deny the newspaper stories. I delighted in learning how my great-grandfather had established a small temple, how he hired many other Jewish immigrants from Chicago to work in his business (a garment factory) and of his prominence in the community. I also laughed out loud when I read that great-uncle Harry's birthday celebration had lasted three days. This is the kind of payoff that makes the research worthwhile.

Once you get bitten by the genealogy bug, you will understand the importance of maintaining good records for your descendants. See the end of this chapter for genealogy resources.

Religious Archives

You can do your religious or spiritual organization a great service by helping maintain a working library and an archive of church records. Your experience as an expert home librarian and archivist (that's right, you can tell other people the best ways to measure shelves and clean leather covers) can be applied to the situations found in religious institutions. Although larger congregations and parishes have paid staff, smaller groups have to rely on volunteer help.

The two most important pieces of advice I uncovered are from the **Archives of the Billy Graham Center,** Wheaton College, Wheaton, Illinois 60187, (708) 752-5910, and come from the notes of a recent public workshop they conducted on the topic of church archives. First, you will need to make the financial support of a library and archives an official part of your religious organization's budget. Otherwise, it will become a second-class concern, fueled with leftovers. Second, archives need to be honest. Mistakes need to be recorded, along with successes. There may be a temptation to rewrite history, to soothe politically powerful people, or to spare the feelings of members of the community. This kind of selective memory is really censorship and hides information that could be very useful to future generations.

Resources for Home Archivists

National Archives

National Archives manage U.S. government records. For home archivists, their main value is as a repository of priceless genealogical data. Here is a list of the regional offices, which are accessible to the public. The one I visited in our region was humming with activity; some of the serious-minded genealogists visit almost daily, according to the staff, and know the collections as well as the employees.

National Archives–New England Region. 380 Trapelo Road, Waltham, MA 02154; (617) 647-8100. *Connecticut, Maine, Massachusetts, New Hampshire, Rhode Island, Vermont.*

National Archives–Northeast Region. Greenwich Village, 201 Varick Street, New York, NY 10014; (212) 337-1300. *New Jersey, New York, Puerto Rico, the Virgin Islands.*

National Archives–Mid-Atlantic Region. Ninth and Market streets, Room 1350, Philadelphia, PA 19107; (215) 597-3000. *Delaware, Maryland, Pennsylvania, Virginia, West Virginia.*

National Archives–Southeast Region. 1557 St. Joseph Avenue, East Point (Atlanta), GA 30344; (404) 736-7477. *Alabama, Florida, Georgia, Kentucky, Mississippi, North Carolina, South Carolina, Tennessee.*

National Archives–Great Lakes Region. 7358 South Pulaski Road, Chicago, IL 60629; (312) 581-7816. *Illinois, Indiana, Michigan, Minnesota, Ohio, Wisconsin.*

National Archives–Central Plains Region. 2312 East Bannister Road, Kansas City, MO 64131; (816) 926-6272. *Iowa, Kansas, Missouri, Nebraska.*

National Archives–Southwest Region. 501 West Felix Street, PO Box 6216, Fort Worth, TX 76115; (817) 334-5525. *Arkansas, Louisiana, New Mexico*, Oklahoma, Texas. (*Most records from federal agencies in New Mexico are at the Rocky Mountain Region office.)*

National Archives–Rocky Mountain Region. Building 48, Denver Federal Center, Denver, CO 80225-0307; (303) 236-0817. *Colorado; Montana, North Dakota, South Dakota, Utah, Wyoming, New Mexico (see above).*

National Archives–Pacific Southwest Region. 24000 Avila Road, Laguna Niguel, CA 92656; (714) 643-4241. *Arizona; Southern California, Clark County, Nevada.*

National Archives–Pacific Sierra Region. 1000 Commodore Lane, San Bruno, CA 94066; (415) 876-9009. *Northern California, Hawaii, Nevada (except Clark County), the Pacific Trust Territories, American Samoa.*

National Archives–Pacific Northwest Region. 6125 Sand Point Way NE, Seattle, WA 98115; (206) 526-6507. *Idaho, Oregon, Washington.*

National Archives-Alaska Region. 654 West Third Avenue, Anchorage, AK 99501; (907) 271-2441. *Alaska.*

Books for Home Archivists

Art supply stores are a good place to find books on taking care of paper and other artifacts. Bookstores that specialize in regional and military history are excellent sources for genealogical information.

Caring for Your Art: *A Guide for Artists, Collectors, Galleries and Art Institutions.* Jill Snyder. Illustrations by Joseph Montague. *Allworth Press, $16.95 paper, ISBN 0-880559-47-1.*
One of the best things about this book is the information on packing paintings and other framed works of art for shipping.

History Comes to Life: *Collecting Historical Letters and Documents.* Kenneth W. Rendell. *University of Oklahoma Press, $29.95 cloth, ISBN 0-8061-2764-3.*
For the person who has everything and is trying to figure out if any of it is worth anything! A history of personal manuscripts and replicas of dozens of autographs, with information about the history of personal manuscripts.

My Family Tree Workbook: *Genealogy for Beginners.* Rosemary A. Chorzempa. *Dover, $2.95 paper, ISBN 0-486-24229-3.*
An inexpensive and easy-to-use introduction to genealogy.

An Ounce of Preservation: *A Guide to the Care of Papers and Photographs.* Craig A. Tuttle. *Rainbow Books, $12.95 paper, ISBN 1-56825-021-5; PO Box 430, Highland City, FL 33846-0430; (813) 648-4420.*
An inexpensive and detail-rich guide to the care of everything from stamps to greeting cards to comic books, with valuable information on simple repair and cleaning of photographs. Although the author provides some historical background, the book is jargon-free and assumes you are a normal human being with a budget and a life.

Organizations for Home Archivists

The historical organizations listed in Chapter II harbor all kinds of archival experts. Here are several specialized groups.

American Association for State and Local History. 172 Second Avenue, Suite 202, Nashville, TN 37201; (615) 255-2971; fax (615) 255-2979.
This group prides itself on its support of the community groups that record and safeguard local history. Write or call for more information.

279

Association for Recorded Sound Collections. Executive Director
Peter Shambarger, PO Box 543, Annapolis, MD 21404-0543;
(410) 757-0488 (home), (410) 956-5600, extension 242 (business); $30/year.
Semiannual journal, quarterly newsletter, biannual membership directory.
Annual midyear meetings.

Association of Records Managers and Administrators. PO Box 8540,
Prairie Village, KS 66208-0540; (800) 422-2762, (913) 341-3808;
fax (913) 341-3742; e-mail: 76015.3151@compuserve.com.
A not-for-profit professional organization offering educational and networking
opportunities to more than 10,000 members worldwide. There are 151 chapters. A
place to meet professionals who can solve your worst record management problems.

Church of Jesus Christ of Latter-day Saints. Genealogy Department,
50 East North Temple Street, Salt Lake City, UT 84150.
This extraordinary genealogy archive is accessible through the church's
branch libraries, which have catalogs that allow you to order specific microfilm
records for the cost of postage. Write for the branch nearest you.

National Genealogical Society. 4527 17th Street North, Arlington,
VA 22207-2399; (703) 525-0050; fax (703) 525-0052; $35/year.
A full-service membership organization with publications, a research service,
and a lending library of family histories.

Society of American Archivists. 600 South Federal Street, Suite 504, Chicago, IL
60605; (312) 922-0140; fax (312) 347-1452; e-mail: info@saa.mhs.compuserve.com.
Members work with records of all types, including letters and diaries, photographs, film, sound recordings, maps, manuscripts, and electronic records. Institutions represented include governmental bodies, colleges and universities,
historical societies, museums, libraries, businesses, and religious institutions. For
more information about the archival profession or SAA, please contact SAA
Membership Services.

Mail-Order Catalogs for Genealogists

Clearfield Company. 200 East Eager Street, Baltimore, MD 21202;
(410) 625-9004.
Genealogical source material organized by state, as well as remaindered
books and reprints regarding genealogy.

Genealogical Publishing Co. 1001 North Calvert Street, Baltimore, MD 21202-3897; (410) 837-8271.

Dozens of family histories, immigration records, and reference directories, partly organized by ethnicity and state.

Genealogical Supply Catalog. Genealogy Unlimited, PO Box 537, Orem, UT 84059-0537; (801) 763-7132.

Genealogical tools, including lineage charts, maps, dictionaries, and some archival-quality supplies.

Mail-Order Catalogs for Archivists and Home Librarians

This is where you find protection for your fragile, rare, valuable, and emotionally precious possessions. Name the artifact, and you will find products designed to protect and preserve. There is some overlap in the products they sell, but each has a distinct market focus and carries exclusive lines.

Gaylord: *The Trusted Source®.* Archival Storage Materials and Conservation Supplies, PO Box 4901, Syracuse, NY 13221-4901; (800) 448-6160 (orders), (800) 634-6307 (customer service); fax (800) 272-3412.

The most user-friendly of these companies, with a strong emphasis on user support and education, particularly for librarians. A general product catalog.

The Hollinger Corporation. PO Box 8360, Fredericksburg, VA 22404; (800) 634-0491; fax (800) 947-8814.

They carry, among other products, fiberboard boxes and sheets. Their products meet the highest technical standards and are designed for serious archivists.

LBS/Archival Products. PO Box 1413, Des Moines, IA 50305; (515) 262-3191, (800) 526-5640; fax (800) 262-4091.

A lovely catalog highlights folders, boxes, and other enclosures, while an equally beautiful newsletter educates customers. This is where you buy your sheet music folders. Also offers a facsimile service for photocopying brittle books.

Light Impressions®. 439 Monroe Avenue, PO Box 940, Rochester, NY 14603-0940; (800) 828-6216; fax (800) 828-5539.

Photography is the focus of this catalog, which includes professional storage materials, albums, framing materials, and books.

Metal Edge West, Inc. 2721 East 45th Street, Los Angeles, CA 90058; (213) 588-2228, (800) 862-2228; fax (213) 588-2150.

Best known for their metal-reinforced archival-quality boxes and their Safe Care line of folders, museum boards, etc.

University Products. 517 Main Street, PO Box 101, Holyoke, MA 01041-0101; (800) 628-1912 (orders), (800) 762-1165 (customer service); fax (413) 532-9281, (800) 532-9281.

A general archival catalog with everything you would need to protect a small museum, including special collection supplies, furniture, and tools.

❖

Glossary

Sharp-eyed readers will notice a laissez-faire attitude in my use of terminology in these pages. The authors who define and document the terms used in the book and library communities do not agree on many usages. And I did not always accept the definitions offered by scholarly organizations as having the force of constitutional law. There was jargon I refused to use, since I believe the words would not offer either precision or clarity. Some experts vehemently insisted that I refer to them and their work in specific ways, even when contradicted by other experts. Also, there are terms, I believe, that are interchangeable.

I apologize in advance for any playfulness on my part that further muddied the waters, and I certainly mean no disrespect to scholars for whom terminology is important. I would not suggest using this book to cram for your Official Book Conservator Badge or to research a doctoral thesis in library science.

acid Chemists describe it in terms of increased hydrogen ion activity, as represented by a number on the pH scale, with *7* being neutral and *0* being the most acid. A booklover will mutter about the "acid burning up my books." Acid, in practical terms, means that, through the careless use of certain products in the manufacturing of paper and books and through the aging process itself, paper and books deteriorate. Combating acid by using products that are buffered or contain little or no natural acid; by keeping books away from moisture, heat, and light; and by using deacidification processes, is one of the main concerns of book conservators.

archival, archive These words are used in two contexts. *Archival* can mean products and processes that combat acid and other damage to books. Since this book is meant for average booklovers managing a home library, the term is not meant to apply to the level of concern that would occur in a museum or rare book library. *Archive* refers to places where books and other artifacts are stored and protected and are less likely to be circulated.

bibliography The term, which literally means "writing about books," can apply to lists of books, the study of book history, or the detailed description of physical and historical facts about a book.

conservation See *preservation* and *restoration*. For the layperson, conservation is interchangeable with preservation, although some would argue that conservation is about all the things you do to prevent damage in the first place.

conservator, book A person with training in chemistry, history, bibliography, and the book arts who knows how to protect a book from damage, prevent further damage, and, if lucky, restore the health and looks of a damaged book. Conservators exist for every kind of artifact.

expert Someone who I and other members of the book and library communities respect, and who, through training and/or experience, has useful opinions about books and libraries.

Gutenberg era Starting in the 1450s, physical memory was defined as a pile of folded, sewn, and/or glued sheets of paper containing images created by a repetitive printing process. The book of this era is mostly what this guide is about.

librarian Someone with a Master's of Library Science (MLS) degree.

library worker Anyone who works in a library, especially one who does not have an MLS. Let me point out that library workers are in the majority compared to librarians.

manuscript A handwritten work. This term is often applied to books produced before Gutenberg. It also refers to the written or typed copy of a book before it has been typeset.

preservation See *restoration* and *conservation*. For the layperson, preservation is interchangeable with conservation, but can refer to actions one takes after the damage has happened in order to prevent further damage.

professional Someone who is paid to work with books and libraries.

real An affectionate term for those people and organizations that conduct business in the library and book community, and who serve public and private interests, as opposed to the home librarians who justifiably serve themselves.

restoration See *conservation* and *preservation*. The latter two terms are more about prevention; restoration is about making a book as close to new as possible. Unfortunately, the likelihood that you can actually fix a book "like new" is slim. A book can be repaired, but it will never be the same once it has been damaged.

❖

Index

Entries in quotes and/or pages numbers in **boldface** indicate the definition of the word.

About the Author

Patricia Jean Wagner has loved books throughout a checkered career as a poet, printer, publisher, bookstore clerk, library clerk, author, small press advocate, bookstore cofounder, writer, book designer, book arts show organizer, typography junkie, and, for the last fifteen years, book reviewer and, more recently, contributing editor for *The Bloomsbury Review*. She and her husband Leif Smith run Pattern Research, a 22-year-old research and educational services company in Colorado, with clients in most states and several countries. She has also conducted workshops for libraries and library organizations since 1979.

About the Illustrator

Sherlock, sometimes known as Sherry L. Watson, is a freelance artist who lives in Texas. She's most active in science fiction fandom, and creates fantasy and humor art in almost any medium. She happily accepts commissions of all sorts in order to keep herself, her van, and her mandatory cat all ready to prowl.

❖

Colophon

This book was the result of the collaboration of high tech, low tech, fine art, good humor, and many months of hard fun.

The book was written and formatted on NeXT computers, running Wordperfect, OpenWrite, Dataphile, FrameMaker®, and NeXTmail.

The book was set in Adobe Garamond and Helvetica.
The book was printed by Gilliland Printing, Inc., Arkansas City, Kansas.
Cover and dust jacket design by Kim Long.
Photograph of Patricia Jean Wagner by Michael N. Flanagan.
The book was produced with the assistance and the guidance of the staff of *The Bloomsbury Review*®.

❖

*W*e take your book
from Concept
... to ...
Finished Product

(and everything in between)

Project Management
EDITORIAL ❁ DESIGN ❁ PRODUCTION
MARKETING ❁ MANUFACTURING

THE FIRST NAME IN BOOK
PRODUCTION SERVICES
IN THE
ROCKY MOUNTAIN WEST,
SINCE 1975

ARGENT ASSOCIATES
❁ 637 SO. BROADWAY, B305 ❁
BOULDER, COLORADO 80303
TELEPHONE 303/447-2320
❁ FACSIMILE 303/447-9710 ❁

ROCKY MOUNTAIN BOOK
PUBLISHERS ASSOCIATION

*T*he largest
professional
organization
of book publishers in the
western United States.
Featuring cooperative
marketing programs, pro-
fessional development
activities, catalog of
books, directory, annual
design contest, and
national conference.

FOR MEMBERSHIP INFORMATION
AND DESCRIPTION OF PROGRAMS,
CONTACT:

RMBPA
Alan Bernhard,
Executive Director
P.O. Box 19013,
Boulder, Colorado 80308
Phone: 303/447-2320
Fax: 303/447-9710

FIRSTS
COLLECTING MODERN FIRST EDITIONS

THE MONTHLY MAGAZINE FOR BOOK COLLECTORS!

Each month FIRSTS is filled with:
- Tips for book collectors
- Catalogue and auction reports
- In-depth discussions of authors and their work
- Book collector's calendar
- Reviews of collectable books
- Expert advice on identifying first editions

Subscriptions to FIRSTS are only $35 dollars per year (II issues).

❏ YES. Please enter my subscription for one year (II issues) of FIRSTS: COLLECTING MODERN FIRST EDITIONS. My payment is enclosed.

❏ U.S. $40   ❏ Mexico/Canada $60   ❏ International $95 U.S.

Name_____

Address _____

City_____ State _____ ZIP _____

❏ Check or money order enclosed.
❏ MasterCard. ❏ VISA Number _____ Exp. Date _____

Signature _____

SEND TO:
FIRSTS MAGAZINE
4445 N. ALVERNON WAY, TUCSON AZ 85718-6139 (520) 529-1355

If you love books,
protect them
with BRODART archival
Book Jacket Covers

Call for a *free* catalog:

BRODART Co. • 1609 Memorial Ave.
Willamsport, PA 17705
800-233-8959 • Fax: 800-283-6087
Internet: www.brodart.com

Rocky Mountain Antiquarian Booksellers Association

℞MABA

An organization of used and rare book-dealers dedicated to stimulating book collecting, promoting ethical trade in all facets of the antiquarian book business, and education of the public in the field of antiquarian books.

Sponsors of the Region's Finest Antiquarian Book Fairs

Rocky Mountain Antiquarian Bookfair in Denver (first week of August, 1997) Pikes Peak Antiquarian Book Fair in Colorado Springs (second week in April 1998)

For Book Fair Information,
please contact Linda Lebsack Books
303-832-7190.
For information about the RMABA,
please contact Polly Hinds
303-329-8011

Celebration Books
Lois J. Harvey

References for Collectors and Professionals, Consultations, Appraisals, Book Events, Buying and Selling Fine Books and Collectables

303-480-5193
celebooklh@aol.com
3617 Meade Street, Denver CO 80211

Open Shop at 32nd & Lowell in Historic Highland Square, Denver, CO
303-561-0035

Small presses and self-publishers:

FREE MONEY-MAKING NEWSLETTER

SPAN (the Small Publishers Association of North America) publishes an information-packed 20-page monthly newsletter. Normally only for members, now you can get a free copy of this profit-making, money-saving tool. SPAN also has many member benefits such as a 58% discount on freight, credit card merchant status, an annual convention, etc.

To get your newsletter call (719) 395-4790, fax (719) 395-8374 or e-mail SPANnet.org

For full membership benefits, visit our Web site:
http://www.SPANnet.org

Karen Jones
Bookbinding
Collections Conservation

3050 W. Denver Place
Denver, CO 80211
303-458-5944

Mad Dog & The Pilgrim Bookshop

Fine Out-of-Print, Used, and Antiquarian books with an emphasis in Children's, Fiction, Military History, Odd topics and Foreign languages, International book-search. Book repair service.

6630 E. Colfax Avenue
Denver, CO 80220
303-329-8011
E-mail: MadDogBks@aol.com

301

Now in Paperback

Women Who Run With the Wolves

Myths and
Stories of the
Wild Woman
Archetype

Over
1,000,000
hardcover
copies
in print

by Clarissa Pinkola Estés, Ph.D.

The runaway bestseller that's become a national touchstone.

Ballantine Books

C.P. ESTÉS GUADALUPE FOUNDATION

From Book Hunter Press

The Used Book Lover's Guide Series
Your guide to over 6,000 used book dealers

✔ Helps you identify dealers likely to carry the kinds of books you're looking for.

✔ Helps you plan your book hunting trips by identifying clusters of shops located near each other.

✔ Easy to follow travel directions take the guess work out of finding out-of-the way shops.

PLUS valuable comments about shops based on the authors' personal visits that help you decide which shops to visit and which to contact by mail or phone.

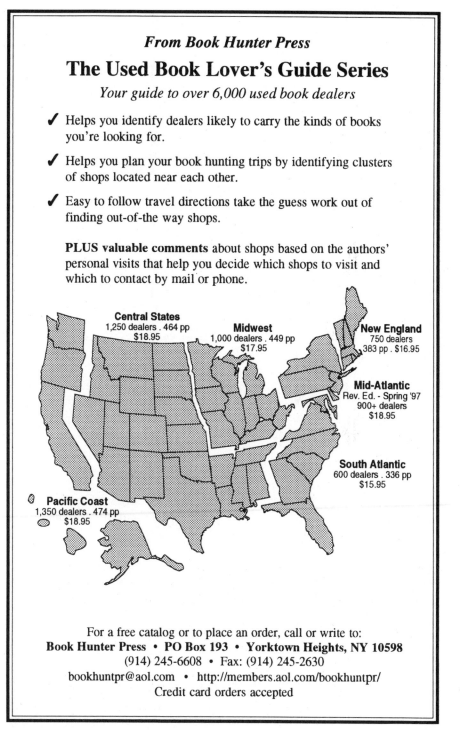

Central States
1,250 dealers . 464 pp
$18.95

Midwest
1,000 dealers . 449 pp
$17.95

New England
750 dealers
383 pp . $16.95

Mid-Atlantic
Rev. Ed. - Spring '97
900+ dealers
$18.95

South Atlantic
600 dealers . 336 pp
$15.95

Pacific Coast
1,350 dealers . 474 pp
$18.95

For a free catalog or to place an order, call or write to:
Book Hunter Press • PO Box 193 • Yorktown Heights, NY 10598
(914) 245-6608 • Fax: (914) 245-2630
bookhuntpr@aol.com • http://members.aol.com/bookhuntpr/
Credit card orders accepted

Grist On-Line

A World Wide Web site for alternative literature that cele-brates books in all their grand diversity: past, present, and future.

*Karl Young's **Light and Dust:** includes samples from books published by Light and Dust with information on ordering, plus the first 80 entries in an ongoing, refreshingly non-sectar-ian anthology of the poetry of the second half of the 20th cen-tury. The site now features over 20 complete books, some of them underground classics, that have gone out of print, as well as cooperative projects with publishers around the world.

*John Fowler's **GOL Publishing** includes complete books by David Ignatow, now an Elder Statesman of American poetry, and Fowler's experiments with hypertext and other forms so new they don't yet have a name. Brief entries from writers as various as William S. Burroughs and Jessica Freeman, Armand Schwerner and Charles Plymell give extra depth to the site.

*Robert Bove's **Room Temperature**—oriented toward short, snappy book reviews, and fast and sharp literary entries, this site serves as an excellent and provocative guide to and sam-pler of many of the cross currents in contemporary literature.

*Jukka Lehmus's **Glossolalia**—Lehmus, a young polymath living in Finland, contributes studies of Shakespeare and extensions of Duchamp, 19th century mystery stories, reports on environmental installation projects, and mail art, as well as contemporary poetry.

Young and Fowler set up their first presses in the 60s, and Young continues to publish books in print, as well as act as a book designer and print broker. These are people whose lives have been completely dedicated to books, and hence ideal guides to the new technologies that will radiate out from books in the years to come.

http://www.thing.net/~grist/page1.htm

From the Award-Winning Author of
Women Who Run With the Wolves

CLARISSA PINKOLA ESTÉS

A Gift That Will Touch the Soul

One of the premier storytellers of our time tells the tale
about how life's difficult transitions and senseless twists of
fate can be met with simplicity and strength of spirit.

HarperSanFrancisco
A Division of HarperCollins*Publishers*
Also available from HarperCollins*Canada Ltd.*

Hardcover
$14.00

Book on tape available from Sounds True Audio at your local bookseller.

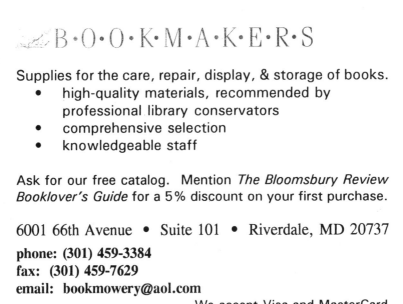

B·O·O·K·M·A·K·E·R·S

Supplies for the care, repair, display, & storage of books.
- high-quality materials, recommended by professional library conservators
- comprehensive selection
- knowledgeable staff

Ask for our free catalog. Mention *The Bloomsbury Review Booklover's Guide* for a 5% discount on your first purchase.

6001 66th Avenue • Suite 101 • Riverdale, MD 20737

phone: (301) 459-3384
fax: (301) 459-7629
email: bookmowery@aol.com

We accept Visa and MasterCard

Call About: Book Collecting Classes

Willow Creek Books

Buy & Sell New, Used, Collectible & Out-of-Print Books

One of the largest literature selections in the Rocky Mountain West: Fiction, Poetry, Literary Criticism, Uncorrected Proofs Western Americana • Illustrated Children's Books

Don Colberg, Ph.D.
Mon-Fri: 11:30-6:00
Sat: 10:00-6:00
Sun: By Appt. Only

8100 S. Akron   Suite 310
Englewood, CO 80112

(303) 790-7530

3 blocks west of I-25 and County Line Road

1-800-891-7530

(in Highland Park)

Used Books & New Books

POWELL'S CITY OF BOOKS

Used Book Buying	Signed First Editions	Corporate Accounts
Rare Books	Author Readings	School & Library Services
Out-of-Print Search	Small Press/Journals	Export Services
Special Orders	Worldwide Shipping	Online Services

1005 W Burnside, Portland OR 97209 · 1-800-878-7323 · Fax 503-228-4631
E-MAIL: ping@powells.portland.or.us **GOPHER:** gopher.powells.portland.or.us **WWW:** http://www.powells.portland.or.us/

Paper Conservation

Evaluation of art, condition reports, and surveys of collections.

Deacidification (wet and dry); dry cleaning of surfaces; patching tests; spot bleaching; bleaching; flattening of documents; mounting to Japanese tissue of posters and weak papers.

Removal of acid backings, glues, and mat boards.

Specialties: Oriental prints, 17th-20th century prints (color and b&w), watercolors, letters, maps, charcoals, and pastels.

Because of the nature of paper and art conservation, Mr. Stone cannot offer evaluations or consulting over the phone. References available on request.

Douglas Stone, PO Box 05147, Milwaukee, WI 53205; (414) 744-6333

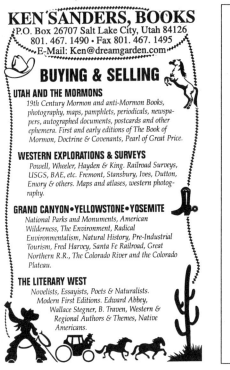

KEN SANDERS, BOOKS
P.O. Box 26707 Salt Lake City, Utah 84126
801. 467. 1490 • Fax 801. 467. 1495
E-Mail: Ken@dreamgarden.com

BUYING & SELLING

UTAH AND THE MORMONS
*19th Century Mormon and anti-Mormon Books,
photography, maps, pamphlets, periodicals, newspapers, autographed documents, postcards and other
ephemera. First and early editions of The Book of
Mormon, Doctrine & Covenants, Pearl of Great Price.*

WESTERN EXPLORATIONS & SURVEYS
*Powell, Wheeler, Hayden & King. Railroad Surveys,
USGS, BAE, etc. Fremont, Stansbury, Ives, Dutton,
Emory & others. Maps and atlases, western photog-
raphy.*

GRAND CANYON•YELLOWSTONE•YOSEMITE
*National Parks and Monuments, American
Wilderness, The Environment, Radical
Environmentalism, Natural History, Pre-Industrial
Tourism, Fred Harvey, Santa Fe Railroad, Great
Northern R.R., The Colorado River and the Colorado
Plateau.*

THE LITERARY WEST
*Novelists, Essayists, Poets & Naturalists.
Modern First Editions. Edward Abbey,
Wallace Stegner, B. Traven, Western &
Regional Authors & Themes, Native
Americans.*

Irene Mitkus
✳
hand Bookbinding
Book Restoration
✳
1145 N. 21st Street
Milwaukee, WI
53233
✳
Since 1974
✳

THE DENVER BOOK MALL

30 BOOKSELLERS
offering a variety of specialties and general stock

IN THE HEART OF DENVER'S BOOK ROW

32 Broadway, Denver 80203 *** (303) 733-3808 *** open 7 days a week

LETTERPRESS PRINTING
• *Business and personal stationery*   • *Broadsides and keepsakes*
• *Announcements for all occasions*   • *Fine printing and design*

ᔕᔭᔬ

Brian Allen *Printer*, Inc.
P.O. Box 533 • 121½ Second Ave. • Niwot Colorado 80544
Telephone: tollfree: 1.888.906.6559   local: 303.652.3130

GUILTLESS PLEASURES

Indulge your passion for fine books with the Daedalus Books Catalog — an irresistible collection of the choicest literary remainders, *all offered at savings of up to 90%*. Seven issues a year featuring hundreds of books on everything from the performing arts to new fiction to science. Each described with uncommon insight and wit. Call for your free catalog today.

DÆDALUS BOOKS

PRICELESS CULTURE.   PRICED LESS.

1-800-395-2665
Call 9:00 am – 6:00 pm EST

Do you remember the first book you really loved?

Relive the experience of two women whose love of books inspired them to open a bookshop in 1916 *(Sunwise Turn: A Human Comedy of Bookselling)*.

Follow the adventures of Roger Mifflin as he travels New England in his book wagon *(Parnassus on Wheels)* or tries to solve the mystery of the disappearing book *(The Haunted Bookshop)* in Christopher Morley's classic tales.

Read about the lives of renowned literary figures, from Robert Frost to Henry Miller, recounted by their booksellers at the *Gotham Book Mart* in New York City; *The Johnny Appleseed Bookshop* in Vermont; *Cody's* in Berkeley; and *Harry W. Schwartz Bookshops* in Milwaukee.

BOOKSELLERS HOUSE titles celebrate your love of books. For more information or to order your copies, contact BPI, c/o American Booksellers Association, 828 S. Broadway, Tarrytown, NY 10591, (800) 637-0037 or (914) 591-BOOK, or visit your local independent bookstore.

Let the adventures begin!

ARCHIVAL QUALITY PERMA/DUR® BOOK JACKET COVERS

...and hundreds of museum quality products for the cleaning, repair, and protection of the books you value most.

Call today for a free catalog...1-800-628-1912

UNIVERSITY PRODUCTS, INC.
Dept. F234, 517 Main Street,
P.O. Box 101, Holyoke, MA 01041-0101

Looking for A Book? Call Us First!

Large Selection — Paperback, hardcover
& out-of-print quality books
at reasonable prices

Knowledgeable, Friendly Booksellers

Open Every Day
10 - 6
Buy & Trade
Every Day

Colfax & Grant
Across from Capitol
Denver, Colorado

Capitol Hill BOOKS

837-0700

MICHIGAN ANTIQUARIAN BOOK & PAPER SHOWS

Spring & Fall
Since 1984
Info:
Curious Book Shop
307 E. Grand River
E. Lansing, MI 48823
(517) 332-0112

120 Dealers

Clips and Quips

Copyright-free Drawings
For Libraries and Schools

*Published by
the Central Colorado
Library System*

Dozens of high-quality cartoon drawings in a convenient notebook

*Drawn by **Sherry L. Watson***

$29.00 includes shipping

*Make checks payable to:
Central Colorado Library System,
4350 Wadsworth, #340,
Wheat Ridge, CO 80033.
Institutional purchase
orders accepted.
ISBN 0-9638913-0-8*

P R O B O O K 303-756-5222

If *your* company, professional society, or organization is producing a book, we can help with design, production, editing, printing, *and marketing.* Our clients include publishers like McGraw-Hill, technology companies Fujitsu and Hyundai, colleges, museums, and artists' estates. For an estimate on your next project, call us!

member
ABPA

Great Gift

Keep track of books the way you do best friends...

BOOKNOTES
THE BOOKLOVER'S ORGANIZER

An address book for books !

Entertaining quotes about reading on every page

•*Order today for you or a friend* •

*Send $12.95 + $2.00 S&H to:
Jackson Creek Press
2150 Jackson Creek Drive
Corvallis, OR 97330*

SERVICE DIRECTORY

Booksellers

ARCHIVES BOOK SHOP
517-519 W. Grand River Ave.
East Lansing, MI 48823
(517) 332-8444
Specializing in rare & unusual books, periodicals, scholarly works, original art, ephemera, history, philosophy, biography & collectible paper items.

CURIOUS BOOK SHOP
307 E. Grand River Ave.
East Lansing, MI 48823
(517) 332-0112
fax (517) 332-1915
Collectable & readable science fiction, mysteries, sports items, movie material, old magazines, pulps, paperbacks, children's books, regional histories and much more!

ARGOS BOOK SHOP
1405 Robinson Rd. SE
Grand Rapids, MI 49506
(616) 454-0111
Large selection of old hard-backs, paperbacks, magazines, including past & present comic books, graphic novels, games & supplies.

ARCHER'S USED & RARE BOOKS
104 South Lincoln St.
Kent, OH 44240
(330) 673-0945
We issue catalogues in: Americana, Baseball, Botany, Gardening, Literature, Mystery, True Crime and nonclassical music.

TAUGHER BOOKS
2550 Somerset Dr.
Belmont, CA 94002
415-591-8366
e-mail: taugher@batnet.com.
I specialize in collectible first editions, especially in modern lit, mystery/detective fiction, Black lit, & books on book collecting. My entire inventory of 1,000 books is on the World Wide Web at www.batnet.com/taugher/.

Editing/Proofreading

CARYL RIEDEL
3233 W. Hayward Pl.
Denver CO 80211
(303) 863-0406
Experienced proofreader and copy editor with more than 18 years experience in typography and publishing. Fast, accurate, and very reasonable rates. I also offer computer keyboarding or word processing services. Excellent grammar, spelling, and punctuationskills.

LORI D. KRANZ
1359 Monroe St.
Denver CO 80206
(303) 388-3837
Fast and accurate. Focus on consistency. Reasonable rates.

Celebrating 16 Years In Publishing

The
BLOOMSBURY
REVIEW
A BOOK MAGAZINE

". . . is the best book magazine in America."
—Tony Hillerman

". . . contains a more balanced examination of current books than any of its glamorous competitors."
—Wallace Stegner

". . . an articulate and beautifully put together magazine."
—John Nichols

"The world of books is the better for it."
—Norman Cousins

BOOK REVIEWS, INTERVIEWS, ESSAYS, PROFILES, POETRY, AND MORE . . .

1762 Emerson Street • Denver, CO 80218-1012 USA • (303) 863-0406 • Fax (303) 863-0408

0475

312

WITHDRAWN
UML LIBRARIES